The McDonaldization Thesis

The McDonaldization Thesis

Explorations and Extensions

George Ritzer

SAGE Publications
London • Thousand Oaks • New Delhi

First published 1998

Reprinted 1998, 1999

SAGE Publications Ltd
6 Bonhill Street
London EC2A 4PU

SAGE Publications Inc
2455 Teller Road
Thousand Oaks, California 91320

SAGE Publications India Pvt Ltd
32, M-Block Market
Greater Kailash – I
New Delhi 110 048

British Library Cataloguing in Publication Data

A catalogue record for this book is available from the British
Library

ISBN 0 7619 5539 9
ISBN 0 7619 5540 2 (pbk)

Library of Congress catalog card number 97–068493

Typeset by Photoprint, Torquay
Printed in Great Britain by Biddles Ltd, Guildford, Surrey

Contents

Preface

Since the publication of the original edition of *The McDonaldization of Society* in 1993 I have been invited to present a variety of papers on, or derived from, the main thesis of that book. Those papers represent the basis of this book which both explores and moves beyond the McDonaldization thesis. To put it simply, that thesis is that the fast-food restaurant, especially the pioneering and still dominant chain of McDonald's restaurants, is the contemporary paradigm of the rationalization process. As a result, that process can be dubbed the "McDonaldization process." Spearheaded by, and modeled after the fast-food restaurant, we have witnessed, are seeing, and are likely to continue to observe a continuation, even an acceleration, of the rationalization process. McDonaldization involves an increase in efficiency, predictability, calculability and control through the substitution of non-human for human technology. While undoubtedly bringing with it many positive developments, McDonaldization also involves a wide range of irrationalities, especially dehumanization and homogenization. It is these irrationalities of rationality (and associated problems) which represent the true heart of the McDonaldization thesis.

While the chapters in this book had their origins as a series of independent essays, efforts have been made to make this volume much more than simply a set of freestanding essays on the McDonaldization thesis. For example, repetition of such things as the basic elements of McDonaldization and the fundamental irrationalities associated with it have been eliminated wherever possible. In addition, there is a logic to the chapters and the book in that efforts to explore various aspects of the McDonaldization thesis are followed by a set of chapters which seek to move beyond, and build upon, that thesis. Thus, this book represents both an extension of earlier ideas into a set of new domains and a platform for planned later work on the "new means of consumption," one of which is the fast-food restaurant.

Chris Rojek, both a fellow sociologist and sociology editor at Sage (London), has been instrumental in bringing this book to fruition. Chris's dual roles make him a unique and particularly rewarding person to work with. He is a valued advisor not only on the book business but also on the most advanced sociological ideas. It has been a pleasure working with him on this and related projects. His brother, and chief aide, Robert Rojek has helped in innumerable concrete ways throughout the course of the writing. Stephen Barr, now in overall charge of London operations for Sage, helped to provide a supportive climate in which this book could be completed. Finally, I would like to thank Alan Bryman of Loughborough University for some very insightful comments on the first draft of the book.

1

Introduction:
McDonaldization and Beyond

This volume may well not be exactly what the reader is expecting. The nature of the book, and the connotation of the title, might lead one to believe that what will follow is a series of chapters extending, defending and applying the McDonaldization thesis. While there *are* several chapters devoted to extensions, justifications and applications, this book has turned out to be more of an odyssey that gradually builds upon, but inexorably moves beyond, the McDonaldization thesis. That is not to say that I am abandoning that thesis, but I am using it as a springboard to deal with a wider range of social phenomena and issues.

Previously, I have focused on fast-food restaurants as a fundamental point of origin of McDonaldization (although, as I point out in *The McDonaldization of Society* (Ritzer, 1983, 1993, 1996a), there were a number of precursors to fast-food restaurants that played important roles in the development of this process). I have also dealt with credit cards (in *Expressing America*: Ritzer, 1995), not only as an example of McDonaldization, but also in relation to a general set of problems associated with them. As this book evolves, the reader will come to recognize that I now see both fast-food restaurants and credit cards as but two specific examples of what I now conceive of as the "new means of consumption," a category which also includes shopping malls, mega-malls, superstores, home shopping television networks, cybermalls, infomercials, and many more. As this book progresses, more and more attention will be devoted to the new means of consumption, and fast-food restaurants and credit cards will come to be treated as just two of its manifestations.

This change in focus at the level of the socioeconomic life-world is closely related to a dramatic change in my theoretical orientation. Clearly, my previous work has been strongly modernist. I looked at fast-food restaurants and credit cards as modern phenomenon and adopted modern theoretical perspectives in examining them. For example, I used Weber's theory of rationalization to examine fast-food restaurants and I employed that theory, as well as a number of other modern theories (Simmel's theory of money, Mill's concern with private troubles and public issues, etc.), to analyse credit cards. I even went so far as to describe credit cards, and especially fast-food restaurants, in terms of a quintessentially modern grand narrative of McDonaldization. While I am not eschewing a modernist perspective in these pages, I am exploring the utility of postmodern theoretical tools in analysing the new means of consumption. I am adopting the view that one need not choose between modern and postmodern theory; we can use *both* in order to enhance our understanding of the social world (Ritzer, 1997). The tilt in the direction of a postmodern orientation in these pages is made necessary, at least in part, by the fact that consumption is so closely tied to the postmodern world. Indeed, to many postmodern society *is* a consumer society (Featherstone, 1991). A focus on the new means of consumption calls for a theoretical perspective well suited to analysing consumption in the contemporary world, and postmodern social theory is that perspective.

All of this could be taken to mean that I have come to think of McDonaldization as a less momentous, or an even an insignificant, process that is subordinate to some broader and more important trend. That is *not* what I intend to imply. I continue to see McDonaldization as a centrally important process that persists in growing exponentially and in extending its reach in various domains of the social world as well as geographic areas throughout the globe. I am more impressed than ever by the durability of McDonaldization and by its capacity to adapt to new domains and settings. And I am even more frightened than ever by the negative byproducts of McDonaldization – the various irrationalities of rationality. In short, my interest in, and concern about, McDonaldization continues unabated.

However, this interest has led me in a series of new directions, directions that will be detailed as this book unfolds. I now see that McDonaldization is not only important in its own right, but it is also intimately related to a series of other developments of great importance to American society and the world. In examining these, and how they relate to McDonaldization, I am drawn in a variety of theoretical directions. But, again, the analysis of these other developments using different theoretical tools should not be taken to mean that I somehow have come to see McDonaldization as a less significant process, problem and theoretical orientation.

This chapter will be both an introduction to a few of the major themes in the chapters to follow and an opportunity to reflect on some of their implications for the McDonaldization thesis. However, since the chapters go well beyond the McDonaldization thesis, this introduction will also range far and wide, both empirically and theoretically.

The theoretical starting point for the McDonaldization thesis is, of course, the work of Max Weber on rationalization. Indeed, McDonaldization can be seen as an effort to "modernize" Weber's rationalization thesis. The use of the term McDonaldization reflects my conviction that the fast-food restaurant, rather than Weber's bureaucracy (and the process of bureaucratization), is the better paradigm for that process in the contemporary world. Weber's work provides a rich resource for anyone interested in the rationalization process, and that richness is greatly enhanced by a large and growing body of work by neo-Weberians.

However, rather than further exploring the work of Weber and the neo-Weberians, I have opted in Chapter 2 to explore the implications of Karl

Mannheim's thinking on rationalization for the McDonaldization thesis.[1] There are three reasons for this. First, a great deal has already been done with the Weberian legacy and the return on our investment would likely be minimal. Second, there are deep problems and profound ambiguities in Weberian theory that make further gains problematic. Finally, Mannheim did a fair amount of work on this issue and it remains a relatively untapped resource. While a number of issues are discussed in Chapter 2, the most important for our purposes is the rethinking of the McDonaldization thesis from the vantage point of Mannheim's theory of rationalization and the conceptual arsenal he developed to deal with that process.

While Mannheim has a great deal to offer to one interested in McDonaldization, his work is not an unmixed blessing. On the negative side is the fact that his early ideas bear little resemblance to, and even contradict, his later, more fully developed conceptualizations. Thus, he does not offer a coherent theoretical perspective; one that developed over the course of his work in a clear and consistent manner. His early ideas on rationalization lead the scholar interested in McDonaldization in one direction, while the later ideas would lead in quite a different direction. Another problem is traceable to the fact that Mannheim's thinking is deeply embedded in the disruption and chaos associated with the Depression, the rise of Nazism and World War II. His theory is so historically specific that it does not travel well and there are grave problems when one attempts to apply it to the contemporary world. For example, Mannheim placed great importance on rational centralized planning as the solution to the irrational chaos and disorder through which he had lived. However, what Mannheim failed to recognize (and Weber had understood) is that such rational centralized planning can be the cause, perhaps even the prime cause, of irrationality, especially the various irrationalities of rationality.

Problems aside, Mannheim does offer ideas that enhance our thinking about McDonaldization. For example, in the terms of his later theorizing, the functional rationalization that would be associated with a process like McDonaldization poses a threat to substantial rationality, or the ability to think intelligently. In this, I think that Mannheim is getting at a major aspect of the dehumanization associated with McDonaldization. That is, McDonaldized systems (through rules, regulations, scripts, and so on) do encroach upon, and ultimately threaten, the ability of those involved in them to think intelligently. It is clearly dehumanizing to find oneself mindlessly functioning like a robot or an automaton in a McDonaldized system.

Mannheim's way of dealing with dehumanization is far neater and less ambiguous than Weber's approach, in which formal rationality is seen as threatening the human values he associates with substantive rationality. The fundamental problem in Weber's approach is that the notion of human values is ambiguous. It can encompass not only positive values like love of humanity, but also negative values like racial superiority. Thus, one would *not* necessarily bemoan the loss of human values (say those associated with Nazism), but virtually everyone would agree that the loss of the ability to think for oneself is a human disaster. While Weber seems ultimately to prefer substantive to formal rationality, in some cases the dominance of formal rationality is preferable. For example, Germany and the world would have been far better off if the functionally rational bureaucracy had not come under the control of the Nazis and their value system, but instead had succeeded in suppressing those values and controlling, if not destroying, the Nazis themselves.

In addition to the ideas of functional and substantial rationalization, Mannheim develops the concepts of self-rationalization and self-observation. These represent higher forms of rationalization in which people come to control themselves better rather than being externally controlled. These ideas, like the others offered by Mannheim, are not unambiguously useful in thinking about the contemporary world. On the one hand, they do not mesh well with the process of McDonaldization, at least as far as employees of such systems are concerned. Such employees are adequately controlled through functional rationality; there is little need for, or interest in, having them engage in self-rationalization and self-observation. However, while the clients/customers/patrons of McDonaldized systems are also subject to the constraints of functional rationality, there *is* a need in their case to supplement that control with self-rationalization and self-observation. So, these concepts are helpful, but certainly not in the way that Mannheim imagined.

Instead of the central, societal-wide planning envisioned by Mannheim, we have seen the emergence of central planning within specific domains of the social world. Successful chains like McDonald's do a great deal of central planning and exert considerable control over their franchisees, employees and customers. The fact is that while such planning is narrow and focused, it undoubtedly exerts far more control, and is far more effective, than the kind of control imagined by Mannheim.

This, of course, brings us back to a Weberian image of the Western world in which there are rationalized sectors, but not all sectors are rationalized (at least to a high degree) so it is possible for the individual to escape at times. This is why Weber preferred capitalism to socialism, which he feared would produce a grand, all-encompassing iron cage from which escape was impossible. However, Weber foresaw a future for capitalism in which more and more sectors of society would fall under the sway of rationalization; escape would become increasingly difficult until we ultimately found ourselves in an iron cage. The cage that Weber imagined is currently being constructed, but it is not being built all at once as the communists in various nations tried to do and failed. Rather, various organizations and institutions are following the McDonald's model and each is, as a result, adding a bar to the emerging cage. The iron cage is being built piece by piece, rather than all at once, but it is being built. Furthermore, being built in this way, it may be stronger, more escape-proof, than even Weber imagined.

Chapter 3 involves, among other things, an application of the McDonaldization thesis to a most unlikely setting – the field of sociology. While we find it easy to understand that fast-food restaurants, or hotels or amusement parks have been McDonaldized, the idea that an academic field like sociology (and sociology is certainly not the only academic field to undergo this process) has been McDonaldized seems hard to accept. After all, academia should be one of the domains that ought to be immune to, or able to resist, McDonaldization. The fact that it (as well as medicine (Ritzer and Walczak, 1988) and law) has been McDonaldized demonstrates the power and reach of the process. This is not to say that sociology has become *as* McDonaldized as, say, fast-food restaurants, but it has become McDonaldized to some degree. This reminds us of the important point that McDonaldization is not an all-or-nothing process; there are degrees of McDonaldization.

This variation can take a number of forms. At the broadest level there are differences in the overall degree of McDonaldization. More narrowly, there is variation in the degree of efficiency (highly efficient to inefficient), predictability (certain to completely unpredictable), calculability (completely reducible to numbers to totally qualitative), and control (fully controllable to uncontrollable). In addition, the irrationalities of rationality can range from totally irrational to hardly any irrationalities at all.

Within sociology, theory is one of the least likely elements to be McDonaldized, yet it too has undergone that process, at least to some extent. We have here another demonstration of the expansionism inherent in McDonaldization. It is relatively easy to understand how statistically oriented empirical research can be McDonaldized (its practitioners are attracted to standardized methods and techniques; it is more team oriented). It is also easy to see why textbooks in sociology (and every other field) fall prey to McDonaldization. But sociological theory? Isn't creative theorizing inherently safe from the mind-numbing routines of McDonaldization? Clearly, the answer is no and the fact that it is not demonstrates how that process sweeps through one domain after another, not only the unlikely field of sociology, but the even more unlikely sub-field of sociological theory.

Another aspect of the expansionism of McDonaldization is its movement from its American roots into other nations. We will encounter this issue again soon, and in Chapter 4 it assumes center stage in the form of a discussion of the concern raised by a German social theorist – Richard Münch – about the McDonaldization of European social theory. Again, this seems surprising. American social theory would appear to be immune to McDonaldization, but one might argue that, well, it is American and therefore more prone to fall victim to this quintessentially "American disease." But European, especially German, social theory? How could a tradition that includes such illustrious thinkers as Marx, Nietzsche, Weber, Simmel and Habermas be threatened by McDonaldization? Yet Münch, himself a noted contemporary German social theorist, fears just such a process and acknowledges that it has already occurred to some degree. Again, one is brought face to face with the question: if something like German social theory is not safe from McDonaldization, then what is?

The answer, of course, is that nothing is safe from McDonaldization as long as there are material interests that push it and stand to benefit from its expansion. In social theory, it is the American creators of what Münch calls "standardized" theory who stand to gain power, prestige and influence if theorists throughout the world come to practice theory in that way. It is they who would become the leaders of this world social theory; they who would become celebrities invited to lecture around the globe on the glories of their approach. More typically, it is economic interests that impel McDonaldization. Those who push it stand to make money, even grow fabulously wealthy, if they can export McDonaldization to previously untouched sectors of society or areas of the world. The only real barrier to McDonaldization is a lack of resources on the part of those who are not McDonaldized. If those pushing McDonaldization have nothing to gain in certain areas, then they will not pursue it in those domains. The poorest areas in the world, and the social venues with little to offer, remain, at least for the time being, safe from McDonaldization. However, as the most rewarding areas become saturated by the process, one can envision a time when even the impoverished domains will seem attractive new venues.

While those sympathetic to the McDonaldization thesis (and thereby sensitive to the irrationalities of McDonaldization) might applaud the absence of the process in these "impoverished" areas,[2] we should not ignore the fact that the denizens of such areas may well feel deprived by the absence of McDonaldization. After all, it has come to be something that is valued in all sectors of society and throughout the world. Those who have not been affected are likely to clamor for the McDonaldization of their societies. However, that is not likely to occur, at least in the short run, or until such time as they are in a position to make it worthwhile to the forces that impel the process.

There is no conspiracy being implied here. Leaders from various arenas are not meeting in secret at Hamburger University to plot the next move in the expansion of McDonaldization. Rather, a number of different individuals, groups and organizations have independently come to recognize that they stand to profit handsomely from the expansion and exportation of McDonaldization. In pursuing their self-interests, they are furthering McDonaldization.

A much less counterintuitive application of the McDonaldization thesis than those made to sociology and social theory involves the jobs and the labor process discussed in Chapter 5. Clearly, the McDonaldization process leads to the creation of what can be termed "McJobs." Such occupations are most obviously found in fast-food restaurants and similar chains, but they are also being found increasingly throughout the work world. As more and more sectors are McDonaldized, they seek to rationalize the work that takes place within them. This brings us more broadly to a concern with the labor process and the literature that deals with that issue, most notably the tradition based on the thinking of Karl Marx and later Harry Braverman. A major weakness in this literature is its narrow focus on the labor process.

McDonaldization permits us to overcome that weakness by examining the labor process within the context of a larger social process.

Such a perspective allows us to shed new light on the labor process. For example, Braverman and his followers have tended to focus on the role played by managerial control in the labor process. However, McDonaldization tends to emphasize other kinds of control. For example, since McDonaldization and its various components have become part of the larger value system, potential employees have internalized many of its expectations long before they take a McJob. They know what they are expected to do and, what is more, they believe in it. As a result, there is relatively little need for managers to control them. More importantly, McDonaldized systems build control into various non-human technologies. It is these technologies, not managers, that control employees. Under this heading we can include such technologies as the drink dispensers that shut off automatically when a cup is full and the french-fry machines that automatically lift baskets out of the hot oil when the fries reach just the right degree of crispiness. With such technologies, there is relatively little need for direct control by managers.

But perhaps the major contribution of the McDonaldization thesis to our understanding of the labor process is the fact that it reveals how patrons/customers/clients have become part of the labor process in McDonaldized systems. We can no longer make a clear distinction between worker and patron. Patrons have become unpaid workers who perform tasks that would otherwise have to be done by paid employees. And since they are part of our McDonaldized society they, like paid workers, generally know what is expected of them and they generally do it (e.g. disposing of their own debris after a meal). In fact, they do it largely on their own, willingly, even almost joyously. Through the McDonaldization process the capitalist has created a new secondary workforce to be exploited in order to enhance profits. In fact, the exploitation of customers greatly exceeds that of workers. Workers must be paid at least a minimum wage that serves to reduce the owner's profits. Customers are paid nothing and *everything* they can be cajoled into doing serves to increase profitability.

In Chapters 6 and 7 the focus shifts to other key aspects of the expansion of McDonaldization under the headings of Americanization and globalization. McDonaldization is certainly not the first process associated with the United States that has elicited anti-American feelings throughout much of the world, especially Europe. In fact, there is a long tradition of a powerful love–hate relationship with the United States and its most distinctive products. To some, they become targets of anti-Americanism, while they are eagerly adopted by many others. A good example of a predecessor to McDonaldization is the interest in, and concern over, coca-colonization that occurred in France in the 1940s (Kuisel, 1993). Here was another American product that was feared and reviled by many, but ultimately embraced by a large proportion of the French population.

However, McDonaldization does represent something quite new in terms of the threat it poses to other cultures. In the past, threats have come from either distinctively American products (like Coca-Cola) or from American business practices (e.g. those associated with Frederick W. Taylor and scientific management). Unlike most of its predecessors, McDonald's embodies *both* threats simultaneously.[3] It threatens to swamp Europe (and the other continents) with Big Macs *and* it brings with it a series of innovations in business practices (e.g. new ways of managing the labor process; of running a huge international operation with a minimal central organization). Furthermore, it is introducing not just a particular set of foods but, much more importantly, the distinctively American way of eating – the idea that food is something to be consumed as quickly, efficiently and inexpensively as possible. Eating is at the heart of most cultures and for many it is something on which much time, attention and money are lavished. In attempting to alter the way people eat, McDonaldization poses a profound threat to the entire cultural complex of many societies. It is little wonder that McDonald's and its many clones have become a focus of anti-Americanism. What is more surprising is that so many people in so many societies are so eager to embrace McDonald's and the process it epitomizes.

Globalization raises similar issues, as well as a number of distinctive ones. Globalization theory has been characterized by its focus on largely autonomous global processes and its adherents have argued that these have become far more important than the practices of any given nation or geographic territory. Theorists associated with this perspective have been especially eager to downplay the role of the United States, and the West in general, in global processes. Related to this has been a rejection of modernization theory with its interest in the ways in which nations throughout the world seek to modernize by emulating the highly developed Western nations.

However, the McDonaldization process points to the fact that globalization theorists have overdone it and ignored the continuing importance of a given nation, in this case the United States, and its economic and cultural products. McDonaldization is, at least to this point, a largely one-way process in which a series of American innovations are being aggressively exported to much of the rest of the world. While there will undoubtedly come a time when other nations produce large numbers of McDonaldized products and systems of their own, at the moment these represent barely a trickle. In our rush to emphasize independent global processes, the McDonaldization thesis indicates the continuing importance of a single nation (the United States), as well as of Americanization and Westernization.

At one level, Chapter 8 is a straightforward application of the McDonaldization thesis to credit cards. The fundamental argument is that credit cards have McDonaldized the process of obtaining and expending loans. More important, at least from the point of view of this book, is the fact that it is here that we begin the move away from a consideration of McDonaldization *per se* and toward an interest in the new means of consumption. While it is an extremely useful idea (at least to me), McDonaldization does not exhaust what we can say about fast-food restaurants and it only scratches the surface as far as credit cards are concerned.

Beyond being the paradigm for McDonaldization, the fast-food restaurant is also one of the new means of consumption leading people to consume food in new and different ways. The credit card is even more significant in this respect. Like the fast-food restaurant, the credit card leads to new and different modes of consumption. But while there is a limited number of foods one can consume in a fast-food restaurant, the credit card permits the consumption of an unlimited range of goods and services. In fact, the credit card might better be seen as a meta-means of consumption, permitting people to use all means of consumption. In this sense, the credit card is far and away the most important of the new means of consumption.

In Chapter 9 we deal explicitly with the wide range of new means of consumption. To the fast-food restaurant and the credit card are now added shopping malls, mega-malls, television shopping networks and cybermalls. America, which is the source of the fast-food restaurant and the credit card, is also the primary source of virtually all of the other new means of consumption. The United States has gone from being the world leader in innovations in production to dominating the world in terms of the creation of new means of consumption. And just as at one time it sought to dominate the world's production, it now seeks to control worldwide consumption by, among other things, creating and exporting these new means of consumption. The creation and exportation of fast-food restaurants and credit cards is part of this wide-ranging process.

If production is associated with modern society, consumption, as we have seen, is often considered the hallmark of postmodern society. Whether or not this assertion is correct, it leads us to a consideration of postmodern social theory as a way of looking at these new means of consumption. This is not to say that they cannot be analysed from a modern point of view; indeed that is what is done in the first eight chapters of this book. However, it is also possible to analyse all of the new means of consumption from a postmodern perspective and that is just what is undertaken in Chapter 9 (and throughout much of the rest of the book). Modern and postmodern social theory can complement one another by leading to different kinds of insights into the same social phenomena.

A number of postmodern ideas are employed in this analysis. To take one example, the new means of consumption are well characterized as what Baudrillard and other postmodernists call simulacra. That is, instead of "real" human interaction and "authentic" products, the new means of consumption tend to be characterized by simulated interactions and products. Thus, the people who serve us in fast-food restaurants, on the phone on behalf of our credit card companies, in the malls, and as telemarketers are all, as a general rule, interacting with us in an inauthentic way. The likelihood is that they have been asked to memorize a series of scripts and sub-scripts and mindlessly recite them at appropriate points in their interaction with us. For our part as patrons, we understand what they are doing and we respond by developing a set of mindless recipes (Schutz, 1932/1967) that we trot out and use in such situations. Interaction is taking place, but it is a simulation and certainly not what we usually think of as genuine human interaction.

Much the same thing can be said about the goods and services offered by the new means of consumption. A perfect example of a simulated product is McDonald's Chicken McNugget. The executives at McDonald's have determined that the authentic chicken,[4] with its skin, gristle and bones, is simply not the kind of product that McDonald's ought to be selling; hence the creation of the Chicken McNugget which can be seen as inauthentic, as a simulacrum. There is no "real" or even "original" Chicken McNugget; they are, and can only be, simulacra. Services can also be simulated. For example, at chains like H&R Block employees offer tax advice and fill out tax forms, often on the basis of a brief training course. In comparison to what may be obtained from a trained and experienced accountant, they can be seen as offering a simulated tax service.

Chapter 10 extends this analysis to a specific sub-type of the new means of consumption, what might be called the new means of tourism. I have in mind here such things as Disney World and other amusement parks, cruise lines, and Las Vegas-type hotel-casinos. Once again we are in a world in which the United States has been a pioneer. In addition, we are in a world that is amenable not only to modern, but also to postmodern, analysis. And from a postmodern perspective the new means of tourism are, like the new means of consumption, well described as simulacra.

This is nowhere clearer than in Disney World. Here virtually all of the rides and attractions unabashedly offer simulations of what was once (and still may be) available in the real world. Furthermore, the employees at Disney World, like their brethren employed by the other new means of consumption (and tourism), interact with us in a simulated, inauthentic way. That is, they follow scripts and have been thoroughly schooled in how to interact with visitors. Not only is Disney a perfect example of the new means of tourism, but it has played the same kind of role in tourism that McDonald's plays in consumption. That is, its success has made it the paradigm within the tourist realm. As a result, it is possible to talk of the "McDisneyization" of tourism.[5]

The idea of the new means of consumption is extended still further in Chapter 11 to what has been termed "McUniversity" (Parker and Jary, 1995; Prichard and Willmott, 1996). Students and their parents are increasingly approaching the university as consumers in much the same way that they approach the new means of consumption like mega-malls. They are looking for things like low price, convenience, efficiency, absence of hassles, and so on. The university is being conceived of as a means of educational consumption. The problem is that the university is a creaky, highly traditional institution that pales in comparison to all of the sparkling new means of consumption. Potential applicants and their parents are comparing the university to these new means and it is generally being found wanting.

With shrinking resources, universities are growing desperate to attract and retain students. To do so, they are going to have to find a variety of new products and techniques. While they could theoretically create many of these on their own, the likelihood is that they will seek to learn from the highly successful new means of consumption. For example, university officials are learning a lesson learned long ago by leaders of many of these new means. Instead of sitting back and waiting for students, they are finding it necessary to go where the students are. For example, following the model of successful chains, more and more universities are opening satellite campuses, often in suburban areas or smaller towns not well served by a central university. These satellites may be found in industrial parks and shopping malls and they adopt many of the trappings of the new means of consumption (e.g. plenty of close-in parking so that students can get in and out quickly). Similarly, universities are using some of the advanced technology associated with the new means of consumption (especially television home shopping networks and cybermalls) by beaming courses to television sets or computers in satellite campuses or even in student homes. (Thus, like Domino's, universities are increasingly in the business of home delivery. Instead of pizzas, they are delivering an education.)

Obviously, such developments serve to radically alter the nature of both education and teaching. Sitting in a satellite classroom or at home and staring at a TV or computer screen is a very different educational experience from interacting directly with a professor in a classroom. Similarly, teaching by TV or computer involves a variety of very different skills and abilities. While a few teachers may become media superstars, most are likely to see their positions become more like McJobs. For example, satellite campuses may employ part-time, poorly paid adjuncts to lead class discussions following the video transmission of a superstar's lecture.

Being conveyed in all of this is a sense not only of enormous social change, but also of a series of social problems associated with these changes. Chapter 12 is devoted to a discussion of various methods of coping with the new means of consumption. I have dealt with this issue in the past from a modern point of view in terms of coping with problems associated with fast-food restaurants, credit cards and other McDonaldized systems. However, a postmodern perspective appears to pose problems to one interested in responses to problematic situations. This is traceable to the fact that postmodernists are often seen as nihilistic, and nihilists have little or no interest in coping mechanisms.

However, it turns out that postmodern social theory is a useful source of rather unusual ideas about responding to the new means of consumption. For example, it can be argued that the problem with the new means is that they are disenchanted. So it is necessary to bring some enchantment to them. Instead of the mechanical exchange of goods for money, we are urged to engage in a genuine, human and truly reciprocal exchange with those who serve us. A wide range of things need to be exchanged (including feelings and emotions) and such an exchange needs to be continuous and reciprocal. Another possibility would be to heap gifts upon those who work in the new means of consumption. Used to giving out goods and services, they are unlikely to know how to respond to receiving gifts. Such gifts bring a new, enchanted dimension to relationships within these settings.

In the concluding chapter we return to a focal concern with the process of McDonaldization. Several new issues are raised including the possibility that we may already be witnessing the de-McDonaldization of society. Then there is a discussion of the relationship between McDonaldization and social stratification on the basis of class, race, gender and age. Also considered is the relationship between McDonaldization and commercialization. The book concludes with a discussion of the fate of McDonaldization in a postmodern society.

A good deal of substantive ground is covered in this book as we move from fast-food restaurants to the means of consumption, from McDonaldization to the implications of those new means for the social world (and back). At another level this book is a journey through many of the leading ideas in sociological and social theory: it is a theoretical and even in some places a metatheoretical odyssey. While this may sound surprising given the highly applied and down-to-earth character of *The McDonaldization of Society*, as well as *Expressing America*, from a different vantage point it is perfectly consistent with most of my other work, which has been highly theoretical and metatheoretical (Ritzer, 1975/1980, 1981, 1991). The following are some of the major theoretical issues dealt with in this book:

- The ideas of a classic, but often ignored, social theorist – Karl Mannheim – are revived and analysed metatheoretically for what they can tell us about McDonaldization.
- The concept of McDonaldization is used as the basis for a metasociological analysis of the discipline as a whole and a metatheoretical analysis of American and European social theory.
- Micro–macro and agency–structure theory is used, specifically in the form of C. Wright Mills's concern with private troubles and public issues, to analyse problems associated with credit cards.
- The Marx–Braverman theory of the labor process is re-examined in light of the rise of McJobs associated with McDonaldized systems.
- Theories of Americanization and globalization are examined in light of the McDonaldization thesis.
- All of the modern theoretical perspectives enumerated above are supplemented by the use of postmodern social theory to analyse the new means of consumption, tourism and education.

In one way or another, this book not only touches on some centrally important developments in the social world, but in doing so also draws upon and engages many of the most important theoretical ideas of the day.

A "Methodological" Note

A social scientist reading this book will note that the format is much like that of a traditional academic monograph. Such a reader with a theoretical bent will notice that there are citations to some of the most dense and sophisticated works in social theory. However, what is clearly missing to even the most casual observer is a series of citations to social scientific research on the topics dealt with in these pages. That is not because I bear some animus in relation to such work, but rather because there is little or no "scientific" research into the topics being dealt with here. Scientifically oriented social researchers have tended not to be interested in the kinds of topics discussed in these pages. Relatively little attention has been paid to topics like fast-food restaurants or credit cards. The more general issue of consumption has received a lot more attention, but *not* by Americans, especially those with a strong social scientific orientation. The sociology of consumption is dominated by European social scientists, especially those from Great Britain. And they tend *not* to approach the issue of consumption from the kind of positivistic standpoint so popular in American social science.

There is great irony here. The United States is the driving force in world consumption and the instigator of most of the major changes in it. However, America's social scientists have devoted virtually no attention to the issue that is virtually the defining characteristic of contemporary American society. This inattention is certainly true of the major topics dealt with here – fast-food restaurants, credit cards, and the other new means of consumption (shopping malls and cruise lines, for example). Accounting for why American social scientists have ignored these questions, and consumption more generally, would probably require a book in itself. Two factors seem most obvious. First, American social scientists, like other Americans, live in the midst of the consumer society and have therefore become desensitized to it as a social phenomenon and issue. Those in other nations tend to see it as a foreign intrusion, even invasion, with origins in the United States, so are more likely to be sensitive to, even jarred by, changes in the world of consumption. After all, many of those changes represent highly American incursions into their indigenous cultures.

This point is beautifully illustrated by the cover painting on the Czech translation of *The McDonaldization of Society*.[6] It depicts a tank in the form of a giant cheeseburger on wheels sporting a cannon against the background of an ancient European town studded with steeples. The sky is an ominous red. The "tank" is rumbling down a cobblestone street both sides of which are lined with people armed with swords. Most of the people are clones (all are wearing dark glasses) and they are leaning on their swords which are pointing down to the ground. They have clearly surrendered to the invasion (do the dark glasses imply that they are blind (to the invasion)?), if not collaborating with the enemy. The only signs of resistance are a seemingly pregnant woman brandishing a sword above her head and a barking dog straining at a leash held by a little girl. It would be difficult to envision such a depiction on the cover of an American version of *McDonaldization*.

Second, topics like consumption, and more specifically fast-food restaurants and credit cards, seem too "trivial" to most American social scientists. The "serious" questions in the economic realm have, since the inception of the discipline, revolved around the issue of production. Examples include Marx on the capitalists and their workers, Weber on the effect of the Protestant Ethic on producers and workers, and Durkheim on the division of labor.[7] While many European social scientists have been able to overcome this productivist bias, this has not been true of the vast majority of their American counterparts.

One would hope for more such social scientific research (not only American, but throughout the world) into the issues of concern in this book. However, even if there is more research of this type, it is still likely to play a secondary role in any works that resemble this one. That is because of the fact, at least part, that it takes too long for a social scientist to identify a problem within this (or any) domain, plan a research project, prepare a submission for (and hopefully get) a research grant, carry out the research, analyse the results, write them up, have an article accepted by a journal and then ultimately published and hopefully read. The topical nature of the subjects dealt with throughout this book makes it necessary that one deal with *the* most recent developments. Research articles, and even worse research monographs, are not good vehicles for learning about the most recent developments in the social world and especially in the domains analysed throughout these pages. As a result, a good deal of the material for this book comes from trade publications, popular books, magazines and newspapers. How can such questionable, journalistic works yield a project to which any self-respecting social scientist would give any credence?

The most positivistic of researchers would, of course, accord such a work little, if any, significance. However, obviously I do think it has much merit, even some social scientific utility. In any case, it simply could not be done, for the reasons discussed above, if one were to rely on scientific research. One who wants to do this kind of work, especially if one wants to range broadly, must rely on the kinds of journalistic sources employed here. However, those sources are not being used as resources for, or statements of, fact. Rather, they are being used to keep one abreast of, informed about, the most recent developments in the social world. They are employed as indicators of various developments, and not as sources of the "truth" about them.

These "data" are material on which to theorize about the social world, especially very recent developments in the realm of consumption. Thus, this book is not necessarily about "truth." It is primarily a theoretical analysis of the changing nature of the social world as reported by, and filtered through, the mainly popular sources employed here. Neither social theory nor popular sources, to say nothing of their combined use, is about truth. They are about creating perspectives that offer new and hopefully profound insights into the nature of the social world. McDonaldization is one such perspective, but many others are developed throughout these pages such as "McDisneyization" and the "new means of consumption." The success of these ideas, and those like them, depends upon whether the reader, and ultimately the larger scholarly community, finds them insightful, useful, and perhaps even the basis for social scientific research. Works like these are to be judged by their theoretical output and not by the nature of the empirical input.

Notes

1. Mannheim could, of course, be considered in some senses a neo-Weberian.

2. In a very real sense, it could be argued that it is the McDonaldized sectors that are truly impoverished.

3. The Ford Motor Company at the turn of the twentieth century posed a similar double-barreled threat (Ford automobiles and Fordist business practices), but Ford cars proved far less mobile than McDonald's hamburgers.

4. Itself, a simulation in this era of factory farming.

5. Las Vegas is another such paradigm and, as we will see, one hears talk these days of the "Las Vegasization" of various aspects of the social world.

6. George Ritzer, *Mcdonaldizace spolecnosti*. Praha: Czech Republic, 1996.

7. The major exception among the classic theorists to this is Georg Simmel and his work on issues like money and the tragedy of culture, both of which can be seen as having much more to do with consumption than production. Veblen, of course, would be another exception, but he is not usually accorded the status granted to Marx, Weber, Durkheim and Simmel.

I
THEORETICAL ISSUES

2

Mannheim's Theory of Rationalization: An Alternative Resource for the McDonaldization Thesis?

Max Weber's (1921/1958, 1921/1968) theory of rationalization lies at the base of the McDonaldization thesis (Kalberg, 1980; Levine, 1981). While that theory provides a rich resource, there are reasons why one might want to look elsewhere for additional theoretical inspiration. For one thing, Weber was far from clear about the rationalization process. One needs to extract a sense of what he meant by it from some often vague definitions of concepts, as well as from his diverse, even divergent, analyses of the various ways in which rationalization played itself out in a variety of domains (religion, polity, law, music, and so on). For another, the wealth of Weberian theory has been exploited to a large degree and further returns on one's investment are likely to diminish. Finally, explorations of other relevant theoretical resources might, at this point, prove far more fruitful in terms of deepening our understanding of rationalization and McDonaldization.

The theory that suggests itself most strongly is Karl Mannheim's thinking on rationality and rationalization. Mannheim's work is based, at least in part, on Weber's ideas (as well as on another under-utilized resource, Simmel's thinking on rationality (Turner, 1986)), but it also goes beyond them in certain ways. In this chapter I want to examine Mannheim's thinking about rationalization, contrast it to Weber's where necessary, and explore the ways in which it does or does not enrich our understanding of the McDonaldization process.

Mannheim's Early Thinking on Rationalization

In *Ideology and Utopia* (1929/1936) Mannheim offered a gross distinction between rationality and irrationality which he both refined and altered dramatically in his later work. This early thinking is reviewed here more as background to, and contrast for, what is to come in a discussion of

Mannheim's later work than for its importance to our focal concerns in this chapter.

At this early stage, the rational sphere of society was defined as "consisting of settled and routinized procedures in dealing with situations that recur in an orderly fashion" (Mannheim, 1929/1936: 113). Such "settled and routinized procedures" are a central component of McDonaldization; McDonaldized systems generally institute such procedures in order to control what employees, customers and many others (e.g. suppliers) do. And those procedures exist in order to deal with recurrent situations (e.g. the ordering of goods or services by customers). To take one example, the following is the original McDonald's procedure for cooking hamburgers:

> Grill men . . . *were instructed* to put hamburgers down on the grill moving from left to right, creating *six rows of six* patties each. And because the first two rows were farthest from the heating element, they were *instructed* (and still are) to flip the third row first, then the fourth, fifth, and sixth before flipping the first two. (Love, 1986: 141–2; italics added)

Employees who follow these procedures are behaving rationally, at least in terms of Mannheim's early sense of such behavior.

Mannheim defines the irrational sphere residually: the irrational must be those domains in which there is an *absence* of settled, routinized procedures for dealing with recurrent situations. Again, from the contemporary perspective, McDonaldization, given its association with such procedures, serves to reduce and ultimately eliminate irrational domains. The objective is to create more and more such procedures to cover as many recurrent situations as possible. (In Weberian terms, the construction of the iron cage of rationality would be complete when all such situations are covered by procedures.) That irrationality which persists is most likely to be found in non-recurrent situations as well as more generally in less and non-McDonaldized sectors of society.

Mannheim (1929/1936: 115) made it clear that at least in his day the irrational spheres continued to predominate over the rational sectors of society: "rationalized as our life may seem to have become, all the rationalizations that have taken place so far are merely partial since the most important realms of our social life are even now anchored in the irrational." While this may still be true, the progress of McDonaldization indicates that the irrational sphere has been reduced, at least to some degree, since Mannheim wrote.

Mannheim discussed several sectors in which he felt irrationality continued to predominate. The economy was still dominated by what he considered to be irrational free competition. Similarly, in the stratification system, one's place continued to be determined by irrational competition and struggle, not by rational objective tests that decided one's position within that system. And in politics, rational planning had not yet been able to eliminate the irrational struggle for dominance at the national and international levels. For Mannheim, the solution to the problem of irrationality lay in greater planning.[1] Planning would provide the routinized and settled procedures (as well as the objective tests needed in the stratification system) that would make greater rationalization possible. While Mannheim was thinking about central planning, McDonaldized systems involve much more, albeit far less centralized, planning than non-McDonaldized alternatives and thereby limit irrationality more effectively.

While the irrational continues to predominate, Mannheim seems to imply (as I do with the McDonaldization thesis) that rationalization is a process that has invaded various sectors of society and that others are likely to come under its sway in the future. In other words, the irrational is likely to retreat in the face of the forward progress of the rational. As Mannheim (1929/1936: 114) puts it, "The chief characteristic of modern culture is the tendency to include as much as possible in the realm of the rational and to bring it under administrative control – and, on the other hand, to reduce the 'irrational' element to the vanishing point."

Mannheim was forced to back away from this optimistic view in his later work in the face of the increasing prevalence of such irrationalities as economic depression, war and Fascism. It became difficult to argue that irrationalities were disappearing. If anything, the opposite seemed to be the case. As we will see, Mannheim came to feel that rationality could not be left to advance on its own, but had to be helped along through planning. Furthermore, as he refined and even altered his sense of rationality, he saw that the progress of at least one type of rationality might in fact be a major *cause* of at least some of these irrationalities (more on this below).

At this early stage in Mannheim's work, rationalization involves behavior that is in accord with some rational structure or framework. Rational actors follow definite prescriptions "entailing no personal decision whatsoever" (Mannheim, 1929/1936: 115). The image is of the actor following the dictates of some larger bureaucratically organized structure (the source of the "administrative control," the settled and routinized procedures, mentioned above) and this image is supported by the examples offered by Mannheim – petty officials, judges and factory workers. As a result of the time in which he wrote, Mannheim (like Weber) overemphasizes the importance of bureaucracies, at least from our contemporary vantage point. McDonald's (as well as most franchisers), for example, has a minimal bureaucratic staff and structure, but it nonetheless has been able to develop and implement "settled and routinized procedures" that it imposes on franchisees, managers and employees. While it is not well described as a bureaucracy, McDonald's has succeeded in developing methods that leave its employees with little or no room for personal decision making.

Mannheim contrasts rational action to *conduct* which begins "where rationalization has not yet penetrated, and where we are forced to make decisions in situations which have *as yet* not been subjected to regulation" (Mannheim, 1929/1936: 115; italics added). In this early work, conduct is associated with the irrational realm and Mannheim holds the view that conduct, like irrationality more generally, will sooner or later come to be limited or even be eliminated by the process of rationalization. In these terms, what McDonaldized systems have succeeded in doing is to greatly restrict "conduct." Rules, regulations, scripts and the like have increased significantly the regulation of the behavior of those associated with McDonaldized systems. Thus, in Mannheim's terms, at least in this early stage in his work, McDonaldization brings with it a decline in irrationality.

There is a conundrum in Mannheim's early thinking on the process of rationalization. On the one hand, he clearly favors the progressive rationalization of sectors that had hitherto been dominated by the irrational. Since they will come to be controlled by administrative dictates, irrational decisions and actions will be reduced or eliminated. On the other hand, can Mannheim really want a world in which all decisions are controlled? in which there is no personal decision making, no personal freedom, whatsoever? We will return to this issue when we discuss Mannheim's views on planning, but before we do we need to get a sense of his later analysis of the nature of rationality (and irrationality).

Mannheim's Later Thinking on Rationality

Mannheim had much more to say about rationality and irrationality, and he said it very differently, in *Man and Society in an Age of Reconstruction* (1935/1940). Mannheim's thinking on rationality had grown far more refined; he differentiated between two types of rationality and two varieties of irrationality. He argued that both rationality and irrationality can be subdivided into the "substantial" and the "functional" (paralleling, at least to some degree, Weber's distinction between substantive and formal rationality). Substantial rationality and irrationality deal with thinking, while functional rationality and irrationality are concerned with action. In this section we will deal with his greatly revised thoughts on rationality, while in the next section we will analyse his similarly modified thinking on irrationality.

Substantial rationality is defined as "an act of *thought* which reveals *intelligent insight* into the inter-relations of events in a given situation" (Mannheim, 1935/1940: 53; italics added). This is clearly very different from the gross definition of rationality adopted in Mannheim's earlier work. Here rationality involves intelligent thought whereas previously his more global sense of rationality (closer to what he now thinks of as functional rationality; see p. 21) implied an almost complete lack of thought.

Substantial rationality is a micro-subjective concept relating purely to individual thought processes (although the larger social setting is clearly implied through the notion of the situation in which the thought takes place).[2] In contrast, Weber's parallel concept of substantive rationality, or the choice of means to ends in the context of larger values, is multi-dimensional. It involves micro-objective action (the choice) and macro-subjective values, as well as, at least implicitly, micro-subjective thought processes leading to the choice of means to ends. Weber's conceptualization is much richer, but that very richness creates problems for those who seek to use it.

The multi-dimensionality of Weber's conceptualization makes it "messy" in the sense that it combines both micro (action, and perhaps thought) and macro (values) elements within one concept. It also does not specify the nature of the relationship between its two (or three, depending on how you count them) elements, especially how much control values exercise over choices, as well as the relationship between thought and action.

Mannheim's substantial rationality is a far neater concept operating purely at the micro-subjective level in terms of individual thought and insight. As a result, there is none of the kind of ambiguity that exists in Weber's parallel concept. There is no need for Mannheim to specify micro–macro relationships, nor the linkage between thought (micro-subjectivity) and action (micro-objectivity), within the concept of substantial rationalization. The simplicity of Mannheim's conceptualization is an asset, especially if one wants to link, as both Mannheim and Weber do, substantive rationality to other concepts, especially functional (or formal) rationality. Because it encompasses several different levels of analysis, Weber's sense of substantive rationality is difficult to relate to, say, formal rationality. Is one relating thought, action, values, or some combination of the three to formal rationality? Depending on which aspect one is linking to formal rationality, one is likely to come up with very different conclusions about the nature of that relationship. On the other hand, given Mannheim's limited conceptualization, it is clear that one is concerned with the impact of substantially rational thought processes on functionally rational systems and the corresponding effect of those systems on such thinking.

The issue of the nature of this relationship is of great importance because in many ways Weber prefers substantive rationality with its human values to formal rationality in which choices are constrained by inhuman rules, regulations and structures. However, because of the complexity of his conceptualization, it is unclear exactly what Weber prefers – substantively rational thought? action? or the larger human values that predominate in substantive rationality? For another, assuming, as most do, that it is the latter, it is very difficult to come down unequivocally on the side of substantive rationality over formal rationality. The problem here is that substantive rationality, in which larger human values predominate, has the potential to lead to far greater inhumanity than formal rationality. History is rife with examples of human destruction that have been animated by so-called human values. Nazism had many such values and some of them led people to take actions that resulted in the destruction of several million people (Bauman, 1989).

While Mannheim, too, prefers substantial rationality, or at least worries about its fate in light of the growth of functional rationality, it lacks the negative possibilities that inhere in Weber's substantive rationality. Indeed, it could be argued that "intelligent insight" would militate against such value-driven excesses as the Nazi Holocaust. Thoughtful, intelligent people would, one assumes, have been better able to see where Nazi values were taking Germany and this would have led them to oppose such a course of action.

Whatever their differences, as well as their relative strengths and weaknesses, both Weber's substantive rationality and Mannheim's substantial rationality are threatened by the development and spread of McDonaldization. We will return to this issue below.

Mannheim comes closer to his earlier, more global sense of rationality in his definition of *functional rationality* as "a series of actions . . . organized in such a way that it leads to a previously defined goal, every element in this series of actions receiving a functional position and role" (Mannheim, 1935/1940: 53). The series of actions is functionally rational in that each has a role to play in the achievement of the ultimate goal, although the goal itself can be either rational or irrational. For example, salvation is defined as an irrational goal, but it can be sought through a series of functionally rational actions. McDonaldized systems are functionally rational with all elements occupying a functional position in a series of actions leading to the objective, say the sale of large numbers of hamburgers to the public.

Mannheim's concept of functional rationality has much in common with Weber's sense of formal rationality. For example, efficiency is a central characteristic of formal rationality from Weber's point of view, and Mannheim (1935/1940: 53) argues that a "functional organization of a series of actions will, moreover, be at its best when, in order to attain the given goal, it co-ordinates the means most efficiently."

However, Weber's concept of formal rationality has disadvantages in comparison to Mannheim's sense of functional rationality and is even messier than his (Weber's) conceptualization of substantive rationality. Like substantive rationality, formal rationality combines micro and macro elements. However, in comparison to substantive rationality which deals solely with values at the macro level, the macro level in formal rationality encompasses "rules, laws and regulations," as well as the macro-objective structures (e.g. bureaucracies) in which they exist. This opens up the possibility of many more interrelationships between the macro and micro and therefore creates even greater ambiguity in the concept. This ambiguity is heightened by Weber's failure to specify the nature of the relationships implied in his multi-faceted conceptualization of formal rationality.

As with substantial rationality, Mannheim's concept of functional rationality has advantages over Weber's parallel conceptualization, especially in its greater clarity and simplicity. Mannheim is working, at least explicitly, at the micro level, this time in terms of micro-objective actions that are arranged in a series with each action receiving a functional position and role. An organization, with rules and regulations, is implied here, but unlike Weber's definition of formal rationality (where do the rules, laws and regulations exist if not in organizations?), it is not integral to the definition.

To Mannheim, as they were to Weber, functional and substantial rationality may be substitutes for, or even in conflict with, one another. For example, the "grill man" described earlier may act in accord with the functional organization of the fast-food restaurant without thinking through the various steps involved in grilling a hamburger. In fact, a functional organization like the fast-food restaurant generally wants its employees to act in accord with its dictates and not to think through such steps on their own; in other words, it ordinarily does not want them to practice substantive rationality.

Mannheim argues that industrialization has led to an increase in functional rationalization, but not necessarily substantial rationalization. In fact, he goes further by arguing that functional rationalization has tended to "paralyse" substantial rationalization by leaving people less and less room to utilize their independent judgment. This seems to be Mannheim's version of Weber's irrationality of rationality. That is, the irrational consequence of the spread of functional rationality is the decline of substantial rationality. Of course, Mannheim (like Weber) was writing before the rise of service industries like fast-food restaurants, but it can easily be argued that substantial rationality is at least as paralysed in those settings as it is by large-scale industry. In other words, the coming of many of the service industries has exacerbated the decline of substantial rationality.

There is one other major point of resemblance between the Weberian and Mannheimian theories of the relationship between these two types of rationality – the progressive disenchantment of the world. In Mannheim's case, this means that we are seeing the disappearance of *both* utopias and ideologies; we are moving toward a world in which "all ideas have been discredited and all utopias have been destroyed" (Mannheim, 1929/1936: 256). In an excellent description, Mannheim depicts the movement toward the "complete destruction of all spiritual elements, the utopian as well as the ideological . . . emergence of a 'matter of factness' . . . in sexual life, art, and architecture, and the expression of the natural impulses in sports" (Mannheim, 1929/1936: 256). This progressive disenchantment of the world is, in Mannheim's view, to be regretted because people need utopias (and ideologies). As Mannheim puts it:

> It is possible, therefore, that in the future, in a world in which there is never anything new, in which all is finished and each moment is a repetition of the past, there can exist a condition in which thought will be utterly devoid of all ideological and utopian elements. But the complete elimination of reality-transcending elements from our world would lead us to a "matter-of-factness" which ultimately would mean the decay of the human will. (Mannheim, 1929/1936: 262)

The world that Mannheim feared is now here in the fast-food restaurant and other McDonaldized systems. For example, such systems strive for a condition in which there is never anything new; that is, where everything is predictably the same.[3] The objective, largely realized, is that each new visit is merely a repetition of all previous visits.

While Mannheim regrets the progressive disappearance of both ideologies and utopias, it is the demise of the latter which is the far greater problem. The reason is that while the death of an ideology would pose a crisis for the social strata espousing it, the disappearance of utopias would have a profoundly negative effect on human nature and on human development as a whole:

> The disappearance of utopia brings about a static state of affairs in which man himself becomes no more than a thing. We would be faced then with the greatest paradox imaginable, namely that man, who has achieved the highest degree of rational mastery of existence, left without any ideals, becomes a mere creature of impulses. Thus, after a long tortuous, but heroic development, just at the highest stage of awareness, when history is ceasing to be blind fate, and is becoming more and more man's own creation, with the relinquishment of utopias, man would lose his will to shape history and therewith his ability to understand it. (Mannheim, 1929/1936: 262–3)

Mannheim is obviously coming very close here to the disenchantment of the world that so interested and concerned Weber.

Weber was also highly interested in the spread of formal rationality in the West and Mannheim has a similar level of concern for, and offers a similar hypothesis about, the spread of functional rationality:

> The more industrialized a society is and the more advanced its division of labour and organization, the greater will be the number of spheres of human activity which will be functionally rational and hence also calculable in advance. Whereas the individual in earlier societies acted only occasionally and in limited spheres in a functionally rational manner, in contemporary society he is *compelled* to act in this way in more and more spheres of life. (Mannheim, 1935/1940: 55; italics added)

There are two aspects of this process, as described here, that relate particularly well to McDonaldization. First, there is the spread of functional rationality (and therefore McDonaldization) to more and more sectors of society. Second, there is the compulsion to act in a functionally rational matter. (McDonaldized systems, as iron cages, in a variety of ways control all of those who find their way into them.) And it is not just the workers who are subjected to such compulsion, but also customers and clients.

While Mannheim and Weber were right to point to the expansion of functional/formal rationality in the West, it is now spreading throughout the world. One example of this is the extension of McDonald's, and the fast-food restaurant more generally, to large portions of the rest of the world.

Both Weber and Mannheim share a sense that over time formal/functional rationality is coming to dominate, squeeze out, "paralyse" substantive/substantial rationality. Further, both accept the view that this development has a series of negative consequences. However, while in Mannheim's schema it is obvious why we should worry about the loss of the individual's ability to think, brought about by the development of functional actions, it is not as obvious why Weber's version of this should concern us. It is difficult to argue against Mannheim's view that society is adversely affected by the declining ability of people to think rationally. However, Weber's assertion that we should fret over the decline of substantive rationality is far more questionable. Again, this depends on the "humanness" of the values in question. A formally rational system with the ability to control, or eliminate, the values associated with Nazism would clearly be preferable to one in which such values dominated formally rational systems (as was true in Nazi Germany).

Mannheim adds needed nuance to the argument by discussing the differential effect of this process on people depending upon their position in an organization. He distinguishes between those at the top of the organization and those below them. Those at the top tend to retain substantial rationality, while the substantial rationality of those below them declines as the responsibility for independent decision making is restricted to those at the top. This has disastrous consequences for a person who does not occupy a high-level, decision-making position:

> He becomes increasingly accustomed to being led by others and gradually gives up his own interpretation of events for those others give him. When the rationalized mechanism of social life collapses in times of crisis, the individual cannot repair it by his own insight. Instead his own impotence reduces him to a state of terrified helplessness. (Mannheim, 1935/1940: 59)

This represents a huge problem if for no other reason than the fact that the vast majority of people occupy subordinate positions. Again, the description offered above applies well to a McDonaldized society, in which the majority of workers (and others) are accustomed to being told what to do and begin to lose the ability to interpret situations for themselves. Should the rationalized system collapse, we can expect such people to be comparatively helpless. However, it should be said that the further development of McDonaldization makes it more unlikely that the system will collapse.

Overall, there is a close correspondence between the Mannheimian and the Weberian approaches as they relate to McDonaldization. In Weberian terms, McDonaldization implies the spread of formal rationalization, while in (later) Mannheimian terms it involves the development, growth and spread of functional rationalization. Also similar is the idea that the spread of functional (and formal) rationalization is serving to choke off the development, even the existence, of substantial (and substantive) rationality. However, while both theorists see this as leading to a kind of disenchantment of the world, the nature of that disenchantment is quite different. For Weber, we suffer a loss of human values, while for Mannheim we suffer the loss of ideologies, utopias, and especially the ability to think.

Both of these perspectives are of utility in thinking about McDonaldization. A McDonaldized world dominated by Weber's formal rationality would be a world devoid of human values. McDonaldized systems, with their emphasis on things like efficiency and profit maximization, have little place for human values such as love or community. Mannheim's version of this is found in his analysis of the elimination of ideologies and utopias in the modern world. However, Mannheim seems more concerned with the elimination of thought than with the demise of ideologies and utopias. And it is even clearer that McDonaldized systems seek to limit, if not eliminate, individual thought. Great control through scripts (Leidner, 1993), non-human technologies and the like is designed to limit the employee's, especially the lower-status employee's, need and ability to think on the job. Thus, the two theorists point to quite different implications of the McDonaldization process. Mannheim's thinking is a useful supplement to Weber's in this case because McDonaldized systems do tend to threaten not only human values, but also the individual's ability to think.

The utility of Mannheim's theorizing is enhanced in this realm because, as we have seen, he points to the fact that one's position in the organizational hierarchy affects one's ability to think. Those at the top are able to limit the effect of external constraints on them, while actively imposing such constraints on those below them in the organization. The result is that the further one descends in a McDonaldized organization, the less the ability of employees to think through their actions on their own. Thus, Mannheim adds an important dimension of stratification to our thinking about McDonaldized systems.

Weber sees larger structures, like bureaucracies, as the source of disenchantment. In contrast, to Mannheim disenchantment involves one type of action (functional) driving out another (substantial). Mannheim lacks an explicit sense that macro-structures are the source of disenchantment and this allows him to propose planning, with the macro-structures that would inevitably accompany it, as the solution to the problem. However, what Mannheim fails to see is that such planning and structures would bring an *increase* in McDonaldization. It is for this reason that Weber opposed socialism and the planning that accompanied it. Thus, Weber's macro-structural perspective gives him a powerful advantage, at least in this instance, over Mannheim's conceptualization.

So cases can be made, pro and con, for both Weber's and Mannheim's thinking about formal/functional and substantive/substantial rationality, as well as the relationships between the two basic types of rationality and irrationality. Both are of utility, and pose problems, for our thinking about McDonaldization.

However, Mannheim went far beyond Weber in his conceptualization of rationalization and it is here, at least potentially, that his greatest advantage lies. The issue is whether the additional conceptual arsenal created by Mannheim furthers our understanding of McDonaldization.

Mannheim goes beyond functional rationalization to posit the intimately related phenomenon of *self-rationalization*, or "the individual's systematic control of his impulses" (Mannheim, 1935/1940: 55). In fact, self-rationalization is sometimes described as a type of functional rationalization and in any case the two are closely linked – "the functional rationalization of objective activities ultimately evokes self-rationalization" (Mannheim, 1935/1940: 56). A high level of overall rationalization occurs when functional and self-rationalization occur together. This is most likely to be found, in Mannheim's view, among the administrative staff of large-scale organizations. Here the external control of the organization's rules and regulations is supplemented by self-rationalization, especially in the case of staff members and their careers. In Mannheim's words, the career prescribes "not only the actual processes of work but also the prescriptive regulation both of the ideas and feelings one is permitted to have and of one's leisure time" (1935/1940: 56). Self-regulation exerts control over matters (ideas, feelings, leisure time) that functional rationalization cannot reach.

Mannheim is quite correct to posit a "deeper" level of rationalization beyond functional rationalization. The latter is designed to exercise largely external control over micro-objective actions and has little or no effect on micro-subjective cognitive processes. In a purely functional system, subordinates cannot be trusted to act on their own accord in the way they are expected to by the organization. A functionally rational system requires rules, regulations, laws, supervision and technological control. However, external control can be extremely costly and far from totally dependable. That is, subordinates are motivated to, and often do, elude these external controls and do not perform as they are expected to by the organization.

The answer, at least in Mannheim's day, was to supplement functional rationality with self-rationalization. For example, the human relations movement, which was in its heyday in Mannheim's time, sought to make workers more satisfied so that they would work harder of their own accord rather than being forced to do so. In other words, the goal of such a management school was the alteration of the consciousness of workers.

Such a movement and a view seem old-fashioned today, as does Mannheim's focus on the importance of self-rationalization as a supplement to functional rationalization. In the McDonaldized world of the fast-food restaurant there is little interest in, or need for, self-rationalization; the emphasis is on honing functional rationality. That is, the goal is the better coordination of actions. As long as those actions are synchronized, there is little need for, or interest in, changing the mind-set of employees.

Why this lack of interest in self-rationalization in McDonaldized systems? For one thing, the employees in such systems are apt to be both part-time and short-term workers; the workforce may turn over two or three times a year. It is impossible to change the cognitive processes of such workers in such a short period of time. Furthermore, even if it could be done, there is little point in doing so since the employees are likely to be gone in relatively short order. Many chains, as well as other types of McDonaldized enterprises, have adopted, at least in part, McDonald's functionally rational approach to managing its workforce. Making this even more necessary is the fact that there has been a vast increase in temporary employees in the economy as a whole. One must rely on functional rationalization to deal with such employees since, again, there is little time for, and interest in, self-rationalization.

However, there are hierarchical differences in the need for self-rationalization. Hence, McDonald's has its Hamburger Universities designed not only to train franchisees and managers in the techniques of running a franchise, and exercising functional control over subordinates, but also to alter their mind-sets so that they can exercise self-rationalization. It is far more important for franchisees and managers to believe in the McDonald's way; they are likely to work harder for the organization when they have such beliefs. Furthermore, it is harder to control them through functional rationality than it is to control their subordinates. Nonetheless, McDonald's does utilize a high level of functional rationalization with its franchisees and managers. There are all sorts of rules, regulations and checks by central management designed to ensure that their actions are coordinated in the way they should be.

Mannheim's point about supplementing functional rationality with self-rationality holds in the case of franchisees and managers and, more generally, for those who occupy higher-level positions in the organizational hierarchy. However, it has little applicability to the vast majority of the employees of modern McDonaldized organizations. The work world has changed dramatically since Mannheim's day, and while his thoughts on self-rationalization may have applied to large-scale productive organizations, they have little relevance to work in today's McDonaldized reproductive organizations.

Nevertheless, self-rationalization does apply, and quite well, to the customers and clients of McDonaldized systems. It is true that there are various external constraints on patrons – drive-throughs, limited menus, hard and uncomfortable seats – but these are supplemented by efforts by McDonaldized systems to "train" consumers to control themselves and to do what is expected of them. How do patrons learn what they are expected to do? Advertisements provide a kind of anticipatory socialization so that customers know, for example, not only what to order, but how to order. Children can be counted on to teach adults (in reverse socialization) what to do (e.g. to clean up their debris). Then there are signs, as well as various physical structures (e.g. visible and readily accessible garbage pails), that serve to indicate what is expected. As a result of all of these things, as well of as their own accumulated personal experiences in McDonaldized systems, the patrons of such systems can be said to be self-rationalized. Indeed, this is a key to the success of McDonaldized systems.

Self-rationalization is *not* the highest and most extreme form of rationalization in Mannheim's theoretical system. That honor goes to what Mannheim calls *self-observation*. Self-rationalization involves a

> process of mental training, subordinating my inner motives to an external aim. Self-observation, on the other hand, is more than such form of mental training. Self-observation aims primarily at inner *self-transformation*. Man reflects about himself and his actions mostly for the sake of remoulding or transforming himself more radically. (Mannheim, 1935/1940: 57)

Once again, Mannheim's thinking seems to be much more a product of his times than a generalization that is fully supportable in today's McDonaldized society. McDonaldized systems are even less interested in the self-observation (that is, self-transformation), than in the self-rationalization, of the bulk of their employees. The fast-food restaurant does not and cannot expect its employees to transform themselves for the sake of a part-time or temporary job. Nor is such a McDonaldized system interested in investing the time, energy and money needed to help ensure such self-transformation. As with self-rationalization, self-observation applies much more to managers and franchisees than it does to the vast majority of employees of McDonaldized enterprises. In Mannheimian terms, there is no need for McDonaldized organizations to seek to have the vast majority of their employees transform themselves. All that is needed is to be sure that their actions are coordinated with those of the others they work with, and then only for a few hours a week and for only the few months that their jobs are likely to last.

And what of the patrons of McDonaldized systems? It could be argued that the broader objective of those systems, and more generally of a McDonaldized society, is just such a self-transformation of those served by them. A McDonaldized system works best when customers have transformed themselves so that they are passive, pliable participants in those systems. That is, they surrender their individuality and move through McDonaldized systems smoothly, efficiently and, above all, quickly. In a sense, they agree to give up their individuality and permit themselves to be treated like, and to be sold the same products as, everyone else.

Mannheim seems to envision a hierarchy, and perhaps even a historical trend, running from substantial rationalization to functional rationalization, self-rationalization and ultimately self-observation. While in the earlier stages of modernity society may have been able to rely on functional rationalization, his view is that more complex and rapidly changing modern societies require self-rationalization and especially self-observation, which control people better and more efficiently and enable them to adapt more readily to complex new situations.

This modern grand narrative is open to question, in part because we are re-examining it in an era when it is difficult to accept grand narratives in light of the postmodern critique (Lyotard, 1979/1984). More importantly for our purposes, it is open to question because developments in much of the work world have not followed the pattern envisioned by Mannheim. He seems to have in mind what was long ago called the "professionalization of the labor force" (Foote, 1953). The idea was that most workers were becoming more and more like professionals. One could and should rely on self-rationalization and self-observation with such "professional" workers, but the professionalized blue-collar workforce that Foote was describing never materialized. More importantly, the blue-collar workforce has shrunk dramatically and become less significant in the era of the downsizing of the organizations most likely to employ them. In their place has arisen a massive number of low-status, low-paid service workers like those found in the local fast-food restaurant and in McDonaldized systems more generally. It is ludicrous to think of counterpeople at the fast-food restaurant subjecting themselves to self-rationalization and self-observation for the sake of a minimum wage, part-time job.

However, returning to a theme that has arisen several times in this section, it may well be that Mannheim's grand narrative applies far better to customers and clients of McDonaldized systems than it does to employees. It is the patrons who can be seen as having lost their substantial rationality in McDonaldized systems where they are dominated by functional rationality. And it is they who can be said to have undergone both self-rationalization and self-observation in McDonaldized societies. With employees of McDonaldized systems well controlled by functional rationality, the focus shifts to customers/clients who are better able to evade such controls. In their case, functional rationality must be supplemented with self-rationalization and self-observation.

Mannheim's Later Thinking on Irrationality

We have already encountered one of Mannheim's implicit, but centrally important, views on irrationality in the discussion of the tendency over time for functional rationality to squeeze out substantial rationality. This idea is in line with Weber's thinking on the irrationality of rationality.

More explicitly, Mannheim offers the concepts of substantial and functional irrationality to parallel substantial and functional rationality. Both notions of irrationality are, however, residual concepts reflecting Mannheim's focal concern with rationality. Given his sense of substantial rationality as rational thought, Mannheim defines *substantial irrationality* as "everything else which either is false or not an act of thought at all (as for example drives, impulses, wishes and feelings, both conscious and unconscious)" (Mannheim, 1935/1940: 53).

This is a very different sense of the irrational than in his earlier work, where Mannheim had associated *rationality* with the lack of thought. Here it is substantial irrationality that involves a lack of thought. However, previously the lack of thought had been linked to administrative control (following prescriptions without any personal decision making), while in the case of substantial irrationality it is tied to drives, impulses, wishes and feelings.

From the point of view of the employees of McDonaldized systems, it is difficult to see much utility in the notion of substantial irrationality. It is certainly the case that McDonaldized systems operate to contain such irrationality among employees, but I do not think that such containment plays much of a role in the planning associated with McDonaldization. Again, the fact that Mannheim was embedded in a world in which such irrationalities were of central importance (for example in the rise of Fascism) served to give this type of irrationality undue importance in his work, at least from the vantage point of the employees of today's McDonaldized systems.

While it is not what he had in mind for the concept, Mannheim's notion of substantial irrationality is applicable to the way in which McDonaldized systems approach their customers/clients. In a variety of ways, but especially through advertisements, McDonaldized systems seek to manipulate the needs, desires and impulses, the substantial irrationality, of customers/clients in order to get them to become devoted, if not habitual, consumers of their products and services. For example, McDonald's utilizes its knowledge of customers' desire to have fun by offering them a carnival-like atmosphere in which to obtain their food. In another realm, malls exploit consumers' fears about shopping in urban stores by offering them a crime-free (or so they would like consumers to believe) environment.

Functional *irrationality* is defined as "everything which breaks through and disrupts functional ordering" (Mannheim, 1935/1940: 54). In contrast to substantial irrationality, this type of irrationality *is* of central importance to McDonaldized systems. Such systems do want to see their functionally rational organizations operate smoothly and, in so doing, seek to limit any outbursts of functional irrationality which threaten that smooth operation. However, I think that McDonaldized systems are far more concerned with ensuring functional rationality than with preventing functional irrationality. In fact, a smoothly running, functionally rational system would tend to militate against functional irrationality.

Mannheim's view that at least one aspect of the irrationality of rationality stems from the fact that great masses of people are crowded together in large cities because of industrialization is quite dated. Mannheim seemed to be arguing that industrialization creates what used to be called "mass society." Thus, paradoxically, as large-scale, industrial society leads to greater functional rationality, self-rationalization and self-observation, it also creates the conditions in mass society for irrational threats to that rational system:

> it produces all the irrationalities and emotional outbreaks which are characteristic of amorphous human agglomerations. As an industrial society, it so refines the social mechanism that the slightest irrational disturbance can have the most far-reaching effects, and as a mass society it favors a great number of irrational impulses and suggestions and produces an accumulation of unsublimated psychic energies which, at every moment, threatens to smash the whole subtle machinery of social life. (Mannheim, 1935/1940: 61)

This image appears to have little to do with what transpires in modern, McDonaldized societies. The machinery of such societies seems in little danger from the kind of emotional mass outbursts of concern to Mannheim. Once again, his thinking seems to be a product of realities that have long since passed into history, at least the history of contemporary McDonaldized societies. Today, most people seem too busy consuming in McDonaldized systems to engage in such outbursts.

Of far greater utility is Mannheim's sense that the functionally rational actions of those in one organization can be functionally irrational from the point of view of those in another organization. For example, when McDonaldized systems produce an abundance of low-skilled McJobs (see

Chapter 5), those actions may be seen as functionally irrational from the perspective of those in the educational system who are seeking to produce a more educated population capable of handling far more complex occupations. Thus, Mannheim (1935/1940: 55) concludes that "'functional irrationality' never characterizes an act itself but only with reference to its position in the entire complex of conduct of which it is part."

In Mannheim's view, the basic sources of the irrational in modern life are the *same* as the sources of the functionally rational. In other words, Mannheim offers a sociological, not a psychological, theory of the origins of both rationality and irrationality. He sees the sources of both as built into the structure of modern society:

> they are driven, now in one direction, now in another by the dual nature of social structure that certain human beings are now calculating creatures who work out their actions to the very last detail, and now volcanic ones who think it right that at a given time they should reveal the worst depths of human brutality and sadism. (Mannheim, 1935/1940: 66)

There is another dialectical aspect to Mannheim's thinking. That is, not only does increasing functional rationality lead to an increase in certain irrationalities, but it also leads to the beginning of a rational sense that *planning* is needed to deal with these problems; not just piecemeal planning, but planning at the level of the whole of society. The rationalization of society, as well as its growing irrationality, have made planning inevitable, but a central issue to Mannheim is who will do that planning? Those who represent narrow interest groups, or those who have the interests of society as a whole in mind? Mannheim prefers that the latter do the planning and they must either be sociologists, or those who have the kind of totalistic perspective that only sociology can offer.

This sense of planning shows once again that unlike Weber, Mannheim does not realize that a fundamental source of the irrationality of rationality, a fundamental problem in society, *is* the organizations that undertake and result from such planning. It is such planning that will lead to greater functional rationalization and therefore to the irrationalities that inevitably accompany it. Thus, Mannheim favors greater functional rationalization even if it comes at the expense of substantial rationalization. He is willing to accept this because in his day, and from his vantage point, the main danger to society stemmed from *ir*rationality. Mannheim's thinking was shaped by the disruptions of the Great Depression and the rise of Nazism. He tended to see these as productive of irrational outbursts, or as irrational in themselves. The answer to the problem of such irrational outbursts is planning which would presumably produce more functionally rationalized systems capable of controlling them.

In the end Mannheim fails to see the key problem that was so brilliantly illuminated by Weber and is so well illustrated by today's McDonaldized systems: that the central problem lies in *the irrationalities of such systems themselves* and not in some irrational force that threatens to disrupt them.

Mannheim's most crucial failure is his inability to see the irrationality that lies at the core of rationality.

Of course, the nature of planning in a McDonaldized system is very different from the kind of planning envisioned by Mannheim. While Mannheim was thinking of centralized planning on a society-wide basis, McDonaldized societies are characterized by a high degree of centralized planning within specific sectors of society. With the death of communism, the kind of centralized planning discussed by Mannheim is of little significance in the modern world. Instead, what we see is an extraordinarily high level of planning within a range of specific sectors as exemplified by the careful and detailed planning associated with the creation and running of each McDonald's outlet. Such planning is far more effective and omnipresent than anything that could have been created through centralized society-wide planning. And the system runs itself rather than requiring a secret police to enforce compliance with its dictates.

For example, McDonald's has recently created a set of business practices in the form of a handbook it calls "Franchising 2000" (Gibson, 1996b). Here are some illustrations of the kind of centralized control exercised by McDonald's over its franchisees:

> One controversial provision requires franchisees to submit annual financial goals to the company's regional managers, who sign off on them. The document also revives annual A, B, C and F grades, with only franchisees receiving As and Bs eligible for more restaurants; some franchisees doubt the system's objectivity.
> In addition, McDonald's is using Franchising 2000 to try to enforce a single pricing strategy, so that a Big Mac, for example, will cost the same almost everywhere. . . . Those who ignore such guidelines and otherwise "seek personal gain and advantage to the detriment of the system," as the new handbook puts it, risk losing their franchise when it expires. (Gibson, 1996b: A10)

This kind of centralized control is characteristic of McDonaldized systems.

Mannheim envisioned a system in which broadly trained sociologists and politicians (schooled in sociological thinking) do the planning for society. However, the fact that this planning occurs in narrow sectors in McDonaldized society means that it is specialists rather than wide-ranging thinkers who do the planning. By its very nature, this kind of planning cannot take the needs of society as a whole into account. In any case, the plans of those in control of one sector can come into conflict with, and act to the detriment of, plans promulgated in other sectors. It is unlikely that this type of planning can accomplish the goals foreseen by Mannheim.

Conclusion

In comparison to its Weberian counterpart, Mannheim's later thinking on rationality has a number of strengths and weaknesses, as well as a number of advantages and disadvantages. Mannheim's conceptualization of substantial and functional rationality is neater and easier to use than the Weberian concepts of formal and substantive rationality. The messiness of the latter concepts makes them more difficult to use, especially in terms of the key issue of relating them to one another. Of perhaps greater importance is the fact that Mannheim's sense of substantial rationality yields a clearer and more defensible problematic than Weber's notion of substantive rationality. To Mannheim, substantial rationality involves rational thought and it is easy to see how that is threatened by the march of functional rationality. Less easy to see, and especially to defend, is Weber's concern over the fact that substantive rationality, associated with human values, is threatened by the advance of formal rationality. It is clear why we should be concerned about the loss of rational thought, but far less clear why we should fret over the decline of value-driven rationality. After all, much harm has been done in the world in the name of such rationality.

While Mannheim's sense of the relationship between substantial and functional rationality is a significant advance, his ideas on substantial and functional irrationality appear to add little, largely because they are defined residually. Of mixed significance, at least from the point of view of McDonaldization, are his notions of self-rationalization and self-observation. These concepts are largely embedded in the era in which they were created and have little to do with the work life realities of McDonaldized society, or at least the McDonaldized sectors of society. However, they do have surprising applicability to the patrons of McDonaldized systems.

The most important issue is: what can we say about McDonaldization in light of Mannheim's conceptualization, in particular his later ideas on rationalization? McDonaldizaton involves an increase in functional rationality at the expense of a decline in substantial rationality. It is this decline, the deterioration of the ability of people in most, especially lower-ranking, positions to think rationally, that is the fundamental irrationality of McDonaldized systems. There is little room for, or interest in, self-rationalization and self-observation in McDonaldized systems, except in higher-level positions. While largely uninterested in the self-rationalization and self-observation of employees, McDonaldized systems have come to place great reliance on self-rationalization and self-observation to get patrons to behave as they are expected to. The kind of centralized planning envisioned by Mannheim would only serve to increase the irrationality associated with the declining ability of lower-ranking employees to think. The local and in many ways more powerful planning of McDonaldized systems has also, in fact, led to an increase in that irrationality.

In the end, our understanding of McDonaldization is enhanced by rethinking it from the point of view of Mannheim's theory of rationality. Its most important contribution is to point us toward the threat to the ability to think, rather than the Weberian threat to human values, as the fundamental irrationality of McDonaldized systems. Clearly, the narrow niches that more and more people occupy within McDonaldized systems provide little scope for thought. We need to devote more theoretical attention to the implications of the declining opportunity for substantial rationality within McDonaldized systems. This is particularly important because side by side with the growth of these McDonaldized systems is the expansion of post-industrial systems demanding the complex thought processes associated with substantial rationality (Hage and Powers, 1992). This brings us to another contribution of Mannheim's approach to this issue – his reminder of the importance of the relationship of social stratification to all of this. We are well on the way to a society differentiated, to a large degree, between high-status, high-paying post-industrial occupations characterized by substantial rationality and low-status, low-paying McDonaldized occupations largely lacking in such rationality.

Mannheim's thinking on rationality and irrationality has a number of weaknesses, most notably the fact that much of it is tied to a particular time and place; in many senses it does not stand the test of time very well. However, in other ways it has strengths and continues to be useful for thinking about contemporary society. All in all, Weberian theory remains the prime resource for thinking about McDonaldization. This is largely because of Weber's realization that irrationality is directly linked to the advancement of formal rationality and to Mannheim's failure to see this, epitomized by his strong case for planning. In spite of this weakness, as well as others, there is much to be gained by supplementing Weberian theory with, and rethinking McDonaldization from, a Mannheimian perspective.

Notes

1. As we will see, planning becomes increasingly central to Mannheim's thinking on rationalization.

2. I am here using a distinction I developed in *Toward an Integrated Sociological Paradigm: The Search for an Exemplar and an Image of the Subject Matter* (Ritzer, 1981) between two microscopic (micro-subjective (consciousness) and micro-objective (action)) and two macroscopic (macro-subjective (norms and values) and macro-objective (social structures)) levels of social analysis.

3. The postmodernist, Jean Baudrillard (1990/1993: 122), describes this as the "hell of the Same."

3

The McDonaldization of American Sociology: A Metasociological Analysis

This chapter has three objectives. The first, and by far the most important, is to apply the concept of McDonaldization to sociology. Second, it seeks to embed this specific work within the sociology of sociology, or metasociology, especially the contributions of Pierre Bourdieu. Third, and much more briefly, this analysis is used to cast some new, or at least different, light on the current "crisis" in sociology.

The Sociology of Sociology and Metasociology

Before getting to the main objective of this chapter, I would like to place this work within the broader context of the sociology of sociology, or what I prefer to call metasociology (Ritzer, 1991, 1992). The sociology of sociology acquired something of a bad reputation in the 1970s and early 1980s, in part through the often trivial, navel-gazing papers (e.g. on citation rates or departmental ratings) that appeared in the original *American Sociologist*.[1] Yet this is an area that can and should be resuscitated through more serious empirical and theoretically based studies and analyses of sociology. Sociologists are in a particularly advantageous position to bring their tools to bear on their own field. In fact, that is what is being done here – the theory of rationalization/McDonaldization is being employed to cast light on, and to critique, contemporary developments in sociology.

This kind of work is in line with what Alvin Gouldner (1970) called the "sociology of sociology" or "reflexive sociology." As he defined it, "reflexive sociology is concerned with what sociologists want to do and with what, in fact, they actually do in the world" (Gouldner, 1970: 489). The individual sociologist is the focus of Gouldner's sociology of sociology.

Pierre Bourdieu also works within the realm of the sociology of sociology as part of his broader concerns with the educational system and cultural capital. In addition to using the term "sociology of sociology," Bourdieu also labels his analyses of sociology "socio-analysis," or "reflexivity" (1984a: 5). Bourdieu (1984a: xii) places the sociology of sociology, as do I, at the very center of the discipline: "social science may expect to derive its most decisive progress from a constant effort to undertake a sociological critique of sociological reasoning." More recently, and more strongly, Bourdieu (Bourdieu and Wacquant, 1992: 68) says, "I believe that *the sociology of sociology is a fundamental dimension of sociological epistemology*. Far from being a specialty among others, it is the necessary prerequisite of any rigorous sociological practice."

Bourdieu's approach is broader and more complex than Gouldner's. While Bourdieu does acknowledge the importance of examining individual sociologists (at least as types), his main focus is on the larger social forces that propel them and become embedded unconsciously in what they do.[2] Sociological reasoning takes place within, and is affected by, structural contexts and it is up to the sociologist to analyse the nature of those structures, or the "social determinants of sociological thought" (Bourdieu, 1990: 184). These social structures are related to the underlying structures of sociological thought which are described as "unthought categories of thought which delimit the thinkable and predetermine the thought" (Bourdieu, cited in Wacquant, 1992: 40). There is a relationship between objective social structures and mental structures and it is up to the sociologist of sociology to uncover the nature of that relationship.

Bourdieu seeks far more than simply the study of the relationship between the social and the mental structures of sociologists. He urges "epistemological vigilance" (1984a: xiii); he instructs the sociologist to use sociology "as a weapon against yourself, an instrument of vigilance" (Bourdieu, 1990: 27). Sociologists are encouraged to be continually sensitive to the way social structures affect, sometimes adversely, what they think and do. Beyond that, the sociologist is encouraged to "try to gain control over the effects of social determinisms which affect both his world, and, unless extreme caution is observed, scientific discourse itself" (Bourdieu, 1984a: xiii).

Looked at in Bourdieu's terms, the objectives of this chapter are to help sociologists to understand how McDonaldization (as a "social determinism") is affecting the field in general as well as the ways in which they think and act, to become more vigilant about these effects, and to enable them to begin to control this impact and to ameliorate its negative effects. But as Bourdieu points out, such effects are felt not only in sociology, but in all scientific fields. Thus, the implications of Bourdieu's approach, and of this chapter, go far beyond sociology.

The term "metasociology" actually predates the widespread use of the "sociology of sociology." Paul Furfey introduced the notion in the early 1950s by making the argument that sociology takes the social world as its subject, "whereas the subject matter of metasociology is sociology itself" (1953/1965: 9). Unfortunately, despite such a useful beginning, Furfey ends up making a false distinction between sociology and metasociology. Working with a positivistic orientation, he argues that sociology is a science and that metasociology is "an auxiliary science which furnishes the methodological principles presupposed by sociology" (1953/1965: 17). Furfey's position is distorted by this bias and by his separation of metasociology from sociology.

In my own work, I use the term metasociology to mean "the systematic study of sociology in general and of its various components" (Ritzer, 1991:

5). This is in line with Furfey's definition, as well as with what both Gouldner and Bourdieu mean by the sociology of sociology. I prefer the term metasociology to the sociology of sociology in order to dissociate it from the trivial studies mentioned above and identified with the latter. Interestingly, while he does not use the term metasociology, and prefers the sociology of sociology, Bourdieu uses "meta" in much the same way it is used here:[3]

> For me, sociology ought to be meta but *always vis-à-vis itself*. It must use its own instruments to find out what it is and what it is not doing, to try to know better where it stands, and must refuse a polemical use of the "meta" which serves only to objectivize others. (Bourdieu and Wacquant, 1992: 191)

There are three basic types of metasociological, especially metatheoretical, types of work. They differ in terms of their fundamental objectives – better understanding, creation of a new theoretical perspective, and creation of a new overarching perspective, or metatheory. This chapter falls within the first category and uses a theoretical idea – McDonaldization – to enhance our understanding of sociology in general, and sociological theory in particular.

McDonaldization and Sociology

In this metasociological exercise, I will try to get at some basic trends in contemporary sociology. It is the thesis of this chapter that sociology can be seen as simply another aspect of the modern world and that it, like almost all others, is undergoing a process of McDonaldization.[4] As Bourdieu (Bourdieu and Wacquant, 1992: 181–2) says, in more general terms, the sociology of sociology "can teach people [i.e. sociologists] always to be aware that when they say or think something, they can be moved by causes as well as by reasons." McDonaldization is one of the key *causes* of some recent developments in sociology. However, not all aspects of the modern world are McDonaldized to the same extent. While sociology is clearly McDonaldizing, it is nowhere as McDonaldized as, for example, fast-food restaurants. In discussing the McDonaldization of sociology we are not saying that it is, or could ever be, fully McDonaldized, but that sociology has come to be characterized, at least to some degree, by the major elements of McDonaldization and that there is evidence that it is moving in the direction of further McDonaldization.

McDonaldization is one of the causes of a variety of *problems* that are plaguing the field. While I will focus on these problems in this chapter, it should be noted that, as with McDonaldization in general (Ritzer, 1996a: 11–13), the rationalization of sociology is far from having only negative effects on the field. Many of the dimensions of McDonaldization to be discussed below bring with them a series of benefits to sociology, but it is unnecessary here to catalogue them since most other sources in the field concentrate on those advantages. The objective here is to highlight the negative aspects.

The key to extending the idea of McDonaldization to sociology is an application of its basic components to an analysis of current trends in the field.[5] These dimensions not only play an important analytic role in the discussion to follow, but the first four (calculability, predictability, efficiency, and increased control over human unpredictability through the substitution of non-human for human technology) also help us to explain *why* sociology, as well as much of the modern world, is McDonaldizing. These dimensions represent advantages to be derived from McDonaldization and, as such, they are sought out by many sectors of the modern world, including sociology. However, they have various disadvantages that will be our focus throughout this discussion. Furthermore, the fifth component, the irrationality of rationality, allows us to get at the negative aspects of McDonaldization more directly.

The remainder of this chapter is divided into three sections. In the first, and longest, I deal with the area of sociology, empirical research, that has been most affected by McDonaldization. I then discuss the McDonaldization of sociology textbooks. Finally, I will turn to a discussion of sociological theory and the ways in which it, too, has undergone this process, at least to some degree.

The McDonaldization of Sociological Research

Calculability, or an emphasis on things that can be quantified, on quantity rather than quality, is manifest in mainstream American sociological research in several ways. First, of course, there is an overwhelming emphasis in the major journals on studies that rely on quantitative, rather than qualitative, data or that are strictly theoretical in nature.[6] Many years ago in *Fads and Foibles in Modern Sociology*, Pitirim Sorokin (1956) labeled this "quantophrenia" and it is far more widespread today than it was in Sorokin's day. Qualitative studies are seen as anachronistic and one finds few of them in the major journals. Even a journal like *Work and Occupations* which was founded, at least in part, to be an outlet for qualitative studies of work has come to find little place for such research in its pages (Abbott, 1993). Journals are likely to include a theory essay or two in most issues, but they rarely occupy center stage.[7] The lack of calculability of qualitative and theoretical essays makes them out of place in a McDonaldized sociology.

Research that is likely to be published in the major journals is apt to involve large rather than small samples. Such studies are not only seen as desirable in themselves, but more importantly they are considered more likely to yield results that are statistically significant. This is the parallel of the Big Mac phenomenon in fast-food restaurants. Just as we assume that a Big Mac is good because it is big, or that McDonald's more generally must be good because it has sold so many billions of burgers, we assume that a research study is important if it involves a large sample and reports strongly significant results. In both contexts quantity becomes a surrogate measure of quality. In other words, in both fast-food restaurants and sociology (at least in terms of correlations and other statistical measures), "bigger is better."

This emphasis is also manifest in the significance placed on obtaining large grants which, at least in part, permit the collection of large data bases. Studies based on these are more likely to be published in the major sociology journals. This is because such studies are seen as desirable in their own right and because they are more likely to be based on large samples and to produce highly significant results.

Furthermore, both sociological research and McDonald's are affected by the idea that it is difficult to assess quality directly, so we must focus on quantity instead. This is another reason for the comparative paucity of qualitative studies and theoretical essays. How is a reviewer to judge the accuracy of ethnographic descriptions or first-person accounts? How is a reviewer to evaluate the adequacy of a new theoretical perspective? Such judgments are made, but they are difficult to make and highly subjective. The result is that reviewers often differ greatly in their evaluations. Faced with widely varying opinions, journal editors are likely to pass when it comes to publishing theoretical essays or qualitative studies. In contrast, because of the objective character of the numbers and the statistics, quantitative studies are more likely to elicit similar judgments from re-viewers with the result that it is easier for editors to decide which quantitative studies should, and should not, be published.

A third, and less important, quantitative factor is that articles tend to be of a fairly uniform length. Those that are very long or very short are less likely to be published.[8] Very short papers are often assumed to lack depth.[9] Very long essays simply do not fit into the rationalized format of most academic journals. Long papers that are deemed publishable are likely to be accepted with the proviso that they be shortened. Such reductions may well result in a decline in quality.

Length is also an important criterion in the publication of research (as well as theoretical) monographs. Given the escalation in the cost of publishing, the decline in the number of publishers in a highly competitive business, and the fact that few sociologists are willing to shell out $50 or more for a book, publishers have become more cost-conscious. Longer books mean higher costs. Publishers who are still willing to publish monographs often insist that lengthy ones be shortened, sometimes quite substantially. Such reductions often hurt the quality of the work (although it is true that cuts sometimes help). In addition, some publishers establish word or page limits even before books are submitted for publication.

Fourth, there is an emphasis among American sociologists on producing large numbers of publishable papers. As Bourdieu (1984a: 125) argues, researchers "sacrifice all to a display of the amount of work accomplished." This is related to the American system of academic tenure and the fact that in many cases more attention is paid to the quantity of publications than to their quality. It is also linked to the fact that it is easy to add up the number of a scholar's publications, but difficult to assess their quality. Not long ago, the then president of Stanford University was disturbed by a report indicating "that nearly half of faculty members believe that their scholarly writings are merely counted – and not evaluated – when personnel decisions are made." He described this as a "bankrupt idea" and sought to "reverse the appalling belief that counting and weighing are important means of evaluating faculty research" (Cooper, 1991: A12). The emphasis on quantity rather than quality exists throughout academia and is not restricted to sociology.

Quantitative factors dominate American sociology just as they define our fast-food restaurants and the rest of our McDonaldizing society. And, while it is not inevitable, the emphasis on quantity often serves to affect quality adversely.

One aspect of the *predictability* of what Mullins (1973) called standard American sociology has already been touched on – research articles tend to be fairly uniform, and predictable, in length. As a result, readers can anticipate with great accuracy how long it will take to work their way through the typical research piece.

More importantly, virtually all research articles have a predictable format – review of the literature, hypotheses, methodology, results, tables, interpretation, conclusion, footnotes and references. Reading the typical American research article offers the same kinds of gratification as eating a Big Mac for lunch. The sociologist knows exactly what to expect and where each component of the article will be found, just as the consumer knows that the Big Mac will include a bun, burger, pickle, relish, and "special sauce," as well as where each element is to be found if one cared to deconstruct the burger. There is great satisfaction in knowing precisely what can be expected in one's lunch and in what one reads before, after, or even with that lunch. Since they are both highly rationalized, a Big Mac and the typical research article in an American journal go well together at lunchtime. (In contrast, it would be ludicrous to try to read the latest, non-rationalized books of Pierre Bourdieu or Jurgen Habermas over such a lunch.) It is nice to know that there will be no surprises – Big Macs and research articles almost always deliver precisely what is expected, no less, but also – and most tellingly and damningly – no more.

The nature of the review process in sociology journals ensures this predictability. Reviewers tend to be leading contributors to the area with which the submission is concerned; in fact, they are often chosen *because* their own work is cited in the article under consideration. Reviewers tend to have a clear sense that a new submission should build upon their work as well as the "intellectual" tradition of which they are part. Works that do not flow out of that tradition, that do not add a slight increment to what is already known about a subject, are likely to be seen as being "off the wall" and rejected out of hand. Truly original pieces of work, those that are "unpredictable," have a hard time finding their way into the journals. The products of normal science, those that offer only slight refinements of the dominant paradigm, are those that are likely to be accepted for publication.

Entire journal issues tend to be quite predictable. We know that each issue will be dominated by quantitative studies. We can also expect that because of criticisms of the pre-eminence of quantitative papers, many issues will have a token theoretical and/or qualitative essay.

The kinds of research articles described above are *efficient* in various senses. They can be read quite expeditiously. Since there is a clear pattern to the articles, the experienced reader can read through them effortlessly. Uniform works can be judged far more quickly than projects that differ wildly from one another in basic structure and format.

Such research articles can also be written efficiently. The author knows the component parts that must be there, and in which order, and those parts can be produced in quite an orderly fashion. In fact, in the likely event that a number of articles are to be produced from the same study, a series of component parts can be "manufactured" and "warehoused" – review of the literature, methods, various tables, references, and so on – and they can be carted out and inserted at the appropriate points in a variety of finished products. If this communicates the feel of an assembly-line process, it is meant to; and this is enhanced when a team of specialized researchers is involved in a project. The various parts can be assigned to team members and each can become a kind of specialist – the library researcher, the data analyst, the computer specialist, the writer, the "theoretician," and so on. This is part of the reason why research articles in sociology seem to involve more and more co-authors.[10] As in the manufacture of automobiles, it is far more efficient for a group of specialists to produce research articles than it is for a single generalist, but such efficiency carries with it, as most studies of the automobile industry have shown, a series of dysfunctions. This perspective is similar to Bourdieu's view and critique of the "*social division of labor* which splits, reifies, and compartmentalizes moments of the construction of the sociological object into separate specialties" (Wacquant, 1992: 32).

All this serves to make for the efficient replication of studies. With all of the component parts included in the published article in the usual order, a researcher can rush to the mail, quickly scan a new journal for relevant studies, hurry off to the computer center in search of the same data set, and rerun the data adding a few new variables. Within a few weeks, a replication of a study, one with a decent chance of acceptance because it is likely to be reviewed by the author of the study being replicated, is in the mail and off to the journal editor. Repeated over and over, we have here a very efficient method for building up a body of "knowledge" on a specific topic.

Implied above is a series of *non-human technologies* that have not only exerted external control over sociologists, but also reduced their importance in the research process. The most notable of these are the computer, the computer program, and the use of increasingly sophisticated statistics. Instead of being done by the sociologist, a large portion of a research study is in the hands of computers, computer programmers, canned programs and

statistical packages. These technologies tend to make studies more quantitative in character, more predictable since large numbers of people have
access to the same non-human technologies, and more efficient to produce
since a good deal of what one needs is in those technologies.

Bourdieu, Chamboredon and Passeron (1991: 5) also describe the contemporary reliance in sociology on "scientific recipes and laboratory gadgets,"
and critique the "blind submission to technical instruments" (1991: 10), as
well as their tendency to reduce or eliminate scientific creativity. They
argue: "Those who push methodological concern to the point of obsession
are like Freud's patient who spent all his time cleaning his spectacles and
never put them on" (Bourdieu et al., 1991: 5).

Research in contemporary American sociology has, and in my opinion to
an increasing degree, the four basic characteristics of McDonaldization
discussed above: sociological research, like most other aspects of contemporary society, has become McDonaldized, at least to some extent. However, as in the rest of society, rationalization leads dialectically to its mirror
image – the *irrationality of this rational system* for producing and dissem-
inating new sociological knowledge.

One of these irrationalities is the leveling of sociology around the world
(see Chapter 4 for a more detailed discussion of this issue, at least as it
applies to sociological theory). McDonaldization, in general, does have such
a leveling effect. For example, the spread of fast-food restaurants throughout
the United States has reduced the significance of regional cuisine. Those
regional cuisines that are McDonaldized become so rationalized that they
lose many of their distinctive characteristics: the Cajun food served by
Popeye's is a far cry from its progenitor in Louisiana. In the same way, in
sociology the model of the American research article has tended to produce
clones throughout the world: the research article published in a European
journal looks much like its American counterpart. Furthermore, the research
teams and the research steps are very much the same on both sides of the
Atlantic.

The most general irrationality of rationality is dehumanization. As Takaki
(1990: ix) put it, as a result of rationalization: "The self was placed in
confinement, its emotions controlled, and its spirit subdued." Fast-food
restaurants are dehumanizing for both workers and diners. The worker is
reduced to a cog in a hamburger assembly line or to a mindless automaton
passing those hamburgers on to customers. Dining, too, is reduced to an
assembly-line like experience – the best example being food obtained at the
drive-through window and consumed on the move while one heads on to
the next rationalized activity. We have already touched on the assembly-line
production of research articles. More generally, what is leeched out of
the research process in a McDonaldized sociology is human creativity, the
creativity of the individual sociologist (again, for more on this, see Chapter
4). Bourdieu is a critic of the loss of the art of sociology in the face of the
spread of numbing sociological routines. For example, he describes French
academia in general as "a world without surprises" (Bourdieu, 1984a: 153).

This is very close to the predictable, McDonaldized world being described here. In contrast, Bourdieu (1990: 26) says, "For me, intellectual life is closer to the artist's life than to the routines of an academic existence." This emphasis on "art" by Bourdieu (as well as by Richard Münch; see Chapter 4) leads to the issue of whether this chapter is just another assault on the increasing emphasis on science in sociology, especially in Kuhn's (1962/1970) terms, on "normal science."

Before we deal with that question, a broader issue needs to be addressed: *is* science itself under attack here? Science does have the basic characteristics discussed above – calculability, predictability, efficiency and substitution of non-human for human technology. This should come as no surprise since science can be seen as one of the precursors of the rationalization process (see Chapter 2 in *The McDonaldization of Society* for a discussion of other precursors). There is no question that science (as well as each of its basic characteristics) has been, in the main, a highly positive development. Indeed, it is always important to recognize that in all realms rationalization and its elements have a wide variety of positive consequences. This should not blind us to the fact that in science in general, and in sociology in particular, rationalization also has negative effects.

The problem is not simply these characteristics, but the excessive reliance on them – an overemphasis on quantifiable research; the quest for ever "bigger and better" studies and results; a careeristic concern with producing large numbers of publishable studies; the slavish dependence on a predictable format in the publication of research results; the over-conformity enforced by excessive reliance on the peer review process; the focus on the production of works that are efficient to write, review and read; an over-elaborate division of labor; too much emphasis on the efficient replication of previously published research; and an increasing reliance on non-human technologies that tend to reduce the role played by human creativity in science.

The problem in sociology is that it has often emulated the worst excesses of scientific rationality. As in all sciences, there are both advantages and disadvantages to rationalization, but in sociology the pendulum seems to be swinging dangerously in the direction of the disadvantages of scientific rationality. It may be that the reason for this is that the elements of scientific rationality work best in normal science. However, to do normal science there must be a paradigm and most observers agree that sociology lacks a dominant paradigm (Ritzer, 1975/1980). Without a paradigm, normal science becomes a kind of parody of itself. The rational trappings are there, but there is no paradigm to flesh out and develop. Furthermore, normal science presupposes previous breakthroughs and presages others. However, sociology lacks the previous breakthroughs leading to a dominant paradigm so it is highly unlikely that normal science will lead to later breakthroughs. In sociology, the ritualistic following of the rational canons of normal science does little more than militate against the kind of "artistic" thinking needed to create a paradigmatic revolution, or more appropriately in sociology, the discipline's first "true," at least in the pure Kuhnian sense, paradigm.

The rationalized practices of science, especially in their excessive forms, are *not* appropriate to contemporary sociology. Of course, they are a disadvantage in any science, but the established sciences can tolerate them better. Sociology seems to have adopted these rationalized trappings without having the knowledge base, or paradigm, to build upon. Whether or not the reader sees sociology as a science in the Kuhnian sense of the term, or agrees that it should be a science, given the realities of contemporary sociology, there is too much reliance on McDonaldized procedures and too little non-McDonaldized artistic creativity. It should not be forgotten, however, that all good science involves a solid mix of artistic creativity (especially during revolutionary periods) and rationalized procedures (especially during the normal science phase).

The McDonaldization of Sociology Textbooks

The preceding discussion has singled out empirical sociology as the bastion of McDonaldization in American sociology. While I think it is, it is also true that other aspects of American sociology have become rationalized. For example, elsewhere (Ritzer, 1988) I have attacked the production of what I called "cookie-cutter" textbooks in sociology, especially introductory texts. Pressures from publishers, reviewers and adopters lead relentlessly to a depressing sameness, a leveling, a high degree of predictability in cookie-cutter textbooks. Publishers are highly attuned to their competitors' bestselling texts. When a particular textbook, such as John Macionis's or Anthony Giddens's in introductory sociology, is a big hit, competitors seek to discover the factors that made it such a success and then set about publishing clones. When a draft of the "new" book is eventually produced, pre-publication reviewers are asked to look for certain things, especially those things that made the leading text such a great success. When reviewers uncover elements that are missing, the authors are pressed by the publisher to include them so that in the end the new text looks depressingly like its successful predecessor. Repeated over and over, many texts come to look like every other one. Adopters also play a key role in the leveling of textbooks. In many cases, adopters prefer to use well-worn lecture notes and this leads them to prefer to continue to use the same text, or if they change, to adopt a text that closely resembles and follows the previously used text.

Textbooks also tend to contain the other elements of rationalization. There is a strong emphasis on quantity in such things as length of chapters, length of the text as a whole, reading level (a 10th- or 11th-grade (16–17 year olds) reading level is preferred), and, most importantly, sales. Books that sell well, irrespective of quality, will go through multiple printings and editions. Books that are high in quality, but low in sales, quickly disappear from publishers' lists. Efficiency is manifest in the emphasis on books that are easier both to produce and to read. The use of several authors and even teams of authors, the construction of so-called customized books with each chapter written by a different author, and production of "managed books" in which professional writers work from notes and outlines provided by one or more sociologists, all reflect the emphasis on efficiency. The books should also be efficient reading. Ideally, students should be able to sail through the text with the same kind of efficiency that permits them to glide past their favorite fast-food drive-in window.

It is difficult for publishers to use non-human technologies to dominate the production of textbooks, but there have been some incursions. For example, the success of an introductory textbook often depends as much or more on the technologies that are available with it than on the quality of the text itself. Such technologies include CD-Roms, computerized testbanks, computerized student projects, video and audio tapes. While these, like all technologies, have been produced by people, they reach students as non-human technologies in which the student is left to interact with a computer-generated multiple choice test, a computer screen, or a video monitor.

This, of course, leads to the irrationality of the rationality of textbooks. Implied above is the dehumanization associated with modern textbooks. Textbooks tend to be products in which all traces of a distinctive authorial voice have been eliminated. A bland, readable, almost mechanical text is preferred to one that reflects an author's distinctive style. Dehumanization can also be associated with the increasing degree to which students interact with computer screens or video monitors, rather than with human instructors. But dehumanization, while it is the most extreme irrationality, is not the only irrationality associated with textbooks. For example, the quantitative pressure to produce books at a 10th- or 11th-grade reading level reinforces student incapacities rather than seeking to elevate them. To take one other example, the need to write down to students reduces the demands on authors and therefore does not fully exploit their capacities as writers and as sociologists. In other words, most textbook writers are capable of doing far more than they are permitted to do in the writing of textbooks. Other irrationalities associated with textbooks could easily be enumerated, but the above suffice for our purposes.

Before moving on it should be noted that textbooks *themselves* are a part of the process of McDonaldization. They reflect the view that it is inefficient for students to have to read original works. Instead, it is left to textbook authors to read those works, to summarize them, and to present them in a palatable way to students. Accustomed to reader-friendly textbook summaries, students will find it difficult, if not impossible, ever to read original works.

The McDonaldization of Sociological Theory

It would be easy to dismiss the views expressed above, especially on empirical sociology, since I am so involved in sociological theory. In order to make those views more credible, and to demonstrate the extent of the

McDonaldization of sociology, let me turn now to its impact on sociological theory. Like Parisian croissants, it is difficult to think of theory becoming McDonaldized, but as with those croissants, that is what has occurred, at least to some extent.

It is possible to trace the current low state of American sociological theory, at least in part, to its McDonaldization. The major American theorists of the recent past were decidedly non-rational in the way they produced theory and in the theories they created. In most cases there seemed to be little concern for the amount of work produced or the maximization of the efficiency of its production. Most of today's non-human technologies were either non-existent, or in their primitive stages, and the technologies of the day (mainly the typewriter) were controlled by the authors rather than controlling them. As a result of the minimal rationalization of theory production, there were few irrationalities of rationality associated with it. In the main, theory emerged, often tortuously, from the creative intellectual impulses of the theorist. For example, George Herbert Mead wrote relatively little in his lifetime; his major work, *Mind, Self and Society*, was produced by his students, from class notes, after his death. Herbert Blumer also produced a relatively small number of essays in his lifetime. Robert Merton, although more productive, often described how slow, laborious and painstaking it was for him to produce his work. Erving Goffman's work is so idiosyncratic that it defies rationalization. Talcott Parsons, of course, produced a voluminous amount of work, but it too is highly idiosyncratic. Furthermore, it is hard to imagine his lengthy, convoluted prose being published today. Modern publishers would have pressed Parsons to shorten his manuscripts dramatically and would have made greater use of copy-editors to make the prose less abstruse and, more importantly, less distinctive.

But how, specifically, is McDonaldization manifest in contemporary sociological theory? After all, it is far more difficult to rationalize a theoretical work than an empirical study. Nevertheless, rationalization *has* affected theoretical works in various ways. For one thing, an array of pressures lead American theorists to devote more attention than their European counterparts to the production of journal articles rather than books. The race for tenure and promotion in American academia is dominated by the model created by empirical researchers and the need to have a certain number of articles in major, refereed journals. To compete with their empirically oriented colleagues, theorists are driven to try to produce a like number of articles. However, theoretical ideas are often difficult to collapse into the page limits imposed by the article format; the natural home for works of theory throughout the history of sociology, and in Europe today, is the book-length manuscript. However, the dictates of an empirically oriented discipline lead to the view that it is the article in a refereed journal that is the "coin of the realm." Furthermore, books are suspect in highly rationalized disciplines. They seem to belong more to less rationalized fields like literature, history or philosophy than to a rationalized science.

Driven to write short articles, American theorists must use a modified version of the rationalized format employed by empiricists. They must take a set of complex ideas and divide them up into a series of bite-sized "theory McNuggets." While they may be tasty, more easily produced and more easily digested, such bits of theory are not likely to be as nourishing as the complex ideas developed in the more substantial theoretical monographs being turned out by their European peers.

In producing articles that include a theoretical nugget or two, and in submitting them to journals, theorists are subjecting their work to the same kind of review process that leads to the rationalization of empirical works. Theoretical essays that represent small increments in knowledge to an extant theoretical tradition are those that are likely to be accepted for publication. To have such works accepted, the author must be careful to till old theoretical ground in the prescribed way and to cite all the "right" sources. In other words, theorists are pressed in the direction of conforming to the dictates of Kuhn's (1962/1970) "normal science." The result is that a good deal of the non-rational art and creativity of theorizing is drained from such work.

Rationalization has also led to the publication in American sociology journals of a particular kind of theory. One rarely sees in those journals original theories, or even novel theoretical ideas. What do get published are metatheoretical works that summarize and/or critique the work of other sociological theorists. Such works are largely exegeses on the work of theoretical ancestors and contemporaries within American or European theory. Such works are about theory, they are studies of theory, rather than being original pieces of theorizing. While new theoretical ideas can come from such exegeses (a good example from the past is Parsons's *The Structure of Social Action*, 1937), the fact is that the return in new theoretical ideas from recent essays of this genre has been slim, if not non-existent.

There is, of course, also a peer review process in the publication of books devoted to theory. However, the nature of that review process is somewhat different, and reviewers of books look for different things than reviewers of essays for the major journals. This is true even when the same reviewer does both. To put it simply, more irrationalities are permissible in book-length manuscripts. Length and format are less important. There is enough space to develop more fully a new theoretical idea or perspective. While, as we saw above, book production has been rationalized, it (especially monograph publishing) has not been McDonaldized to nearly the degree that article production has been rationalized. The fact that American theorists are forced to devote far more attention to writing essays for journals, and less to book-length manuscripts, helps to account for the rationalization of American theory and explains why it has suffered in comparison to European theory.

Another aspect of the McDonaldization of American sociological theory is the fact that to succeed, an American theorist has had to be seen as part of an extant tradition. Historically, this has led to specialization within socio-logical theory: a theorist was identified as a structural functionalist, a conflict theorist, a symbolic interactionist, an exchange theorist, and so on. One worked within a theoretical tradition and built on it, again in the manner of normal science in empirical sociology. This specialization tended to rationalize the process of theory development. For example, it was highly efficient to add increments of knowledge to the tradition in which one was embedded. However, such specialization also had its limitations. To the degree that one was exposed to other theories, one was inclined to critique them, rather than to try to integrate their useful derivatives into one's own theoretical perspective.

European theory has rarely had such clear theoretical boundaries. As a result, European theories have traditionally been a blend of ideas drawn from many traditions. The emphasis is more on the production of truly original works that are distinguished by the fact that they are clearly different from their theoretical ancestors and from other contemporary theoretical products. This is best seen in French social science where the overwhelming pressure is to be different; to be original (Lemert, 1981).[11] The result is that that tradition has, in recent years, given us the very inventive and distinctive contributions of social theorists like Bourdieu, Foucault, Derrida, Lyotard, Baudrillard and Virilio. The idiosyncratic character of much of this theoretical work stands in stark contrast to the careful and measured extensions offered by the vast majority of contemporary American theorists. It is difficult, if not impossible, to think of a contemporary American theorist whose work rivals that of the best contemporary Europeans in originality and distinctiveness.

Of course, there are important changes taking place in contemporary American theory. We are witnessing the end of the clear boundaries around theories and the emergence of more synthetic theories (Ritzer, 1990). However, even here these syntheses are occurring from a base in one of our traditional theories. The best example of this is the work of Jeffrey Alexander (Alexander and Colomy, 1990) who is seen as being part of, and building on, the structural-functional tradition with his neofunctionalism. Similar extensions are being made by Fine (1990) from within symbolic interactionism, Cook et al. (1990) from a base in exchange theory, and many others. Like contributions to empirical knowledge, these are more like comfortable increments to extant theories, than creative new theories that ignore all boundaries.

Sociological theorists not only specialize in a particular kind of theory, but more generally they specialize in theory; that is, they often do theory to the exclusion of empirical research.[12] Bourdieu is a severe critic of this specialization, believing that "social theory has little to expect from ventures in 'theoretical logic' that are not grounded in a concrete research practice" (Wacquant, 1992: 32). While I disagree with Bourdieu here and feel that pure theorizing can produce, and more importantly *has* produced, important advances in sociology, I do agree that the tendency to specialize in *either* theory *or* research has had adverse effects on sociology.

Conclusion

While the thrust of this chapter has been to describe the McDonaldization of sociology, sociology has not, and can never be, McDonaldized to the degree that fast-food restaurants and other aspects of modern society have been. Yet the process has affected sociology and its impact is continuing to spread. The point of this discussion is both to describe this process for the general reader and to warn sociologists about what is occurring and to urge them to practice, in Bourdieu's terms, vigilance concerning this development. Above all, again following Bourdieu and Wacquant (1992: 183), "you [the sociologist] must learn to *avoid being the toy of social forces in your practice of sociology.*" Given its breadth and power, it is possible to become a mere toy in the larger process of the McDonaldization of sociology.

This brings us to the final objective of this chapter – its contribution to our understanding of the current crisis in sociology. There are some who see the closing of one sociology department, and reductions in the size of others, as signs of deep problems in the field. These difficulties are seen as making sociology very vulnerable in a period of academic cuts resulting from budget shortfalls. While these fears are, in my opinion overstated,[13] there *are* problems in sociology and McDonaldization is one of them. Briefly, the forward march of McDonaldization will lead sociology further away from creativity and more toward the predictability and uniformity of work on the "academic assembly line." To the degree that the work of sociologists becomes predictable and uncreative, more and more administrators will ask why they need such people, or at least why they need so many of them. Creative scholars are indispensable, but as on the nation's automobile assembly lines, the value of those who perform highly routinized work can be questioned more easily *and* they are easier to replace.

While the thrust of rationalization theory leads to pessimism, this author hopes that the theory is wrong, at least in this regard. After all, it is human beings who lie behind the production of a rationalized society in general, and a rationalized sociology in particular. Humans produced this world historically, and they reproduce it on a daily basis. Hence, they have the capacity to change those products. Reified social structures have been produced, but as the history of the former Soviet Union demonstrates, reified structures can be demolished. However, it is important to note that Soviet structures were distinctly non-rationalized and it may have been this that made them relatively easy to bring down. Rationalized structures, following Weber, are far more difficult to destroy. Sociologists *can* bring down those structures; they can in Goffman's term be "dangerous giants." In fact, it may be that because they understand the social processes involved, because they can bring sociological tools to bear on sociology, they are in a truly distinctive position to destroy the structures produced, or at least to mitigate their worst effects. Sociologists often inveigh against a public that mindlessly accepts the rationalized structures in which they exist. However, those critiques cannot be seen as credible until sociologists themselves act to overcome the rationalized systems that constrain them and their work. Indeed, such actions may be the first of what could ultimately become a wide-scale assault on the rationalized systems that increasingly control every facet of our lives. I would be the first to accept the idea that such a scenario is far-fetched. However, a basic premise of sociology is that all social systems are human constructions and that they can therefore be deconstructed!

Unlike many similar efforts, the goal of this critique is not to bring sociology to its knees; there are already too many people and forces intent on attaining that objective. In line with Wacquant's (1992: 36) contention about Bourdieu's metasociology, this chapter "seeks not to assault but to *buttress the epistemological security of sociology*." The ultimate objective here is to help build sociology by warning of the process of McDonaldiz-ation and suggesting that its adverse effects can be minimized and con-trolled. In terms of his work, Bourdieu (Bourdieu and Wacquant, 1992: 211) says: "I continually use sociology to try to cleanse my work of the social determinants that necessarily bear on sociologists." Put in those terms, the object of this chapter is to help sociologists "cleanse" the negative effects of one of the major contemporary determinants – McDonaldization – of what is taking place in the modern world in general, and modern sociology in particular.

Finally, a word about the sociology of sociology, or metasociology, and its bad name in the discipline. As pointed out above, the sociology of sociology contributed to its poor reputation with the triviality of many of its works. However, there is another factor in its lack of acceptance – sociologists have long been resistant to applying their own tools to them-selves; to seeing themselves as being affected by the same social forces that affect everyone else. Wacquant (1992: 43–4) makes this point in discussing Bourdieu's approach:

> Sociological reflexivity instantly raises hackles because it represents a frontal attack on the sacred sense of individuality that is so dear to all of us Westerners, and particularly on the charismatic self-conception of intellectuals who like to think of themselves as undetermined, "free-floating," and endowed with a form of symbolic grace.

This chapter, as well as the sociology of sociology implied in it, is likely to "raise the hackles" of sociologists by associating them with a trend of which most of them are likely to be critical and with which they do not wish to be associated. Yet, it is necessary for sociologists to recognize that they are not immune to this wide-reaching trend and that in order to begin to counteract it, they must be aware of its incursions into the heart of their own discipline. A greater awareness of this will help sociologists to see the importance – indeed, the necessity – of turning their intellectual tools on themselves.

Notes

I would like to thank Mark Abrahamson, JoAnn DeFiore and Ken Kammeyer for a number of useful suggestions on an earlier draft of this chapter.

1. One exception to this (and there are others) is the work inspired by Thomas Kuhn's (1962/1970) philosophy of science, especially Robert Friedrichs's (1970) book (which, incidentally is entitled *A Sociology of Sociology*). See also my own work on the paradigmatic status of sociology, especially *Sociology: A Multiple Paradigm Science* (Ritzer, 1975/1980) and *Toward an Integrated Sociological Paradigm* (Ritzer, 1981).

2. In fact, Bourdieu criticizes as "narcissistic" those metasociologists who focus exclusively on the individual sociologist.

3. However, it should be pointed out that Bourdieu (Bourdieu and Wacquant, 1992: 191) uses "meta" to mean above, while I use it to mean coming after. Nevertheless, as is clear from the following quotation, the kind of analysis contemplated is the same in both cases.

4. Or, depending on one's perspective, the postmodern world (Lyotard, 1979/1984; Shelton, forthcoming). For more on the postmodern view, see Chapter 9.

5. It should be noted that the trends to be discussed below represent, in the main, my subjective views about them. It would be useful for others to undertake research studies aimed at ascertaining their validity as well as the validity of the overall thesis about McDonaldization.

6. There are American journals such as *Qualitative Sociology* that publish qualitative studies and there is greater emphasis on such work in other countries (e.g. Great Britain).

7. One exception is the June 1992 issue of *Social Psychology Quarterly* devoted to theoretical essays.

8. Although, short research articles may be published as research notes.

9. Interestingly, sociology lags behind even more rationalized social sciences like psychology on the issue of paper length. In psychology the norm tends to be very short, highly routinized research papers that can be read very quickly and efficiently.

10. Once again, more rationalized fields like psychology seem to be "ahead" of sociology on the number of articles co-authored by long lists of people.

11. Although, as we saw earlier, Bourdieu is also critical of French sociology for being a world without surprises.

12. There are, of course, exceptions to this (for example the work of Joseph Berger and his colleagues on expectation states: Berger et al., 1989), as well as all other generalizations made throughout this chapter.

13. As I was quoted in an article on the state of the field, "There's no question that there are problems in the field. . . . But I don't think they are problems that represent the imminent demise or dissolution or decline of sociology" (cited in Coughlin, 1992: A6–A7).

4

Munch(ing) on McDonald(ization) of
Social Theory

Richard Münch (1991, 1993) draws on my work to argue that American social theory has been McDonaldized.[1] Within that context he is concerned with the fact that it has, in his view, been standardized (in much the way the Big Mac is made to uniform standards around the world). Of even greater concern to Münch is the fact that American sociology is busy exporting its standardized approach to social theory to the rest of the world, especially Europe. This line of argument fits in very well with two of my general arguments about McDonaldization. First, the McDonaldization process is affecting many different sectors of society, including academia in general and social theory in particular. Second, the principles that lie at the base of the success of the American fast-food industry are being exported to many other societies.

Münch (like me) is not merely describing a benign process, but critically analysing one with a series of unfortunate consequences. While in many ways highly desirable and alluring, the principles of McDonaldization bring with them a series of irrationalities. What Münch has done is to emphasize one of those irrationalities – the loss of creativity. On the one hand, Münch is arguing that American social theory has already lost much of its creativity. On the other hand, the exportation of the American way of doing theory is threatening the creativity of theorizing in other parts of the world, especially Europe.

Münch is interested specifically in the Americanization of European social theory since the end of World War II. He is animated by what he sees as the "detrimental effects" of American hegemony on social theory throughout the world. In his view, these detrimental effects are largely the result of the negative impact of professionalized American sociology on the "more artistic works" of European sociologists. More specifically, he argues that "professional" American sociologists have produced a standardized, "quality-approved" product (especially articles in the *American Sociological Review* and the *American Journal of Sociology*) and they have disseminated that product around the world. Münch links this directly to the idea of McDonaldization:

> Each article has the same format and quality guaranteed by a professional system of editors and reviewers. The effect on world sociology is the same as that of McDonald's worldwide supply of the same quality-approved hamburger for the world economy . . . the standardized article of the *American Sociological Review*

is the common life-world of sociologists throughout the world just as McDonald's hamburger is the common life-world of fast-food consumers everywhere. Indeed, Ritzer (1983) has referred to the phenomenon as the "McDonaldization of the world."[2] Here we can speak of the *McDonaldization of world sociology* originating from the highly professionalized and standardized work produced by American sociology departments.

One can continue the analogy by saying that the average American sociologist works like an employee of McDonald's: a team-worker who is dedicated to producing one hamburger-like article after another, according to the same quality standards. The consequence is a much greater standardization of sociological products than exists in European sociology, a levelling in which there is no place for the exceptional. (1991: 318; italics added)

Turning to more recent developments in American sociology, Münch underscores the rise of the economic paradigm in general and rational choice theory in particular.[3] This, too, is, in his view, associated with McDonaldization:

There is also a "McDonald's effect" associated with the success of rational choice theory. Because it is the most exactly and precisely formulated theory, it can be reproduced and applied to a great variety of social phenomena in the same way and without any difference in quality all over the world. It is a standardized product that can be reproduced and applied everywhere with only minimal training in theoretical skills. The theory does not require a deeper study of its cultural and philosophical background because the culture of economism has expanded throughout the world. McDonald's is now present all over the world and everyone understands the nature of economic transactions. . . . The final triumph of Western capitalism over the Communist world has broken down the last barrier to the culture of economism; that is why rational choice theory will be even more successful in the coming decades. (Münch, 1991: 319)

Münch is critiquing the McDonaldization of sociology in much the same way that other Europeans have attacked the more general spread of McDonaldization to the continent (see Chapter 6). For example, in a critique of another leading aspect of our McDonaldizing world, amusement parks, especially those created by Disney, a French socialist politician said at the opening of Euro Disney that it "will bombard France with uprooted creations that are to culture what fast food is to gastronomy" (Riding, 1992: A13). Extending this, one could say that Münch's essential point is that American sociology is an "uprooted creation" that is to its European counterparts what McDonald's is to European cuisine.

He seems to see some hope in American sociology, especially in the work of American theorists embedded in the European tradition and in that of Europeans working in American sociology. However, both of these bases for optimism are viewed as transplants and not as native American products. Thus, they are not accorded much of a chance of stemming the tide in the direction of rationalization. "The highly professionalized American system of sociology will *inevitably* exert its standardizing effects on the European implants" (Münch, 1991: 330).

Münch (1991: 329) concludes that Europe must resist the McDonaldization of social theory: "European sociology needs to resist this trend just as Europe inevitably has to resist McDonaldization of its culture as a whole in order to preserve diversity for itself and for the world." However, this resistance is not going to be easy because, among other things, "European sociology . . . now has indigenous McDonald's simply because of the domination by American sociology" (Münch, 1991: 330). Weakening the ability of European sociology to resist is the existence of a "Trojan horse" in its midst in the form of social theorists who have been afflicted by the "American disease."

Given the standardization of American social theory, Münch pins his hopes on the "interrelated diversity" of European, and more generally world, sociology. While Münch recognizes that European theory needs to emulate the Americans and become more professionalized, it also must seek "an intensification of exchange, competition, communication, and cooperation among the relatively divided parts of Europe, yet without replicating the American path of professionalization by standardization" (Münch, 1991: 329). European theorists are urged to draw on the diverse resources of the variety of national traditions to be found on their continent. In effect, the answer to the uniformity of American social theory is the diversity of European theory, albeit in a professionalized form.

Münch's argument is in many ways a legitimate extension of the McDonaldization thesis to social theory in general, and European social theory in particular. As is clear in the preceding chapter, I am sympathetic with Münch's interest in the process and his concern about its negative effects. However, his argument is not without its weaknesses. For example, his description of the standardized American journal article applies far better to those reporting on empirical research than it does to theoretical essays. Theoretical essays are far *less likely* to follow a standard pattern; far *less likely* to be mere clones of one another. Indeed, Münch (1981, 1982) is well aware of this since he published a lengthy and highly unusual two-part essay on Parsonsian theory in the *American Journal of Sociology*. His description of American sociologists as teamworkers putting together sociological works in a manner similar to the way McDonald's employees assemble hamburgers also applies far better to empirical researchers than to theorists. One is hard-pressed to think of many, if any, theoretical "teams" involved in putting together a series of works.

However, my major disagreement with Münch is over his contention that professionalization is linked to the standardization and more generally to the McDonaldization of American social theory.[4] I do not see professionalization as an integral part of the process of rationalization; indeed, in many ways they are in conflict. Rationalization is often linked to bureaucratization; in fact, the two are closely intertwined in Weber's work. However, bureaucracies and professions are in many ways different methods of organizing work. For example, bureaucracies seek top-down control, often by nonprofessional managers, while the professions seek autonomy and self-control. The professions have often resisted bureaucratization, and rationalization more generally. When they do fall prey to these twin processes, the result is often a process of deprofessionalization. In other words, rationalization leads to the loss of at least some degree of profession-alization (Ritzer and Walczak, 1988). It is not professionalization, but rationalization, that is the source of the problems in American sociology discussed by Münch.

In support of this view is the fact that fast-food restaurants, and most other McDonaldized systems, are not havens of professional employment. Rather, they are characterized by "McJobs" (see Chapter 5) and in most, if not all, senses of the term, "professional" occupations are the antithesis of McJobs. For example, those who hold McJobs have virtually no autonomy while those who work in the professions seek and, at least traditionally, have a high degree of autonomy. For another, the professions possess, at least ideally, general systematic knowledge, whereas McJobs involve, at best, the specific knowledge associated with, for example, flipping hamburgers.

However, it is worth noting that there are signs that the professions are not immune to McDonaldization. In medicine, for example, the dramatic in-crease in "managed care" is pushing physicians to operate more efficiently, to make their activities more calculable and predictable, and in the direction of being more controlled by non-human technologies. We even have the increasing presence of McDoctors, or drive-in medical centers that in many ways resemble fast-food restaurants. While the professions may be under-going McDonaldization, they are *not*, as Münch suggests, an integral part of the process of rationalization.

Criticisms like these aside, evidence to support Münch's basic thesis abounds in contemporary social theory. On the one hand, American social theory has been adversely affected by the standardization described by Münch. As pointed out in the preceding chapter, it is difficult to think of more than a few, if any, contemporary American social theorists who are doing the kind of innovative, ground-breaking work that is likely to have a powerful influence on the course of social theory (viewed universally) over the next several decades. On the other hand, there is a relatively long list of innovative European thinkers who are likely to have a powerful impact on world social theory. Most of them either did the bulk of their work before the McDonaldization of the continent was far advanced or were able to evade the impact of standardized American sociology. Of course, Münch's fear is that McDonaldization will serve to choke off this innovativeness and it is that which he is struggling to prevent.

Why has American social theory lost its pre-eminence in recent decades? Why has social theory come, once again, to be dominated by Europeans? There are undoubtedly many reasons for this, but at least one of them *is* the McDonaldization of American society in general and academia in particular. In fact, the rise and spread of this process in the 1950s and 1960s is coincident with the beginning of the demise of the hegemony of American social theory. I am certainly not suggesting that McDonaldization is the sole cause of this decline, but there is an interesting correlation between them.

Münch has touched on only one factor in this decline in his discussion of the standardization of American sociology. This is a factor internal to sociology, but there are many other internal factors that he could associate with the McDonaldization of American social theory. More importantly, Münch has had nothing to say about the McDonaldization of the larger society in which American theorists operate. Today's American theorists have been raised in a McDonaldized society, trained in McDonaldized schools and universities, employed by McDonaldized institutions of higher learning, and are participants in the increasingly McDonaldized discipline of sociology. The result is a strong propensity to do their own theorizing in a highly rational way. This leads to the need to create a large amount of theory as quickly and efficiently as possible. This, in turn, leads to an emphasis on producing a large quantity of work that tends to suffer as a result in terms of quality. It also often results in the use of shortcuts in the production of theory (not carefully and systematically reading the work of predecessors, spending less time than is needed to carefully craft a theoretical piece) and these, too, negatively affect quality. The tenure system at American universities, with its emphasis on number of publications, exacerbates this problem.

So there are many reasons for the comparative lack of creativity in American social theory. In fact, Münch has focused on the one that happens to be of comparative *in*significance to American social theorists. As indicated above, the pressure to produce the standard journal article falls much more on those who are doing empirical sociological research than social theory. There is far greater variation in the structure and length of the typical theory article and, in any case, important theory work is at least as likely to appear in book form as it is to find its way into sociology journals. I think Münch is largely right about American social theory, but for the wrong reason.

Of course, a key part of my thesis (and Münch recognizes this) is that McDonaldization is not only spreading throughout American institutions, but it is also making significant inroads throughout the world. Furthermore, the future is likely to bring with it a great increase in McDonaldization. The implication is that European sociologists are likely to lose at least some of what Münch regards as their comparative advantage as their societies, and their sociologies, grow more McDonaldized. As European societies become more homogenized as a result of the process of McDonaldization (and many others), the possibilities of cross-fertilization among the theorists of different nations extolled by Münch are likely to be greatly reduced. If Münch is right about American social theory, and I am right about the process of McDonaldization, then European social theorists are in the early stages of the "American disease." Furthermore, it should be borne in mind that the roots of the theory of McDonaldization lie in the work of Max Weber and it was Germany that produced the early paradigm for the rationalization process – the bureaucracy. One could envision a scenario in which Germany once again takes the lead in the rationalization process with powerful effects on social theory not only in Germany, but throughout the rest of the world.

In one of the critiques of Münch's thesis, Jeffrey Alexander (1994) excoriates Münch for focusing on the nation-state and for ignoring global-ization (see Chapter 7). To Alexander, the globalization process, as it is manifest in social theory, serves to erode the significance of the nation-state as a force in molding social theory (and, for that matter, many other things). While globalization theory is hot in world sociology today, I think it underestimates the continuing significance of the nation-state. My focal interests – the fast-food restaurant, the credit card (see Chapter 8) and other new "means of consumption" (Chapter 9) – are, and in many ways could only be, products of the United States. For example, in *Expressing America* (Ritzer, 1995; see also Chapter 8 of this volume) I discuss the spread of credit cards around the world explicitly in terms of Americanization. Credit cards (like fast-food restaurants) are rapidly Americanizing the way much of the rest of the world consumes.

In spite of the growing influence of global processes, the nation-state continues to be of continuing importance in shaping social theory. To take another example, poststructural and postmodern social theories are heavily dominated by French social theorists (Ritzer, 1997). In many ways, it is only French society and the French intellectual community that could have created these theoretical perspectives (Lemert, 1981).

I am not suggesting that McDonaldization is the only, or even the central, factor in the problems confronting American, and increasingly world, social theory. However, it does offer us an interesting way of connecting issues of concern to the theoretical community to broader social trends. Once known for its steel and automobiles, America has come to be known for its junk food. Once known for the work of thinkers like Parsons, Merton, Mead and Homans, is American social theory destined to suffer a similar fate and come to be known for the theoretical equivalent of junk food? More importantly, is Münch right? Is American sociological theory leading theorizing throughout the world in the same, potentially disastrous, direction?

Notes

This chapter is based on "Münch(ing) on McDonald(ization) of Social Theory", *Swiss Journal of Sociology*, 22, 1996: 247–50.

1. In particular, my early essay on McDonaldization (Ritzer, 1983). Here I shall focus on social theory rather than sociology as a whole because that is clearly Münch's major concern.

2. I discuss the "McDonaldization of society," and the idea that it is coming to encompass the world is certainly explicit in my work.

3. While I agree that rational choice theory has an affinity with McDonaldization, I do not think that doing rational choice theory inevitably involves such rationalization. For example, rational choice theorists can operate in a highly creative manner. While the triumph of rational choice theory may increase the likelihood of the rationalization of theory, it is far from the only force pushing theory in that direction and it is not the only theory being subjected to that process.

4. Part of the problem is that Münch is not using the term "professionalization" in its formal, sociological sense (Abbott, 1988; Macdonald, 1995), but in an informal way which includes only some of the elements of the formal definition (professional association with strong leadership, leading professional journals, peer review of articles for those journals, and a specialized graduate curriculum).

II
THE EXPANSION OF McDONALDIZATION

5

McJobs: McDonaldization and Its Relationship to the Labor Process

In recent years the spread of McDonaldized systems has led to the creation of an enormous number of jobs. Unfortunately, the majority of them can be thought of as McDonaldized jobs, or "McJobs." While we usually associate these types of positions with fast-food restaurants, and in fact there are many such jobs in that setting (over 2.5 million people worked in that industry in the United States in 1992 (Van Giezen, 1994)), McJobs have spread throughout much of the economy with the growing impact of McDonaldization on work settings which had previously experienced relatively little rationalization.

It is worth outlining some of the basic realities of employment in the fast-food industry in the United States since those jobs serve as a model for employment in other McDonaldized settings (Van Giezen, 1994). The large number of people employed in fast-food restaurants accounts for over 40 percent of the approximately 6 million people employed in restaurants of all types. Fast-food restaurants rely heavily on teenage employees – almost 70 percent of their employees are 20 years of age or younger. For many, the fast-food restaurant is likely to be their first employer. It is estimated that the first job for one of every 15 workers was at McDonald's; one of every eight Americans has worked at McDonald's at some time in his or her life. The vast majority of employees are part-time workers: the average work week in the fast-food industry is 29.5 hours. There is a high turnover rate: only slightly more than half the employees remain on the job for a year or more. Minorities are over-represented in these jobs – almost two-thirds of employees are women and nearly a quarter are non-white. These are low-paid occupations, with many earning the minimum wage, or slightly more. As a result, these jobs are greatly affected by changes in the minimum wage: an upward revision has an important effect on the income of these workers. However, there is a real danger that many workers would lose their positions as a result of such increases, especially in economically marginal fast-food restaurants.[1]

Although the McDonaldization of society is manifest at all levels and in all realms of the social world, the work world has played a particularly pivotal role in this. On the one hand, it is the main source of many of the precursors of McDonaldization, including bureaucracies, scientific management, assembly lines, and so on. More contemporaneously, the kinds of jobs, work procedures and organizing principles that have made McDonald's so successful have affected the way in which many businesses now organize much of their work. In fact, it could well be argued that the primary root of the McDonaldization of the larger society is the work world. On the other hand, the McDonaldization of the larger society has, in turn, served to further rationalize the work world. We thus have a self-reinforcing and enriching process that is speeding the growth and spread of McDonaldization.

The process of McDonaldization is leading to the creation of more and more McJobs.[2] The service sector, especially at its lower end, is producing an enormous number of jobs, most of them requiring little or no skill. There is no better example of this than the mountain of jobs being produced by the fast-food industry. However, new occupational creation is not the only source of McJobs: many extant low-level jobs are being McDonaldized. More strikingly, large numbers of middle-level jobs are also being deskilled and transformed into McJobs.

McJobs are characterized by the five dimensions of McDonaldization. The jobs tend to involve a series of simple tasks in which the emphasis is on performing each as efficiently as possible. Second, the time associated with many of the tasks is carefully calculated and the emphasis on the quantity of time a task should take tends to diminish the quality of the work from the point of view of the worker. That is, tasks are so simplified and streamlined that they provide little or no meaning to the worker. Third, the work is predictable; employees do and say essentially the same things hour after hour, day after day. Fourth, many non-human technologies are employed to control workers and reduce them to robot-like actions. Some technologies are in place, and others are in development, that will lead to the eventual replacement of many of these "human robots" with computerized robots. Finally, the rationalized McJobs lead to a variety of irrationalities, especially the dehumanization of work. The result is the extraordinarily high turnover rate described above and difficulty in maintaining an adequate supply of replacements.[3]

The claim is usually made by spokespeople for McDonaldized systems that they are offering a large number of entry-level positions that help give employees basic skills they will need in order to move up the occupational ladder within such systems (and many of them do). This is likely to be true in the instances in which the middle-level jobs to which they move – for example shift leader, assistant manager or manager of a fast-food restaurant – are also routinized and scripted. In fact, it turns out that this even holds for the positions held by the routinized and scripted instructors at Hamburger University who teach the managers, who teach the employees, and so on. However, the skills acquired in McJobs are not likely to prepare one for, help one to acquire, or help one to function well in, the far more desirable post-industrial occupations which are highly complex and require high levels of skill and education. Experience in routinized actions and scripted inter-actions do not help much when occupations require thought and creativity.

After this brief introduction to McJobs, we turn to a more theoretical issue: what relationship, if any, exists between the McDonaldization of society and the changing nature of what a number of theorists and re-searchers, following the work of Karl Marx and Harry Braverman, have called the "labor process"? These analysts adopt a critical orientation: they tend to look at the labor process from the point of view of things like managerial control over what workers do, technological advancement and control, deskilling and exploitation. The labor process associated with the McJobs described above certainly has these characteristics and therefore falls within the purview of those associated with this approach.

The labor process, at least in the sense of the term as it is used above, was not the central concern of *The McDonaldization of Society*. Nonetheless, a critical approach to the labor process, at least as it occurs in McDonaldized settings, is very much in evidence throughout *McDonaldization*. And while the literature on the labor process was not a crucial resource in that book, some of the key people and central ideas associated with that literature – Frederick W. Taylor (1947), Henry Ford (1922; as well as Fordism and post-Fordism: Clarke, 1990), scientific management, deskilling, control (Edwards, 1979), and so on – are found throughout *McDonaldization*. Nonetheless, there is no mention of *the* central figure in the labor process tradition, Harry Braverman (1974; Smith, 1994). Furthermore, the ideas of Karl Marx (which lie at the base of Braverman's thinking as well as of the labor process literature in general), while generally important in my own thinking, are also not mentioned;[4] the book is overwhelmingly Weberian in character.[5] Thus, the best that *can* be said is that there are a number of concerns that are common to *McDonaldization* and the labor process literature. However, more *could* be said about the relationship between these phenomena. The issue here, then, is what does the McDonaldization thesis have to say, explicitly or implicitly, about the labor process?

The major contribution, at least potentially, lies in dialectically linking a larger and broader social process (McDonaldization) to the way in which the labor process is organized. Leading to an interest in such a relationship is the tendency of analysts to deal with the labor process in isolation from larger social developments. An interest in exploring such linkages has existed in the labor process literature for some time. For example, it is expressed at a general level by Littler (1990) and more specifically by Strinati (1990) in his work on the state. McDonaldization can be seen as one such large-scale social process encompassing a wide array of cultural and structural changes that is affecting (and being affected by) changes in the labor process.

At the cultural level, large numbers of people in the United States, and increasingly throughout much of the rest of the world, have come to value McDonaldization in general, as well as its fundamental characteristics. McDonaldization, as well as its various principles, has become part of our value system. That value system has, in turn, been translated into a series of principles that have been exported to, adopted by, and adapted to, a wide range of social settings. These principles have been institutionalized at the structural level in an array of social structures, the rules, regulations and physical characteristics of which have been affected by these principles. Thus, McDonaldization is manifest at the macro level in both culture and social structure.

What is of greater interest is the way in which these macro-level phenomena are affecting the micro level, especially, at least from the point of view of this chapter, the labor process. However, this large-scale development is affecting a wide array of more micro-level processes, not just the labor process, and all of them are being affected in similar ways. For example, the behavior of customers at fast-food restaurants is being affected in much the same way as the behavior of those who work in those restaurants. Thus, McDonaldization allows us not only to link the labor process to larger social changes, but also to see that workers are far from alone in being affected by these changes. Furthermore, the impact on employees and customers is being felt throughout a society in which sector after sector is undergoing McDonaldization.

The constraints on the behavior of employees and customers in McDonaldized systems are of both a structural and a cultural nature. Employees and customers find themselves in a variety of McDonaldized structures that demand that they behave in accord with the dictates of those structures. For example, the drive-through window associated with the fast-food restaurant (as well as other settings such as banks) structures both what customers in their cars and employees in their booths can and cannot do. They can efficiently exchange money for food, but their positions (in a car and a booth) and the press of other cars in the queue make any kind of personal interaction virtually impossible. Of course, many other kinds of behavior are either made possible, or prohibited, by such structures. In Giddens's (1984) terms, such structures are both enabling and constraining.

At a cultural level, both employees and customers are socialized into, and have internalized, the norms and values of working and living in a McDonaldized society. Employees are trained by managers or owners who are likely, themselves, to have been trained at an institution like McDonald's Hamburger University (Schaaf, 1994). Such institutions are as much concerned with inculcating norms and values as they are with the teaching of basic skills. For their part, customers are not required to attend Hamburger University, but they are "trained" by the employees themselves, by television advertisements, and by their own children who are often diligent students, teachers and enforcers of the McDonald's way. This "training," like that of those employees who attend Hamburger University, is oriented not only to teaching the "skills" required to be a customer at a fast-food restaurant (e.g. how to queue up in order to order food), but also the norms and values of such settings as they apply to customers (e.g. customers are expected to dispose of their own debris; they are not expected to linger after eating). As a result of such formal and informal training, both employees and customers can be relied on to do what they are supposed to, and what is expected of them, with little or no personal supervision.

The preceding discussion of the impact of structure and culture is very much in line with Braverman's focal concern with control. Recall that he defined management as "*a labor process conducted for the purpose of control within the corporation*" (Braverman, 1974: 267). To Braverman, that control is exercised and extended through such mechanisms as the specialization of work, scientific management's "*dictation to the worker of the precise manner in which work is to be performed*" (Braverman, 1974: 90), and the use of non-human technologies. All of these can be seen as part of the process of McDonaldization. Scientific management is, as we have seen, one of the precursors of McDonaldization and its basic principles continue to inform that process. Control through non-human technologies is one of the basic elements of McDonaldization. And the specialization of work furthers rationalization by making work tasks more predictable, efficient and calculable. While McDonaldization encompasses these forms of control, it highlights other elements of that control based on larger structural and cultural factors.

While Braverman was right to emphasize the importance of management to control, McDonaldization points to other factors as being central to the control of employees (and customers). In light of the increasing importance of these factors, it is likely that the role played by management in control is less today than it was when Braverman wrote. The control exercised by culture and structure makes management a less powerful force. In many ways, such control is more effective *and* less expensive than control exercised by managers. And employees are less likely to rebel against the impersonal control exercised by drive-through windows and social norms.

Neither Marx nor Braverman fully anticipated the rise of the kind of service worker who has come to dominate McDonaldized systems. While they have much in common with them, McJobs are not simply the deskilled jobs of our industrial past in new settings; they are jobs that have a variety of new and distinctive characteristics. While those who hold McJobs are controlled in many of the ways explored by Marx and Braverman, there have also emerged many distinctive aspects of the control of these workers. Industrial and McDonaldized jobs both tend to be highly routinized in terms of what people do on the job. However, one of the things that is distinctive about McDonaldized jobs, especially since so many of them involve work that requires interaction and communication, especially with consumers, is that what people *say* on the job is also highly routinized. To put this another way, McDonaldized jobs are tightly scripted: they are characterized by *both* routinized actions (for example, the way McDonald's hamburgers are to be put down on the grill and flipped: Love, 1986: 141–2) and scripted interactions (examples include, "May I help you?"; "Would you like a dessert to go with your meal?"; "Have a nice day!"). Scripts are crucial because, as Leidner (1993) points out, many of the workers in McDonald-ized systems are interactive service workers. This means that they not only produce goods and provide services, but they often do so in interaction with customers.

The scripting of interaction leads to new depths in the deskilling of workers. Not only have employee actions been deskilled; employees' ability to speak and interact with customers is now being limited and controlled. There are not only scripts to handle general situations, but also a range of sub-scripts to deal with a variety of contingencies. Verbal and interactive skills are being taken away from employees and built into the scripts in much the same way that manual skills were taken and built into various technologies. At one time distrusted in their ability to *do* the right thing, workers now find themselves no longer trusted to *say* the right thing. Once able to create distinctive interactive styles, and to adjust them to different circumstances, employees are now asked to follow scripts as mindlessly as possible. In Braverman's terms, just as management has long "conceived" what employees are supposed to do, it now "conceives" what they are supposed to say and how they are supposed to say it, and in both action and interaction employees have little choice but to "execute" management's demands.

In her analysis of Combined Insurance, Leidner (1993) found that this company went even further and sought to transform and thereby control its employees' selves.[6] This is consistent with Arlie Hochschild's (1983) discovery that airlines sought to manage the emotions of their employees. These findings seem in tune with the efforts of labor process thinkers and researchers to extend their concerns from objective realities to employee subjectivities. What we have evidence of here is a series of unprecedented efforts to control employees. It is not simply what people do and say on the job that many organizations now seek to control, but also how they view themselves and how they feel.

However, Combined Insurance is not a good example of a McDonaldized firm and Leidner's findings cannot be extended to most such settings. The fact is that McDonaldized systems have little interest in how their mainly part-time, short-term employees feel about and see themselves. These systems are merely interested in controlling their employees' overt behavior for as long as they work in such a system. This point was made, in a different way, in Chapter 2 in which it was argued that Mannheim's concepts of self-rationalization and self-observation are dated and have little relevance to employees of McDonaldized systems.

One very important, but rarely noted, aspect of the labor process in the fast-food restaurant and other McDonaldized systems is the extent to which customers are being led, perhaps even almost required, to perform a number of tasks without pay that were formerly performed by paid employees. For example, in the modern gasoline station the driver now does various things for free (pumps gas, cleans windows, checks oil, even pays through a computerized credit card system built into the pump) that were formerly done by paid attendants. In these and many other settings, McDonaldization has brought the customer *into* the labor process: the customer *is* the laborer! This has several advantages for employers such as lower (even non-existent) labor costs, the need for fewer employees, and less trouble with personnel problems: customers are far less likely to complain about a few seconds or minutes of tedious work than employees who devote a full work day to such tasks. Because of its advantages, as well as because customers are growing accustomed to, and accepting of, it, I think customers are likely to become even more involved in the labor process.

This is the most revolutionary development, at least as far as the labor process is concerned, associated with McDonaldization. As a result of this dramatic change, the analysis of the labor process must be extended to what customers do in McDonaldized systems. The distinction between customer and employee is eroding, or in postmodern terms "imploding," and one can envision more and more work settings in which customers are asked to do an increasing amount of "work." More dramatically, it is also likely that we will see more work settings in which there are no employees at all! In such settings customers, in interaction with non-human technologies, will do *all* of the human labor. A widespread example is the ATM in which customers (and the technology) do all of the work formerly done by bank tellers. More strikingly, we are beginning to see automated loan machines which dispense loans as high as $10,000 (Singletary, 1996). Again, customers and technologies do the work and, in the process, many loan-officer positions are eliminated. Similarly, the new automated gasoline pumps allow (or force) customers to do all of the required tasks; in some cases and at certain times (late at night) no employees at all are present.

In a sense, a key to the success of McDonaldized systems is that they have been able to supplement the exploitation of employees with the exploitation of customers. Lest we forget, Marx "put at the heart of his sociology – as no other sociology does – the theme of exploitation" (Worsley, 1982: 115). In Marxian theory, the capitalists are seen as simply paying workers less than the value produced by the workers, and as keeping the rest for themselves. This dynamic continues in contemporary society, but capitalists have learned that they can ratchet up the level of exploitation not only by exploiting workers more, but also by exploiting a whole new group of people – consumers. In Marxian terms, customers create value in the tasks they perform for McDonaldized systems. And they are not simply paid less than the value they produce, they are paid *nothing at all*. In this way, customers are exploited to an even greater degree than workers. As is true of the exploitation of workers (Marx, 1867/1967: 550), owners are unaware of the fact that they are exploiting customers. But knowledge of exploitation is not a prerequisite to its practice.

While we have been focusing on the exploitation of customers in McDonaldized systems, this is not to say that employers have lost sight of the need to exploit workers. Beyond the usual exploitation of being paid less than the value of what they produce, McDonald's employees are often not guaranteed that they will work the number of hours they are supposed to on a given day. If business is slow, they may be sent home early in order that the employer can economize on labor costs: this reduces their take-home pay. As a result, employees often find it hard to count on a given level of income, meager as it might be, each week. In this way, and many others, employees of McDonaldized systems are even more exploited than their industrial counterparts.

This discussion brings together the two great theories in the history of sociology – Weber's theory of rationalization and Marx's theory of capitalist expansion and exploitation. Rationalization is a process that serves the interest of capitalists. They push it forward (largely unconsciously) because it heightens the level of exploitation of workers, allows new agents (e.g. customers) to be exploited and brings with it greater surplus value and higher profits. This discussion adds a needed corrective to Braverman's perspective which focused on control and had little to say about the dynamics of economic exploitation. We can see here how rationalization not only enhances control, but also heightens the level and expands the reach of exploitation.

In various ways, McDonaldization is imposed on employees and even customers. They often have no choice but to conform, even if they would prefer things to be done in other ways. However, it would be a mistake to look at McDonaldization as simply being imposed on workers and customers. As discussed above, the basic ideas associated with McDonaldization are part of the value system: many workers and customers have internalized them and conform to them of their own accord.

Furthermore, through their actions both workers and customers can be seen as actively "manufacturing" or "subjectifying" McDonaldization (Burawoy, 1979; Knights, 1990). By acceding to the constraints placed on them, by creating new and idiosyncratic ways of McDonaldizing their actions and interactions, and by extending McDonaldization to other aspects of their lives, workers and customers can be seen as actively involved in the manufacture, the social construction, of McDonaldization (Berger and Luckmann, 1967). This is another aspect of the way in which McDonaldization is not simply imposed on people. Workers and customers often both buy into McDonaldization and are actively involved in its creation.

The emphasis on the McDonaldization of work (like that on deskilling) tends to emphasize only one side of the dialectic between structural changes, especially those imposed by management, and the significance of the responses of employees, which are consistently downplayed. But as Leidner takes great pains to point out, the employees of McDonaldized systems often exhibit a considerable amount of independence, perhaps even creativity, on the job. Leidner also points out that in our rush to condemn, we must not ignore the advantages to both employees and customers of the routinization, even the scripting, of work.

Although it had precursors in the bureaucracy, the assembly line and scientific management, and so on, McDonaldization had its proximate source in the fast-food restaurant. Continuing changes in the way such restaurants operate are serving to both reinforce and alter the nature of the larger process of McDonaldization. Not only does this larger process affect employees and customers in the fast-food restaurant, but that type of business was and is a major source of McDonaldization. There is a true dialectic here between the fast-food restaurant and McDonaldization.

There is also a dialectic between living one's life in a McDonaldized society and working in a McDonaldized job. These are mutually reinforcing and the net result is that if most of one's life is spent in one McDonaldized system or another, then one is less likely to feel dissatisfied with either one's life or one's job. This helps to account for Robin Leidner's (1993) finding that McDonald's workers do not evidence a high level of dissatisfaction with their work. This, perhaps, is one of the most disturbing implications of the McDonaldization thesis. If most of one's life is spent in McDonaldized systems, then there is little or no basis for rebellion against one's McDonaldized job since one lacks a standard against which to compare, and to judge, such a job. More generally, there is little or no basis for rebelling against the system or for seeking out alternative, non-McDonaldized systems. McDonaldization then becomes the kind of iron cage described by Weber from which there is no escape and, worse, not even any interest in escaping.

This also undermines one of Braverman's (and Marx's) fundamental assumptions that when all is said and done workers remain at odds with the kind of work that is being imposed on them and are a threat to those who are imposing the work. To Braverman (and Marx), there is a creative core (Marx's species being, for example) lying just below the surface that is ever-ready to protest, or rebel against, the rationalized and exploitative character of work. However, can that creative core survive intact, or even at all, in the face of growing up in a McDonaldized world, being bombarded by media messages from McDonaldized systems, and being socialized by and educated in McDonaldized schools?

Braverman argued that the kinds of trends discussed above and in his work are occurring not only among lower layers in the occupational hierarchy, but also in the middle layers. McDonaldization is something that those at the top of any hierarchy seek to avoid for themselves, but are willing and eager to impose on those who rank below them in the system. Initially, it is the lowest level employees who have their work McDonaldized, but, as Braverman argued, it eventually creeps into those middle layers.

While guilty of exploiting and controlling employees, franchise operators are, in turn, controlled and exploited by franchise companies. Many franchise operators have done well, even becoming multi-millionaires controlling perhaps hundreds of franchises (Tannenbaum, 1996), but many others have staggered or failed as a result of high start-up costs and continuing fees to the franchise companies. (The inducement to the franchisor to open as many outlets as possible threatens the profitability and even the continued existence of extant franchise owners: Gibson, 1996b.) The operators take much of the financial risk, while the franchise companies sit back and (often) rake in the profits. In addition, the franchise companies frequently have detailed rules, regulations, and even inspectors that they use to control the operators.

While no class within society is immune to McDonaldization, the lower classes are the most affected. They are the ones who are most likely to go to McDonaldized schools, live in inexpensive, mass-produced tract houses and work in McDonaldized jobs. Those in the upper classes have much more of a chance of sending their children to non-McDonaldized schools, living in custom-built homes, and working in occupations in which they impose McDonaldization on others while avoiding it to a large degree themselves.

Also related to the social class issue (see Chapter 13) is the fact that the McDonaldization of a significant portion of the labor force does not mean that all, or even most, of the labor force is undergoing this process. In fact, the McDonaldization of some of the labor force is occurring at the same time that another large segment is moving in a post-industrial, that is, more highly skilled, direction (Hage and Powers, 1992). Being created in this sector of society are relatively high-status, well-paid occupations requiring high levels of education and training. In the main, these are far from McJobs and lack most, or all, of the dimensions discussed at the beginning of this chapter. The growth of such post-industrial occupations parallels the concern in the labor process literature with flexible specialization occurring side by side with the deskilling of many other jobs. This points to a bifurcation in the class system. In spite of appearances, there is no contradiction here; McDonaldization and post-industrialization tend to occur in different sectors of the labor market. However, the spread of McJobs leads us to be dubious of the idea that we have moved into a new post-industrial era and have left behind the kind of deskilled jobs we associate with industrial society.

Finally, it may well be that the focus on the labor process, in fast-food restaurants and elsewhere, ignores what labor process theorists call "the full circuit of capital" (Knights and Willmott, 1990: 13). Although it does not relate to *McDonaldization*, but to my work on credit cards (see Chapter 8; also Ritzer, 1995) it should be pointed out that the focus in contemporary capitalism, at least in the United States, seems to have shifted from the valorization and control processes, indeed from production as a whole, to consumption. The essence of modern capitalism, at least as it is practiced in the core nations, may not be so much maximizing the exploitation of workers as the maximization of consumption. What the credit card (and other modern innovations in credit) indicates is that capitalism can no longer survive in its present form by convincing consumers to spend all of their resources at hand. What it must do is to come up with a constant set of innovations designed to get consumers to spend not only everything at hand, but also an increasingly large proportion of money they have not yet earned.

In a telling and startling reversal of what we usually mean by the term, the credit card companies refer to those who pay their bills in full each month as "deadbeats." From the warped perspective of the credit card industry, a deadbeat is so designated because he/she does not allow the industry to earn the large profits derived from charging usurious interest rates to those who revolve their accounts (about two-thirds of all users). The message, clearly, is that it is our duty to go into debt so that the credit card firms can earn extraordinary profits.

More generally, the message is that if we want the capitalist system to continue to prosper, we must continue to increase our level of indebtedness not only to the credit card companies, but also to the banks and other agencies that hold our mortgages, home equity loans, car loans, and so on. Banking used to be primarily about saving; profits were earned from the difference in the rate paid to savers and the rate the banks earned by lending the money to others. However, in recent years banks have learned that it is far more profitable to be in the loan business. Massive efforts have been made to get us to borrow money in various ways, while inducements to save have all but disappeared. For example, several billion pieces of mail were sent to American homes in 1995 (about 25 per household) urging and inducing (with low introductory rates, free offers) people to sign up for yet another credit card. How many pieces of mail arrived urging, let alone inducing, those same people to save at their local bank? The answer may well be zero. This disparity in mailings tells us where the priorities of today's banks lie.

Capitalism has found that it is imperative for people to consume far beyond their cash at hand. In a sense, there is a new law of capitalist accumulation operating here. While not ignoring international expansion of their markets, capitalists have discovered a new way to increase their markets at home. They have done this, as the postmodernists suggest, by eliminating the constraints and boundaries of time (Harvey, 1989). Capitalism can only grow so far by getting us to spend everything we have, so it has found a way through credit cards and other types of readily available loans to get us to spend money we have not yet even earned. Capitalist growth is dependent on the finding of ever new and more refined ways of getting us to spend money that is not to be earned until farther and farther into the future. The goal, to use a phrase from an earlier period of capitalism, is to get all of us to "owe our souls to the company store."

While the American capitalist will not ignore today's international markets (and will even export modern credit instruments to them), those markets have more vagaries than the future market at home. The economic crisis in Mexico in the mid-1990s pointed, once again, to these dangers. Capitalists today appear to be driven more by intensifying the market at home in terms of time than they are in making the markets for their products more geographically (spatially) extensive.

It could be argued, as many have, that the focus in modern capitalism has shifted from the control and exploitation of production to the control and exploitation of consumption. While that may well be true, the fact is that capitalists do not, and will not, ignore the realm of production. As *McDonaldization* shows, the nature of work is changing and capitalists are fully involved in finding new ways of controlling and exploiting workers. Further, they have discovered that they can even replace paid employees not only with machines, temporary workers and so on, but also with customers who are seemingly glad do the work for nothing! Here, clearly, is a new gift to the capitalist. Surplus value is now not only to be derived from the labor time of the employee, but also from the leisure time of the customer. McDonaldization is helping to open a whole new world of exploitation and growth to the contemporary capitalist.

Notes

This chapter combines a paper, "McJobs," published in Rich Feller and Garry Walz (eds), *Career Transitions in Turbulent Times*. Greensboro, NC: ERIC/CASS Publications, 1996 and the Invited Plenary Address, International Labour Process Conference, Blackpool, England, April 1995.

1. Although a study by Katz and Krueger (1992) indicates an employment *increase* accompanying a rise in the minimum wage.
2. As we will see below, other kinds of high-status, high-paying post-industrial occupations are also growing.
3. There are, of course, many other factors involved in turnover.
4. For example, Marx's ideas lie at the base of my sense of an integrated sociological paradigm (Ritzer, 1981).
5. Although the ideas of a few Marxists do receive some attention.
6. Much like Mannheim's self-observation.

6

McDonaldization:
The New "American Menace"

McDonald's, fast-food restaurants and the process of McDonaldization are all largely, if not exclusively, American phenomena, at least in terms of their origin. The export of these interrelated phenomena can therefore be viewed as an example of Americanization. In this way, we can link the process of McDonaldization to that of Americanization.[1] While such a linkage exists, it is by no means a simple one. McDonaldization does have various non-American roots, most notably the German bureaucracy analysed so famously by Max Weber. In addition, many cultures throughout the world have their own varieties of what is now called "fast food." Thus, we are not discussing an exclusively American phenomenon. In addition to McDonaldization, Americanization involves many other things (the export of movies, popular music, credit cards, and so on). Complicating matters is the issue of which of the two is the broader and the more important process. McDonaldization is but one of many processes emanating from the United States that can be subsumed under the heading of Americanization, yet in other ways McDonaldization may be seen as broader and more important since it has succeeded, at least to some degree, in disengaging itself from its American roots (for example many nations now have indigenous clones of McDonald's) and becoming an influential worldwide process operating independently of Americanization. In spite of these complexities, *one way* of looking at McDonaldization is as a form of Americanization and that is the way it will be approached in this chapter.

My specific objective here is to examine McDonaldization, its spread, and its irrationalities from the point of view of Europe's long-running love (but especially) hate relationship with the United States.[2] As Richard Kuisel (1993: 3) has recently put it, "America appeared [to the French, and Europeans in general] as both a model and a menace." Turning this around slightly, the theme of this chapter might be described as the *menace* posed to Europe by America's McDonald's *model*.[3] The "hate" has often taken the form, especially (but not exclusively) in France, of fear and loathing of Americanization. According to Edward McCreary (1964: 1), Americanization is "a catchall for anything of which the speaker morally and emotionally disapproves."

There are a number of books dealing with the American influence in Europe, including *America the Menace* (Duhamel, 1931), *The American Invasion* (Williams, 1962), *The Americanization of Europe* (McCreary,

1964), *The Rebirth of the West: The Americanization of the Democratic World* (Duignan and Gann, 1992), *Seducing the French: The Dilemma of Americanization* (Kuisel, 1993), and the best-known of such works, *The American Challenge* (Servan-Schreiber, 1968).[4] Many of these were written during a period when the United States was *the* dominant economic power in the world, Europe was comparatively weak and fragmented, and a titanic struggle for political supremacy was underway between communism and capitalism. Of course, none of these realities exist any longer – the United States faces serious competition in the world economy, Europe is stronger and more unified, and communism has disappeared as a serious competitor to capitalism. In these and other ways, there is a new world order in which to address the nature of the American "menace" to Europe.

In the old days, the American menace was largely seen in business, economic and industrial terms. This is reflected in the now quite amusing opening line of Servan-Schreiber's (1968: 3) *American Challenge*: "Fifteen years from now it is quite possible that the world's third greatest industrial power, just after the United States and Russia, will not be Europe, but *American industry in Europe.*" The ludicrousness of that vision, in light of current industrial and economic realities in the United States, Europe and especially Russia, should give pause to all of those (including this author) with an interest in social forecasting.

While no industrial pygmy today, the United States, to say nothing of Russia, does not represent a serious threat to European industry and business practices. There is undoubtedly far more concern in Europe about an invasion of Japanese industry and business practices (what has been termed "Toyotaization" or "Japanization:" Elger and Smith, 1994), than such an American incursion into Europe (Womack et al., 1990). But does the comparative weakness of American industry mean that the American menace to Europe (and elsewhere) has ended? It is my thesis that rather than ending, the American menace has, from the vantage point of Europe, taken a new, more insidious, and in many ways more dangerous form. Rather than being led by dour business executives, this phase of the invasion is being spearheaded by such "leaders" of American society as Mickey Mouse, Madonna and her most recent MTV video, the announcers on CNN and, most importantly from my point of view, clowns like Ronald McDonald. (It says much about the decline of America's traditional industrial base that Europe has more to fear from clowns, hamburgers and the techniques involved in making and selling them than it does from the American steel and automobile industries.)[5] This is not merely an invasion of the board-rooms and factories of European businesses; it is an invasion into every nook and cranny of European popular culture; it is an incursion into the day-to-day, the most mundane, activities of modern Europeans. Thus, Francis Williams (1962: npi), in *The American Invasion*, came far closer to hitting the mark than did the better-known Servan-Schreiber by subordinating the industrial challenge posed by America to the cultural challenges emanating from it: "The American invasion is going on all over the world: American ideas, American methods, American customs, American habits of eating, drinking and dressing, American amusements, American social patterns, American capital."

Stemming, as they do, from the early 1960s, Williams's concerns show that hand-wringing over an invasion by American popular culture is far from new. Europeans have been worried about this for many decades, perhaps even before they grew concerned about the American industrial and economic invasion. This concern has been especially strong among the French, perhaps because, as Kuisel (1993: 127) points out, the United States and France are the only two Western nations "that harbor universal pretensions." For example, as early as the early 1930s Georges Duhamel (1931: 215) wrote, "American civilization . . . is already mistress of the world. . . . There are on our continent . . . large regions that the spirit of old Europe has deserted. The American spirit colonizes [or 'taints'] little by little such a province, such a city, such a house and such a soul." It is this American colonization, this fear of a loss of traditional European spirit; of a "tainting" of the European "soul," that, in light of the massive spread of McDonaldization, is even more of an issue today in France (and elsewhere) than it was in Duhamel's time.[6]

There was an important precursor to today's concern about McDonaldization in the 1940s when a furor arose in France over the marketing of Coca-Cola. French communists (and others) grew concerned about what was termed the "coca-colonization" of France. Here was a product intimately associated with American culture that was to be marketed in France. It represented the importation of the American love of soft drinks and it posed a threat, at least in the eyes of some in France, to a way of life – wine drinking and the café life associated with it – that was the essence of French culture. Protests were mounted, but in spite of them Coca-Cola eventually came to France in 1949. The nation, its culture and its love of wine and cafés seem to have survived the onslaught.[7] Other European societies have embraced Coca-Cola and many other American exports far more eagerly, and to a greater degree, than France and they, too, have survived.

More recently, there was the furor over another very American phenomenon – Euro Disney. Here was another element of Americanization that was perceived by the French, and others, as a profound threat. One French socialist politician linked Euro Disney directly to the threat of concern in this chapter: that posed by fast-food restaurants.[8] He warned that Euro Disney would "bombard France with uprooted creations that are to culture what fast food is to gastronomy" (Riding, 1992: A13). Disney, like fast food, is seen as being imported from the United States and threatening to degrade French culture. To another critic, it represented the first step toward the homogenization of Europe. A government minister worried that it might be the first indication of an American takeover of the European leisure industry. Still another critic described Euro Disney as "a cultural Chernobyl" (Kraft, 1994: H1). Such an image brought to mind a French culture decimated by an explosion of Disney products. Now, with a bit of hindsight, we can see that

France has survived the Disney invasion just as it did coca-colonization. In fact, resistance was so strong that the question was, at least for a time, whether Disney could survive in France. While Euro Disney has survived (but not without a massive bailout) and is even prospering, French culture has persisted, and will persist.

Having survived Coca-Cola and Disney, the lesson of history seems to be that French (and more generally European) culture and society are far tougher and more resilient than they are sometimes given credit for. As one American sociologist has pointed out, America's cultural exports do not tend to replace extant cultures, but coexist with them, becoming in a sense "everyone's second culture" (Gitlin, in Kuisel, 1993: 230). If that is the case, then why this chapter? Why ask readers, especially those in Europe, to be concerned about McDonaldization, when fears about coca-colonization and, dare we say it, "Disneylandization," among others, have proven to have been way out of proportion?

The reason, I think, is that McDonaldization, as a form of American-ization, *does* represent something unique and more threatening than all of its predecessors that were seen as imperiling Europe. McDonaldization does have at least the potential to be more than a second culture; to be a kind of cultural Chernobyl. One of the things that makes McDonaldization unique is that it brings together in one package a threat to both European business *and* cultural practices. Previous manifestations of the American menace have tended to represent one or the other, but not both. While the invasion of, for example, Harvard Business School techniques and a corporation like DuPont represented a threat to European ways of doing business, they had relatively little impact on European culture in general. In contrast, the coming of MTV, Coca-Cola and Disney threaten to homogenize culture, but they do not greatly affect European business practices. McDonaldization involves *both* a revolutionary set of business practices *and* a revolution in one absolutely key element of culture – the way in which people eat.

Taking the issue of business practices first, Leidner (1993: 47) argues that McDonald's "is often represented as emblematic of American capitalist know-how." In many nations it is seen as a model of capitalist efficiency. Relatedly, one of the things that McDonald's stands for is running a far-flung empire with a minimal central organization. In contrast, French organizations, for example, are often run by huge and cumbersome bureauc-racies (Crozier, 1964). Adding greatly to the threat posed by McDonald's in this realm is the fact that its principles and business practices can be, and in many cases already have been, extended beyond restaurants to many other types of business.

Within the realm of culture, Kuisel underscores the centrality of eating and the threat to its indigenous forms posed by McDonaldization: "how could the French accept American economic aid and guidance; borrow American technology and economic practice; buy American products; imitate American social policy; even dress, speak, and (*perhaps worst of all*) *eat* like Americans and yet not lose their Frenchness?" (1993: 3; italics added). To illustrate, eating long meals with many courses, often involving high-quality ingredients and sophisticated recipes, is central to French culture. The Americanization of eating, as exemplified by the fast-food restaurant, brings with it quick meals using basic ingredients and simple recipes. Just as in the case of organizational philosophy, there is a direct antithesis between the American and the traditional French way of eating. And the issue of eating is just one part, albeit an important one, of the larger threat posed by American culture to French culture.

It is not just the specifics of the McDonald's approach that are seen as so threatening. There is the more general fact that what McDonald's seeks, at least implicitly, is to standardize the way people work and eat (at least in its outlets) throughout the world. Writing from the vantage point of Great Britain in the early 1960s, Williams (1962: 146) got to the heart of the matter by linking standardization and Americanization:

> What American experience suggests, however, is that if the pressures toward standardization – standardization of production, standardization of consumption, standardization of executive and administrative practices – are permitted to gain too great a hold on a society, then it is exactly such an intrusion into intellectual and emotional life that is to be feared. You come to a stage where if you want all that a completely unfettered deployment of the resources of modern civilization can offer in the satisfaction of material appetites you must be prepared to pay the price.

The price of McDonaldization is an intrusion into, a standardization of, the lives of people throughout Europe, and much of the rest of the world.

If Europe wants the fruits of McDonaldization, it must be willing to accept its costs. Yet, few Europeans seem willing to pay the price, if they are conscious of the price to be paid. For example, Kuisel (1993) argues that the French wanted all the benefits of Americanization without all the costs. It is highly unlikely that any nation can have the fruits of McDonaldization without paying at least some of the attendant costs.

To put this in the terms of the McDonaldization thesis, Europe and the rest of the world are moving toward business and cultural worlds dominated by the principles of efficiency, predictability, calculability, and control through the substitution of non-human for human technology. In other words, we are moving toward a world in which business and culture in one region will be indistinguishable from the business and culture of every other.

Several decades ago, Williams argued that what Europeans had to fear was a "loss of national personality" and that is far more true today since it is precisely what McDonaldization offers, or threatens, depending on one's perspective. Williams (1962: 11–12) goes on:

> The impact of American ideas, and still more of American ways of life, is now so large, the drive of America so great, that to ask how much of what is specifically English in our civilization will remain in a decade or two if the trend continues is by no means absurd . . . the danger of swallowing wholesale American ideas, American methods, and American values is [that] . . . in the process we may kill much that gives to English life its colour and zest and character.

The challenge to England and the rest of Europe then, and even more so today, is how to borrow and adapt what is useful about McDonaldization, without being swamped by it; without losing national identities.

McDonaldization also poses the threat of the loss of individuality. Of course, this is also a danger in the United States, but our main focus here is on Europe. As Duhamel (1931: 48) put it, "America seems bound to lead the rest of humanity along the path of the worst experiments. Today, America affords us a measure of how complete the effacement of the individual . . . can become." Or, in Francis Williams's (1962: 11–12) words, "an all-American world would be the last sad surrender to conformity."

There are two reasons why McDonaldization is in an unprecedented position to cause such a loss of national identity and individuality; such a dehumanized world. First, as pointed out earlier, unlike many of its predecessors it has an impact on both the business world and the larger culture. Second, it represents a set of principles that in both the business and cultural world can be completely disengaged from their original source in McDonald's and, more broadly, American society. This may be part of a broader process since Kuisel (1993: 4) argues that "Americanization . . . has become increasingly disconnected from America." As a disembedded set of principles (Giddens, 1990), McDonaldization can be applied to any business or cultural setting. Once materialized in indigenous forms, it becomes difficult to identify these principles as originating in McDonald's or in the United States. As a result, it becomes more difficult to oppose McDonaldization, let alone to mount anti-American sentiment against its various manifestations. In contrast, American exports like Coca-Cola and Euro Disney are merely products that retain their American identity, even when they are produced or exist in Europe.[9] While the McDonald's franchise, the Big Mac and so on also have this character, McDonaldization as a process is able to escape its specific material manifestations and invade any indigenous entity. Of course, it does not do this on its own. Entrepreneurs who see profits to be gained through McDonaldization are eager to apply its principles to more and more settings.

Take the example of a recent Russian chain called "Russkoye Bistro" (Specter, 1995; Hockstader, 1995). Modeled after McDonald's (which has been enormously successful in Moscow with more customers in the 1990s than tourists who visit the city's major tourist attractions), this new chain plans to have 200 outlets in Moscow by 1997. Instead of hamburgers and french fries, Russkoye Bistro sells traditional Russian food like pirogi (meat and vegetable pies), blini (thin pancakes), and Cossack apricot curd tart, as well as vodka. That this is all part of the process of McDonaldization is made clear by an executive associated with the new chain:

> "Every day in Russia we are trying to adapt to the Western experience, Western living standards, Western clothes – everything. And a Western diet as well. . . . Now we need to create fast food here that fits our lifestyle and traditions. . . . We see McDonald's like an older brother. . . . We have a lot to learn from them." (Hockstader, 1995: A13)

As a set of disembedded principles, McDonaldization is capable of overcoming one of the essential problems of transplanting such ideas to other societies. As Williams (1962: 147) put it, "Too facile a transplantation can produce, at the best, no more than an inferior version of the original. . . . What often strikes one is not the likeness to America but the extent to which the slickness and efficiency, the vigour and exuberance of the original have been lost in the transfer." However, what is striking is not only how similar McDonald's operations are around the world, but also how indigenous clones in many nations (like Russkoye Bistro) not only measure up to, but sometimes outstrip, their American source. McDonaldization has solved the transplantation problem!

Recently, Talbott (1996; see also Waters, 1996; McKay, 1996) has challenged this view, emphasizing the idea that local reactions to McDonaldization foster heterogeneity rather than homogeneity. There are clearly such local reactions and they do sometimes foster heterogeneity. However, the fact that those in specific sectors of society, and in many countries around the world, react, sometimes vociferously and violently to it, underscores the power of McDonaldization. People are reacting to the strength of that process, and the dangers it poses to their way of life. They are being deeply affected; their lives are likely to be McDonaldized to some degree. Even the counter-reactions to McDonaldization speak to its power and importance.

Talbott also makes the point that McDonald's in Russia operates very differently than the McDonaldization thesis would suggest. Part of this is a result of the fact that McDonald's, at least in recent years, always *adapts* to the local environment. In addition, we are still in the early stages of this incursion into Russia and assuming that there is no return to communism, McDonald's in Russia is likely to grow more like the model. It will always differ in some ways (now it offers Russian pirozhok-potato, mushroom and cheese pies: McKay, 1996), but I take the adaptations made in Russia, the development of indigenous Russian fast-food restaurants like Russkoye Bistro, as well as similar developments throughout the world, as evidence *for*, not against, the McDonaldization thesis.

In addition to the specific threats discussed throughout this chapter (e.g. homogenization, loss of individuality), McDonaldization also promises to bring to Europe and the rest of the world all of the irrationalities it has already brought to the United States. The most important of these is the dehumanization associated with working in, and dealing with, McDonaldized settings.

Writing for a European audience, Servan-Schreiber (1968: 2) argued: "It is time for us to take stock and face the hard truth. . . . If we are to be master of our fate, we will need a rude awakening." That rude awakening proved not to be, as Servan-Schreiber thought, the pre-eminence of American industry in Europe, but it may be a McDonald's, or one of its clones, on every major street corner throughout Europe. Unfortunately, if one waits for that to occur, it will be too late to stem the tide of McDonaldization. To paraphrase Max Weber, by that time all of us will be well ensconced in the "iron cage" of McDonaldization, with the result that not summer's bloom will lie ahead of us, but a polar night of icy darkness and hardness.

While I have focused on Europe in this chapter, the threat of McDonaldization is certainly not restricted to that continent (for example Russia which, of course, is also part of Asia). Take the case of the opening of a new McDonald's in Jerusalem, one of 14 currently in Israel (Lancaster, 1995). A kosher inspector of Jerusalem's restaurants had the following to say of that opening:

> "This leads to bank robberies, murders, decadence and corruption. . . . When a Jew, a pure soul, eats an impure animal, it destroys his soul and he becomes a jungle man, an evil animal. . . . This causes people to leave the homeland, and mixed marriages. It's worse than Hitler. McDonald's is contaminating all of Israel and all of the Jewish people." (Lancaster, 1995: A14)

Lest we dismiss this as the view of an extremist, take the following comment by the President of Israel after three Israeli teenagers were killed following a stampede at a rock concert:

> "The Israeli people are infected with Americanization. We must not be concerned for culture only as culture, but understand what is Israeli culture, Israeli religion. *We must be wary of McDonald's*; we must be wary of Michael Jackson, we must be wary of Madonna." (Lancaster, 1995: A14)

An Israeli professor recognized the threat posed by McDonald's, and other American institutions, to the distinctive character of Israeli society:

> "Residents and visitors have found renewal in this atmosphere for millennia, and now, more than in any recent time, this legacy faces a grave threat. . . . With the imminent opening in midtown Jerusalem of mega-businesses such as Tower Records and Blockbuster Video, the preservation of the city's unique significance takes on a new urgency." (Lancaster, 1995: A14)

The Israeli case shows that the spread of McDonaldization, and fears about it, are far from restricted to Europe. But rather than end on such a dark note, let me conclude with three more optimistic points.

First, on a more pro-American note, Francis Williams (1962: 12) argued that "the best of America . . . is not for export . . . what too often moves across the world in the wake of American money and American knowhow is what is most brash and superficial." Not too many years ago, Japanese exports were synonymous with junk, but today Japan is known for the high quality of its exports. Perhaps this is another way that America can follow the Japanese model and concentrate in the future on exporting "the best of America" and not just the "salty candy" that is McDonald's trademark. However, while high-quality Americanization is to be preferred to a low-quality version, it is still Americanization.

Second, also following Williams (1962: 146), "It is probably true that complete Americanization of any country other than America itself is impossible." More recently, Kuisel (1993: 233) concluded, "Americanization neither obliterated French independence nor smothered French identity." And even more recently, McKay (1996) found that Russia is backing away, at least to some degree, from Americanization and returning to Russian goods and popular culture. One can go further and say that not only is the complete McDonaldization of Europe (and elsewhere) impossible, but even the United States can never be completely McDonaldized (although it is in danger of coming awfully close). The issue is how much McDonaldization European business and culture can tolerate without losing their distinctive characteristics.

Third, there is hope in the distaste for standardization and homogenization in France, Great Britain, the Netherlands and elsewhere. The cause for optimism is that those with a strong dislike for standardization, as well as other dimensions of McDonaldization, will stand up, at least in part, to its onslaught.

McDonaldization is a powerful, perhaps even an inexorable force, but it is not too late to prevent it from overwhelming every facet of European society, as well other parts of the world. It probably cannot and should not be completely repelled, but it can be contained. However, to retain pockets of society free from McDonaldization, large numbers of people must first come to recognize that it represents a profound threat. Bathing itself in bright colors and a carnival-like atmosphere, selling salty candy, and using a clown as its representative, McDonald's seems to be anything but an American menace. But lift up the circus tent, wipe off the sugar and salt and strip off the clown suit and what you will find just beneath the surface is the cold skeletal framework needed for construction of the iron cage of rationalization.

Notes

This chapter was the basis of the Burgerzaal Lecture presented at the invitation of the Mayor of Rotterdam, the Netherlands, on 22 October 1993. It was published in pamphlet form by the city of Rotterdam.

1. In Russia, nationalists have labelled this incursion "Snickerization" to reflect the popularity of the American candy bar (McKay, 1996).

2. Much of this analysis applies, as well, to many other parts of the world.

3. As is my usual pattern, I will not dwell on the positive, the "model," side of McDonaldization.

4. Among the classical sociologists, Georg Simmel (1991: 27) was concerned with the growing "Americanism" of his day. To him, Americanism stood for the "enormous desire for happiness of modern man" and, more negatively, for "modern 'covetousness.'" While we will employ more proximate sources for this discussion, it is interesting to note that Simmel anticipated the issue of Americanization.

5. Of course, there has been a corresponding rise of other industries, most notably those associated with computer technology.

6. See Chapter 4 for a discussion of a similar point made by Richard Münch about the tainting of European social theory by the American model.

7. Although France does not seem to have been as successful in resisting McDonaldization as represented by the proliferation of fast-food restaurants and croissanteries modeled after them in France.

8. Disney and McDonald's have recently announced plans for a series of joint undertakings.

9. Although in the case of Euro Disney it may be possible to talk in terms of "Disneyization" or "McDisneyization" (see Chapter 10).

7

Globalization, McDonaldization and Americanization

Globalization has emerged as a central concern in sociology and other social sciences in the last few years. While a focus on the globe and global issues is welcome, many globalization theorists have been premature in their rejection of other substantive focuses and of alternative theoretical orientations. This is apparent not only in my work on fast-food restaurants and the McDonaldization process, but also in my more recent work on credit cards and the process of Americanization. The objective in this chapter is to re-examine some of the basic tenets of globalization theory not only in light of this work, but also as it relates to the new "means of consumption" (see Chapter 9) emanating, in large part, from the United States.

While there are significant differences among globalization theorists, most if not all would accept Robertson's (1992: 61, 64) advocacy of the idea that social scientists adopt "a specifically global point of view," and "treat the global condition as such." Elsewhere, Robertson (1990: 18) talks of the "study of the world as a whole." More specifically, Robertson (1992: 60) argues, "there is a general autonomy and 'logic' to the globalization process, which operates in *relative* independence of strictly societal and other conventionally studied sociocultural processes." Similarly, Featherstone (1990: 1) discusses the interest in processes that "gain some autonomy on a global level."

Virtually all globalization theorists, and even many of those operating with other theoretical orientations, are able to accept such generalizations. However, it is a different matter when one gets into the specifics of these approaches. They are open to serious debate and disagreement not only from outsiders, but also from within globalization theory itself (for example, Robertson's critiques of Wallerstein's world-systems version of globalization theory).

What is of interest to us here is not so much the nature of globalization theory, but the many things it appears to reject. In fact, it sometimes seems as if globalization theorists spend almost as much time critiquing alternative perspectives and focuses as they do developing the theory itself. While they may disagree on the specifics of the approach, they do agree much more on ideas to which they are opposed. Among the things that tend to be rejected are:

1   a focus on any single nation-state;
2   a focus on the West in general, or the United States in particular;

3   a concern with the impact of the West (westernization) or the United
    States (Americanization) on the rest of the world;
4   a concern with homogenization (rather than heterogenization);
5   a concern with modernity (as contrasted with postmodernity);
6   an interest in what used to be called modernization theory (Tiryakian,
    1991).

Let us look at each of these as well as what the work on fast-food restaurants
and credit cards (and later on the new means of consumption) tells us about
them.

First, the focus on the globe as the unit of analysis is generally coupled
with a rejection of a focus on the nation-state (and related phenomena).[1] This
is a result of a Durkheimian sense of emergence, or the view that "the global
whole . . . is more than a collection of juxtaposed particularities" (Beyer,
1994: 14). Therefore, globalization theory involves a "shift in unit of
analysis" (Beyer, 1994: 14). More negatively, Beyer argues that "we must
make the primary unit of analysis the global system and *not* some subunit of
it, such as the *nation*, the *state*, or the *region*" (1994: 2; italics added). Even
more strongly, Beyer argues: "Globalization means, for instance, that we
cannot conceive the whole in terms of one of its parts, say the First or Third
worlds, or as a composite system of logically prior nation states" (1994: 7;
italics added).

This change in the unit of analysis is sometimes seen as a result of the fact
that there has been a historical shift and the nation-state is no longer the
major player on the globe. Anthony Smith (1990: 174), for example, argues
that "the era of the nation-state is over." This change is seen as leading to a
shift in the main focus of sociology. For example, in Archer's (1990: 133)
view, the "globalisation of *society* means that *societies* are no longer the
prime units of sociology." Indeed, classical and contemporary sociology are
often castigated for their near-singleminded concern with the nation to the
exclusion of an interest in global processes. Globalization theorists seem
intent on righting this wrong by moving our focus away from the nation and
to the globe. While they may be right about a traditional imbalance in
sociological concerns, and the contemporary importance of global processes,
this is not to say that the nation-state has ceased to be of great, if not
paramount, importance in the contemporary world.

In a related, but more general, argument, Appadurai (1990: 301) contends
that deterritorialization "is one of the central forces in the modern world." In
such a deterritorialized world, "money, commodities and persons are involved in ceaselessly chasing each other around the world" (Appadurai,
1990: 303). While this view well describes fast-food restaurants and credit
cards, the "territory" from which they emanate, largely the United States, as
well as the territories to which they are exported, remains of central
importance.

In practice, however, globalization theorists *do* have a great deal to say
about territories and nation-states, but they tend to be *different* territories and

states than those of interest in traditional sociology. That is, to use the concepts of Immanuel Wallerstein (1974, 1980, 1989), while traditionally sociologists have focused on "core" nations (and territories) and their impact on "peripheral" nations, globalization theorists seem much more interested in peripheral nations and the way they resist or modify that which emanates from the core nations (Smart, 1994).[2]

So, as even many globalization theorists implicitly acknowledge, the nation-state remains important today. However, it is certainly not just the peripheral nations that are of significance; needless to say, core nations like the United States are of great, if not overwhelming, importance. In our rush to focus on the globe, we should not lose sight of the importance of nation-states, *both* core *and* periphery.

The fast-food restaurant and the credit card are both very distinctive products of the United States, that is, of a single nation-state. While it had precursors, the first truly important chain of fast-food restaurants, McDonald's, opened in the United States in 1955. Similarly, while it, too, had predecessors, the first modern "universal" credit card, Diners Club, was first issued in the United States in 1950 and the first modern bank card was created by the Franklin National Bank of Long Island in 1951. Bank-Americard (later Visa) was originally issued in California in 1958 by the Bank of America. Master Charge (later MasterCard) was founded in 1966 by several large Chicago banks. In many ways, these innovations in the means of consumption (and many others to be discussed below) could *only* have emerged from a specific nation. They were generated by the affluence and the mobility, especially via automobile, that are so much associated with the post-World War II United States. Thus, while we certainly need to concern ourselves with global processes, we must also be attuned to the specific nature of a given nation in order to understand its role and place in the global society.

While fast-food restaurants and credit cards are products of a single nation, they are certainly global in character. In fact, with their American markets becoming more and more crowded and saturated, the fast-food and credit card companies are focusing on international expansion. For example, McDonald's is now opening more outlets overseas each year than it is in the United States and half its profits come from overseas operations. Similarly, with the American market moving toward saturation, the credit card companies are concentrating on international expansion. Nevertheless, their point of origin was the United States.

A concern with the products of the United States, even if they are global in character, stands in opposition to the rejection by globalization theorists of a focus on the United States or the West in general, as well as on the processes of Americanization or westernization (Robertson, 1992; Friedman, 1994). For example, Featherstone (1991: 127) critiques the idea that "consumer culture on a global scale parallels the expansion of the power of the United States over the world economic order. Here consumer culture is seen as destined to become a universal culture which destroys each country's own national culture." Featherstone (1991: 142) also critiques a more general focus on the West: "if we consider the relations between nation-states and power blocs on the global level, it can be argued that a shift is taking place away from the West." Pieterse (1994: 163) criticizes the notion of westerniz-ation for offering "a narrow window on the world, historically and cultur-ally." Such rejections are traceable to the fact that much thinking about international processes was, in the past, biased in the direction of America and the West: Americanization and westernization. Globalization theorists argue that such perspectives were misguided and ethnocentric.

Furthermore, even if such theorists are willing to admit (and they aren't) that Americanization and westernization adequately described the past, they argue that the world has changed, has become more "compressed" and subject to multi-dimensional and multi-directional processes. Smith argues that today's global culture has become decentered: "Today's emerging global culture is tied to *no place* or period. It is context-less, a true melange of disparate components drawn from everywhere and nowhere, borne upon the modern chariots of global telecommunications systems" (1990: 177; italics added).[3] In light of the demise of communism, Friedman (1994: 99) sees a crisis with the breakdown of the global order and "declining centers of the world system." Thus, from the point of view of globalization theorists, a focus on America and the West, or Americanization and westernization, would be both far too restrictive and out of touch with contemporary global realities.

Again, while there is much truth in this, it remains the case that there *is* a disproportionate amount of goods, bodies of information, and other cultural products emanating from the United States and the West: a great deal more than there is flowing into them. More generally, much of the rest of the world is subject to westernization and Americanization. In fact, with the death of communism, with the end of the only viable large-scale alternative to Western/American-style capitalism, the world is more open and vulner-able to this than ever before. The main opposition to these processes will come from local cultures (McKay, 1996) and it remains to be seen just how capable many of these cultures will be of warding off such incursions on their own.

The fast-food restaurants are bringing to the rest of the world not only Big Macs and french fries, but more importantly the American style of eating on the run. The fast-food restaurant brings with it the idea (and the structure to implement it) that eating is something to be completed as quickly and effortlessly as possible. Similarly, credit cards make it easier to purchase American goods like Levis and Pepsi and, more generally, the American consumer culture.[4] Fast-food restaurants and credit cards are beginning to flood the globe, and to bring with them the Americanization of local cultures. This judgment is in line with Dezelay's (1990: 281) conclusion, in another domain, that "the globalization of the market for legal services . . . is for the most part an Americanization." To paraphrase Dezelay, the world-wide spread of fast-food restaurants and credit cards is primarily an Americanization of the world.

This focus on Americanization (and westernization) is not to deny the independent importance of local cultures. As we have seen, McDonald's routinely adapts itself to local markets and for their part the locals adapt these restaurants to their cultures. While McDonald's sells products like Big Macs and fries throughout the world, it also sells products adapted to the needs and demands of local markets. Take the following, for example:

In Norway, McDonald's sells McLaks, a grilled salmon sandwich with dill sauce on a whole-grain bread.
In the Netherlands, a groenteburger (or vegetable burger) is on the menu.
Uruguayan McDonald's sport McHuevo (hamburgers with poached egg) and McQuesos (toasted cheese sandwiches).
Thai McDonald's offer Samurai pork burgers marinated in teriyaki sauce.
In Japan, we find a Chicken Tatsuta sandwich, fried chicken spiced with soy sauce and ginger, with cabbage and mustard mayonnaise.
Finally in the Philippines, McDonald's offers McSpaghetti, with tomato sauce and a meat sauce with frankfurter bits (Sullivan, 1995).

Local cultures have produced their own versions of fast-food restaurants such as Lebanon's Juicy Burger and India's Nirula's (as well as Russkoye Bistro, discussed in Chapter 6). Furthermore, American fast-food restaurants may have a very different meaning in other societies: dinner at McDonald's may be considered an elegant and expensive date or a family outing that requires months of saving.

Appadurai (1990: 295) argues that the "central problem of today's global interactions is the tension between cultural homogenization and cultural heterogenization." Most globalization theorists argue that we are witnessing greater heterogenization, while the spread of fast-food restaurants and credit cards around the world points toward increased homogenization. Thus, Featherstone (1991) devotes a chapter to the "globalization of diversity." Pieterse (1994: 161) rejects a singleminded focus on homogenization and argues "for viewing globalisation as a process of hybridisation which gives rise to a global melange." As examples of cultural hybridization (he is also interested in structural hybridization), Pieterse offers the following: "Thai boxing by Moroccan girls in Amsterdam, Asian rap in London, Irish bagels, Chinese tacos and Mardi Gras Indians in the United States" (Pieterse, 1994: 169).

In fact, of course, it is possible for *both* things to be true. That is, we can have the greater homogenization of some aspects of our lives along with the greater heterogenization of other aspects. This is the position taken by Giddens (1990: 64): "Globalization can thus be defined as the intensification of worldwide social relations which link distant localities in such a way that local happenings are shaped by events occurring many miles away and vice versa." Robertson (1992: 132) takes a similar position on this issue: "In the ideal-typical form of my conception of the global human condition it is possible for there to be an equal emphasis upon societal uniqueness, on the one hand, and the commonality of mankind, on the other." Similarly, Friedman (1990: 311) contends, "Ethnic and cultural fragmentation and modernist homogeneization are two constitutive trends of global reality." Smart (1994: 157) argues that "global transformations have led simultaneously to the dispersion of some common forms, commodities and ideas and yet, in so far as they are received, interpreted, adapted and utilised in potentially radically different cultural contexts, have contributed to the (re)production and (re)constitution of difference and diversity." Similarly and more specifically, Beyer (1994: 3) argues,

> the global system corrodes inherited or constructed cultural and personal identities; yet also encourages the creation and revitalization of particular identities as a way of gaining control over systemic power. It is in the context of this last feature that religion plays one of its significant roles in the development, elaboration, and problematization of the global system.

King (1990: 410) concludes that the world's cities are growing simultaneously more "similar to, and different from, each other." In fact, as we have seen, a number of globalization theorists argue that it is homogenization that tends to bring forth heterogenization as a response to it.

The coexistence of homogenization and heterogenization is manifest in the concept of "glocalization," reflecting a complex and reciprocal relationship between the global and the local (Robertson, 1992: 173). Similarly, Friedman (1994: 12) focuses on the "ongoing articulation between global and local processes." More specifically, he argues that "the local is itself a global product" (Friedman, 1994: 198) and contends that we have both the "cultural pluralization of the world" and the "formation of a single world culture . . . the things and symbols of Western culture have diffused into the daily lives of many of the world's peoples" (Friedman, 1994: 100). This is similar to Robertson's view that we have witnessed both the "particularization of universalism" (the world as a single place) and the "universalization of particularism" (the global expectation that societies should have their own distinctive identities). Robertson is right in his view that local cultures are not crushed by global phenomena. However, the spread of fast-food restaurants and credit cards indicates that such global processes *are* having a powerful homogenizing effect on them. I would take issue with Friedman's (1994: 239) contention that Western products have not led to homogenization, "but ha[ve] supplied raw materials for new local variations." While Friedman offers some important examples, I am hard pressed to see McHuevos, McLaks or elegant dates at fast-food restaurants as significant local variations on the homogenizing process of McDonaldization.

More generally, Robertson is correct in pointing to the global importance of factors like ethnicity, nationalism, race and gender. These can, and do, retard the progress of McDonaldization and Americanization.[5] At the same time, the forces behind the latter processes actively seek to neutralize such factors by co-opting them into the system. For example, advertisements are tailored to the needs and interests of different ethnic and national groups, different races, and both genders.

Most globalization theorists also reject modern theories and favor postmodern approaches (Smart, 1994). Beyer (1994: 8) argues that "this global spread has resulted in a new social unit which is much more than a simple expansion of Western modernity." However, fast-food restaurants and credit cards can be seen as highly modern phenomena.[6] For example, to use the concept – rationality – most often associated with modernity, they are highly rational, emphasizing the most efficient ways of obtaining a meal, purchasing goods and services, and getting credit. Furthermore, these and other rational phenomena are of increasing importance in the West and are spreading throughout the rest of the world. This stands in contrast to various ideas associated with postmodernism. Postmodernists would argue that the world is growing less rather than more rational and that local cultures are of greater importance than such a homogenizing trend as increasing rationalization. Furthermore, the rationalization thesis implies a grand narrative which is rejected by postmodernists in favor of local or even individual narratives.

Featherstone (1990: 2) argues that postmodernism rejects the idea of "proto universal culture riding on the back of Western economic and political domination." This involves a rejection not only of westernization and Americanization, but also of the ideas of cultural imperialism and the exportation of mass consumer culture. Yet what the fast-food and credit card industries represent is precisely that. They *are* involved in a general effort to export American culture with the aim of gaining control over indigenous cultures. More specifically, they are involved in the exportation of America's mass consumer culture. One of the things that distinguishes these efforts from previous efforts such as coca-colonization (Kuisel, 1993), is that America is not merely exporting products, but also, and more importantly, the means to consume those and other products.[7] Fast-food restaurants and credit cards are better seen as means of consumption than as consumer products: they can be used as means to consume anything and everything. They are more important than products that preceded them into the international marketplace such as Coca-Cola and Levis since they are not merely altering what is consumed in other cultures, but also the *way* in which they and many other things are consumed. In that sense, their impact is far greater and far more pervasive.

In addition, Featherstone (1990: 3) argues that postmodernism assumes "that we have moved beyond the logic of the universal 'iron cage' rationalization process." Of course, the opposite thesis, the greater proximity of the iron cage as time passes, is precisely the point of my work on fast-food restaurants. Similarly, credit cards represent the rationalization of the loan process (see Chapter 8) and have, in turn, helped to further rationalize all types of consumption.

Finally, globalization theorists contrast their perspective to the modernization theory that was popular several decades ago (Archer, 1990). Featherstone (1990), for one, argues that Western modernity, and therefore implicitly modernization theory, is exhausted. However, the spread of fast-food restaurants and credit cards seems to support modernization theory. While there is some overlap between the thesis about the growth of these phenomena and that theory, there is at least one absolutely crucial difference. Modernization theorists tended to laud Western developments and to urge the rest of the world to move in this direction. In contrast, my work on fast-food restaurants and credit cards has been highly critical of these developments. Most of these criticisms are subsumed under the heading of the irrationality of rationality. There are many irrationalities associated with these systems, especially dehumanization. From a global perspective these rational systems tend to bring about homogenization, and an increasingly homogeneous world is a less human world. Other nations are urged to resist such incursions, or at least to try to adapt them to the local culture. In fact, given its focus on formal (or instrumental) rationality, and its critical character, my approach is closer to that of anti-American thinking and critical theory than it is to modernization theory (see Chapter 6).

Critical theorists were concerned with the rise of instrumental rationality and its extension from production to consumption (Featherstone, 1991). It could be argued that what I am doing is extending this critique from consumer goods to the means of consumption. This would seem to be in line with the postmodern critique of consumer culture, but there is an important difference. Postmodernists such as Baudrillard are focally concerned with the consumption of signs and not of use values as material utilities. In contrast, my main concern is the effect of such material realities as fast-food restaurants and credit cards (and other means of consumption) on consumption. My position can also be broadly contrasted with the "cultural turn" in the social sciences and seen as a reassertion of the importance of material realities in consumption.

Thus far, I have made this argument in largely negative terms. That is, I have been critically analysing the rejection by globalization theorists of various perspectives and social realities. By way of summary, let me now turn things around and put the case I am making more positively.

- The development and growth of fast-food restaurants and credit cards indicate that the nation-state continues to be important in sociological analysis.
- More specifically, the West in general, and the United States in particular, continues to be central to global analyses.
- Relatedly, the processes of westernization and Americanization continue to have a profound effect on the world economically, politically and culturally.

- The spread of fast-food restaurants and credit cards indicates that there are powerful homogenizing trends in the world today, although that does not deny a parallel trend in the direction of heterogenization.
- The developments of concern in this chapter, especially given their highly rational characteristics, indicate that we continue to live in a world with many modern characteristics; it is premature to declare the end of modernity and the dawning of postmodernity.
- These developments seem supportive of what used to be called modernization theory. However, it is important to remember that one is not necessarily describing desirable developments when one talks of modernization. Modernization can and does have undesirable, irrational consequences for societies.

Points of Agreement

While I have emphasized areas of disagreement with globalization theorists, there are several points of agreement between our perspectives. For example, I would agree with Featherstone (1990: 12) that we can anticipate "continuing struggles to define the global cultural order." Similarly, I accept Robertson's contention that the global order is "up for grabs." Where I differ with Featherstone and Robertson is over the nature of the struggle. From my perspective, it is a struggle in which the West in general, and especially the United States, holds the upper hand. With the death of communism, there is no large-scale alternative to international capitalism. Local cultures will certainly continue to be important and will remain capable not only of generating their own ways of life, but of modifying and altering the imports from other societies, especially the United States (McKay, 1996). Some may even succeed in exporting significant elements of their culture to large portions of the rest of the world. But they will also continue to be bombarded, and greatly altered, by exports from the West in general and the United States in particular.

I tend to agree with Featherstone's contention (1990: 10) that "there is little prospect of a united global culture, rather there are global cultures in the plural." Smith (1990: 171) makes a similar argument, contending that "the idea of a 'global culture' is a practical impossibility." Hannerz is on target when he says:

> There is now a world culture. . . . It is marked by an organization of diversity rather than by a replication of uniformity. No *total* homogenization of systems of meaning and expression has occurred, nor does it appear likely that there will be one anytime soon. But the world has become one network of social relationships, and between its different regions there is a flow of meanings as well of people and goods. (Hannerz, 1990: 237; italics added)

However, while we will continue to see global diversity, many, most, perhaps eventually all of those cultures will be affected by American exports; America will become virtually everyone's "second culture."

While I see a strong trend in the world at the moment toward American-ization, I do not think that that trend will last forever. In fact, there is evidence that in Russia the initial love affair is ebbing and there is a resurgence of interest in things Russian (McKay, 1996). In his discussion of the global market for legal services, Dezelay sees it as dominated by Americanization, but he also argues that this is merely a "historical interlude" resulting from the head start of American lawyers (Dezelay, 1990: 287). We are in a similar interlude in American hegemony in fast-food restaurants, credit cards and other means of consumption. Eventually, much of the rest of the world will catch up in these areas (as they have in production) and not only become better able to control their own societies, but begin exporting their creations to other societies.

While I have focused on differences between globalization theory and a perspective derived from my work on fast-food restaurants and credit cards, there are ways in which the latter phenomena can be dealt with under the heading of globalization theory. For example, Robertson (1992: 8) defines globalization as a process encompassing "the compression of the world" and "the intensification of consciousness of the world as a whole." The world-wide presence of fast-food restaurants and credit cards has served to compress the world, and those who utilize them are certainly made more conscious of the global system.

Globalization theorists also emphasize the development of third cultures within the global system (Robertson, 1992). These are partially autonomous cultures that transcend national boundaries and exist on a global basis. Appadurai (1990) has identified several. For example, there is the global "finanscape" dealing with the "movement of megamonies through national turnstiles at blinding speed" (Appadurai, 1990: 298). Clearly, the credit-card industry is part of the finanscape.[8] It, and the fast-food industry, are also part of the ethnoscape, involving the movement of large numbers of people via tourism (see Chapter 10). And both industries, especially the credit-card industry, are part of the technoscape employing technologies that girdle the globe.

Globalization theorists recognize the importance of economic and polit-ical factors, but give special attention to cultural factors and the emergence of a "global culture" (Robertson, 1992: 114). However, to Robertson (1992: 135), the global culture is not normatively binding, but simply a "general mode of discourse about the world as a whole and its variety." Clearly, fast-food restaurants and credit cards are not only of economic significance; they also are of great cultural significance. They are certainly influencing the world's mode of discourse, but I also think, in contrast to Robertson, that they are creating normative constraints on the way people eat and con-sume.

Friedman (1994: 103) argues that consumption is "an aspect of broader cultural strategies of self-definition and self-maintenance." Credit cards profoundly alter the way in which things are consumed. Friedman singles out eating as of central cultural importance and the fast-food restaurants are radically altering the way in which many people in many cultures eat. In doing this, credit cards and fast-food restaurants are changing, at least to some degree, people's definitions of self.

Means of Consumption

Fast-food restaurants and credit cards are far from the only American exports that are radically altering the globe. Furthermore, it is not just that the United States is producing consumer goods that are being exported to the rest of the world. What fast-food restaurants and credit cards show is that the United States is now in the business of creating, producing and exporting dramatic new means of consumption.[9] Once the center of revolutionary new developments in the means of production, the United States is now better described as the center of the creation of radically new means of consumption. Exporting the means of consumption to other societies, often along with the goods to be consumed by them, is of far greater importance than simply exporting such goods alone. This radically alters not just what people consume, but the ways in which they consume.

The notion of means of consumption is derived from Marx's concept of the means of production, or the tools, machines, raw materials, and so on owned by the capitalist and needed by the proletariat in order to be productive. Means of consumption can be defined as those things owned by capitalists and rendered by them as necessary to customers in order for them to consume. The chains of fast-food restaurants and the credit-card system clearly fit this definition. Like Marx's means of production, means of consumption should be seen as material phenomena.

Fast-food restaurants and credit cards are not the only new means of consumption being generated by the United States. We can include under this heading such predecessors as the supermarket (Walsh, 1993) and the shopping mall (Kowinski, 1985). Of greater interest are the means of consumption emerging in the United States today and still in the very early stages of being exported to the rest of the world. Take, for example, the TV shopping channels such as Home Shopping Network (HSN). For those of you unfamiliar with it, HSN is a 24-hour a day, seven-day a week, television network devoted to nothing but shopping. Goods are displayed and viewers are given phone numbers to call in order to place their orders. This development, by the way, is made possible by the existence and widespread use of credit cards. HSN (and the other similar networks) is revolutionary in that it breaks down space, and especially time, barriers to consumption. Now goods from anywhere in the world can be purchased at any time of the day or night; no more frustration over being unable to consume because the shops are closed. We are already beginning to see more global versions of HSN.

Another development worth noting is the ongoing fusion of consumption and entertainment – the goal of entertainment has become consumption; consumption must be entertaining. In a sense, there is nothing new here.

Fairs, for example, have long been both markets and sites of pleasure. The pre-industrial "carnivalesque tradition" has long been incorporated in the modern world (Featherstone, 1991). However, this fusion of consumption and amusement has become far more widespread and it has been rationalized (manufactured, sanitized, homogenized). The old "ordered disorder" of fairs has been transformed into much order and woefully little, if any, disorder.

For example, amusement parks like Disneyland and Disney World , while they are ostensibly about entertainment, can be seen as really shopping malls for the vast array of Disney products (Fjellman, 1992).[10] Shopping malls themselves are coming to look more and more like amusement parks: the huge malls in Bloomington, Minnesota and Edmonton, Canada literally encompass amusement parks complete with rollercoasters and ferris wheels. Lured to the malls by the amusements, many consumers stay to shop, eat, drink, see a movie, visit a fitness center, and so on. Featherstone (1991: 103) has described an English version of such a mall, Metrocentre at Gateshead: "The Metrocentre has promoted itself as a tourist attraction with its 'Antiques Village', fantasy fairytale 'Kingdom of King Wiz', Ancient Roman Forum gallery. . . ."

Malls are also being transformed by encompassing more businesses, most of them chains, devoted exclusively to entertainment (Pressler, 1995a). There are the often franchised play centers (Discovery Zone, for example) where parents can leave their children while they go shopping. The big growth area, however, is in the adult play centers (Dave and Buster's, Q-Zar) of various types proliferating throughout the malls of America (Pressler, 1995b). Dave and Buster's "is adult entertainment '90's style, with dozens of specially made billiard tables and shuffleboards, carnival games, play-for-fun blackjack, state-of-the-art electronic simulators and virtual reality pods where players can fight virtual pterodactyls or one another" (Pressler, 1995a: D1). Q-Zar is a 15-minute game of laser tag played by two teams with up to 20 players on each team. Each player has a laser gun and wears a vest with laser-sensitive panels.

> Music pounds overhead while the players weave and dart toward each other's home base looking for the enemy. . . . Players know they have "tagged" a member of the opposite team when a computer voice from the gun exclaims, "Good shot!" The target's vest vibrates when it is hit. Computers track each player's ammunition level and hit ratio. (Pressler, 1995b: D1)

Drawn to the malls to "play," adults not only spend large sums of money at these centers, but stay on to spend even larger sums at the malls' many shops.

By the way, some of the earlier innovators in the means of consumption have long recognized that they are in the business of using fun to sell goods. Supermarkets use games, clowns, and "fun foods" (Count Chocula breakfast cereal, for example) to help market their wares. Fast-food restaurants know that what they are selling, given the mundane character of their food, is "fun." Thus, they are characterized by bright lights, garish colors, clowns and cartoon characters, and above all the kind of finger food one associates with amusement parks.

Featherstone (1991: 103) has offered the following overview of developments in shopping centers, malls and department stores:

> Within these sites it is apparent that shopping is rarely a purely calculative rational economic transaction to maximize utility, but is primarily a leisure-time cultural activity in which people become audiences who move through spectacular imagery designed to connote sumptuousness and luxury, or to summon up connotations of desirable exotic far-away places, and nostalgia for past emotional harmonies. In short, shopping has become an experience.

While fast-food restaurants and supermarkets may not conjure up a sense of luxury, they do seek to make the customer's visit an "experience."

As for credit cards, they represent the ideal way to pay. They are seemingly magical keys that open the doors to all of these wondrous experiences. Not only do they allow one to partake in all of them, but it all appears, at least for the moment, to be free. Credit cards are *meta-means*: means that make possible the other means of consumption. We are likely to see expansion in other meta-means of consumption (debit cards, electronic funds transfers) in the future.

We are now even witnessing the emergence of *meta-meta-means*. Take, for example, Hospitality Franchise Systems, an organization that provides services to franchises. For example, for the hotel chains that it owns (e.g. Ramada, Days Inn), it provides marketing services and centralized reservation systems. It has recently agreed to buy the largest residential real estate chain in the USA, Century 21, and will provide it with a similar set of services (McDowell, 1995).

Returning to the central theme, fast-food restaurants and credit cards are just two of a steady stream of innovations in the means of consumption that one can expect from the United States in the coming years. They are not simply aberrant phenomena; they are part of a long-term process that is altering the way people consume and live.

Lest the reader still be wary of the conclusions being drawn here, let me close with yet one more example of a revolution in the means in consumption, this time one which is as yet in the very earliest stages of development. This is the emergence of "cybermalls" on the Internet. While the wrinkles are still being worked out (for example, Visa and Mastercard are currently ironing out the details on how to pay for the products purchased since credit card numbers can easily be compromised on the Internet), it is just a matter of time until more and more purchases will be made via the cybermalls on the Internet. What is striking about this development is its global implications. There will come a time when anyone with a computer any place in the world can tap into the Internet and its cybermalls. We will witness an unprecedented level of homogenization of consumption around the world; the world will in effect have its own shopping mall. Created in America, and undoubtedly dominated at least initially by American technology and

American businesses, the cybermalls will lead to yet higher levels of Americanization and homogenization.

Notes

This chapter is the text of a paper presented at a plenary session of the meetings of the International Institute of Sociology, Trieste, Italy, in July 1995. A version was published as "The McDonaldization Thesis: Is Expansion Inevitable?" *International Sociology*, 11, 1996: 291–308.

1. The rejection of a focus on the nation-state is but part of a broader rejection of prioritizing all global subunits: "*ethnies*, nations, states, organizations, movements, or religions . . . [are] no longer conceived simply as logically pre-existing social unities" (Beyer, 1994: 14). Featherstone (1991: 146) defines ethnie as "the set of symbols, myths, memories, heroes, events, landscapes and traditions woven together in popular consciousness . . . the ground for a common culture."

2. I use the terminology of world-systems theory here even though, as mentioned above, that theory is often heavily criticized by other globalization theorists.

3. It might well be that the thinking of globalization theorists has been distorted by their focus on telecommunications which lend themselves quite readily to globalization. Other international processes, like those taking place in the fast-food and credit card industries, do not lend themselves as easily to globalization, at least as that process is conceived by globalization theorists.

4. However, credit cards can be, and are, used to purchase indigenous goods and services.

5. As pointed out in the preceding chapter, there is not a simple one-to-one relationship between these two processes. McDonaldization has origins outside the United States and Americanization involves much more than McDonaldization.

6. Although, as we will see later, they can also be analysed from a postmodern perspective.

7. Another, as we saw in the preceding chapter, is that they also involve the exportation of McDonald's business practices.

8. The fast-food industry fits here, too, in the sense that a portion of the profits earned in other countries is making its way back to the United States.

9. This can be differentiated from Featherstone's (1991: 16) "modes of consumption," or "socially structured ways in which goods are used to demarcate social relationships."

10. For more on this, see Chapter 10.

8

Credit Cards, Fast-Food Restaurants and Increasing Rationalization

Both the credit card and the fast-food restaurant were products of post-World War II changes in American society and both have greatly contributed to an accelerating rate of change in recent years. The concern in this chapter will be with the similarities and differences between these two seemingly mundane, but nonetheless enormously important, social and economic developments. After dealing with some initial comparisons, the main focus of the chapter will be on the degree to which the two are part of the general process of the McDonaldization of society. We will pay special attention to what C. Wright Mills (1959) called the "private troubles" and the "public issues" that accompany the rationalization process as it is being manifest in the credit card industry.

Mills's views are important here for two reasons. First, in 1953 Mills co-authored with Hans Gerth a now almost-forgotten exemplar of integrative micro–macro theoretical work, *Character and Social Structure* (Gerth and Mills, 1953). As the title suggests, the authors were interested in the relationship between micro-level character and macro-level social structure. According to Gerth and Mills (1953: xvi), one of their goals was "to link the private and the public, the innermost acts of the individual with the widest kinds of socio-historical phenomena." Thus, Gerth and Mills's thinking is in line with some of the most recent developments in sociological theory (Ritzer, 1996b: 489–525), developments that will inform this analysis.[1]

Of related, even greater and more direct importance here is Mills's now famous distinction between micro-level personal troubles and macro-level public issues. *Personal troubles* are problems that affect an individual and those immediately around that individual. *Public issues* are problems that affect large numbers of people and perhaps society as a whole. While there are many different relationships that could be examined within this context (Münch and Smelser, 1987), our focus will be on the credit card industry as an element of social structure and the way it generates both personal troubles and public issues.

There is a useful parallel here between the credit card and the cigarette industries. The practices of the cigarette industry create a variety of personal troubles, especially illness and early death. Furthermore, those practices have created a number of public issues (the cost to society of death and illness traceable to cigarette smoke) and many people view a number of those practices as themselves public issues. Examples are the aggressive marketing by American companies of cigarettes overseas where restrictions on such marketing are limited or non-existent, as well as the way they market cigarettes to young people in this country (for example, the recent controversy over the advertisements in the USA featuring "Joe Camel").

Similarly, the practices of the credit card industry help to create a variety of personal problems for people (e.g. indebtedness) and public issues (e.g. the nation's relatively low savings rate). Furthermore, some industry practices have themselves become public issues. One such practice that has come under attack is the aggressive marketing of credit cards to teenagers.

One of the premises of this chapter is that we need the same kind of critical outlook toward the credit card industry that we utilize in scrutinizing the cigarette industry. Interestingly, some years ago Galanoy suggested a warning label for credit cards like the ones found on cigarette packs:

> *Caution. Financial experts have determined that continued bank card use can lead to debt, loss of property, bankruptcy, plus unhealthful effects on long-lived standards and virtues.* (Galanoy, 1980: 110)

Similarly, in *The McDonaldization of Society*, I suggested that the following warning label be affixed to fast-food restaurants:

> Sociologists warn us that habitual use of McDonaldized systems are destructive to our physical and psychological well-being as well as to society as a whole. (Ritzer, 1996a: 1)

The ideas of C. Wright Mills, in combination with Max Weber's theory of rationalization, give us the remarkably contemporary theoretical tools that we need to undertake a critical analysis of the credit card industry and the problems generated by it.

Some General Similarities

Both credit cards and fast-food restaurants are products and producers of radical changes in American society. Yet, despite their revolutionary character, neither was highly innovative. Here is what Lewis Mandell (1990: 11) has to say on this score about the "invention" in 1949 of the first important universal credit card, Diners Club:

> The founders of Diners Club introduced no radically new ideas. Rather, they combined a number of well-known and widely used techniques for extending credit and changed the way credit service was delivered to the customer. The key to their success was their recognition of the need and untapped demand for a mobile credit device.

Compare this to what I have had to say previously about Ray Kroc and his franchising of the first McDonald's in 1955, six years after the founding of Diners Club:

> Kroc invented little that was new. Basically, he took the specific products and techniques of the McDonald brothers and combined them with the principles of other franchises (food-service and others), bureaucracies, scientific management, and the assembly-line. Kroc's genius was in bringing all these well-known ideas and techniques to bear on the fast-food business and adding his ambition to turn it,

through franchising, into a national, then international, business. *McDonald's and McDonaldization, then, do not represent something new, but rather the culmination of a series of rationalization processes that had been occurring throughout the twentieth century.* (Ritzer, 1996a: 31)

It is striking that two of the most far-reaching social and economic developments of the twentieth century were so lacking in innovativeness.

More specifically, both the credit card and the fast-food industries were not innovative technologically. Mandell (1990: 11) says: "Innovations in the credit card industry have developed slowly. . . . Existing technology has usually been adapted to fit the needs of the developing industry." Similarly, McDonald's has preferred to rely on traditional technologies and labor-intensive processes rather than labor-saving advanced technologies.

The fast-food restaurant's lack of innovativeness has not been restricted to technology: "McDonaldized institutions have also not developed notable new products" (Ritzer, 1996a: 124). Similarly, there has been relatively little in the way of innovative new products in the modern credit-card industry since its inception in 1949.

Still another similarity between credit cards and fast-food restaurants is their heavy reliance on advertising. This is especially true of the leaders in the two fields – Visa, MasterCard and American Express in credit cards and McDonald's, Wendy's and Burger King in fast foods. The essential point is that since their products or services are relatively indistinguishable from those of their competitors, the dominant firms have sought to achieve pre-eminence through the employment of costly and elaborate advertising campaigns. The leaders have spent many billions of dollars on advertisements designed to manufacture a sense of difference. This is made even more necessary by the fact that the dominant companies in both industries, at least until recently, have not wanted to compete on a price, or more precisely a price-cutting, basis.

In recent years *both* credit card and fast-food firms have been forced to forgo their near-exclusive reliance on competitive marketing and engage in price competition. The hamburger chains, for example, have faced severe competition not only from each other, but also from chains purveying fried chicken, pizza and tacos. To meet the threat, McDonald's and the other chains have been forced to do such things as create low-priced specials and "value-meals." For their part, the major credit card companies and banks have had to deal with competition from the entry of "non-banks" like AT&T and General Motors and their co-branded cards into the credit card business. They have been forced to compete by slashing interest rates and reducing or eliminating annual fees.

The dominant companies in both industries would prefer not to engage in price competition since it cuts directly into profits. In contrast, the costs of competition through marketing and advertising efforts can be passed on to the consumer in the form of higher prices, fees and interest rates. Price competition has been more or less forced on the leading players by the exigencies of the two businesses.

Both fast-food restaurants and credit-card companies have devoted considerable attention to expanding upon their original base. For charge card companies like American Express that base was businesspeople, especially those associated with large and successful companies. Later, American Express sought to attract less affluent and less successful businesspeople. Since most American Express cards were held by men, attention turned to attracting females to what the company would like to be known as "the Card." Low-key ads aimed at females and featuring young female executives and professionals led to the statement by feminist Gloria Steinem that American Express "now makes women feel welcomed and invited" (Friedman and Meehan, 1992: 110). As a result of such efforts, by 1984 one-third of new cardholders were women. The fast-food chains have sought at various times to attract every conceivable group, including very young children, grandparents, "thirtysomething" married couples, and so on.

Credit card firms and fast-food restaurants have sought to expand in other ways, as well. For example, fast-food restaurants have moved on to college campuses (Whitefield, 1987) and are even beginning to make inroads in the nation's high schools (Meier, 1992). Credit card firms have sought to move out of their adult base of customers and attract college and even high school students. Fast-food restaurants have devoted great energy to moving beyond their traditional foundation of teenage customers. Another route for expansion for both the fast-food industry and credit cards has been overseas.

Both businesses have sought to expand into their competitors' domains. For example, American Express began its Optima card in 1987 in order to compete more directly with Visa and MasterCard. Expansion also took place in the other direction. American Express's Gold Card had ceased to be distinctive because the banks expanded into the Gold Card market. For example, Visa began offering Gold Cards in 1988. An illustration of this phenomenon in the fast-food industry is the fact that most, if not all, hamburger chains now handle many of the products that were at the root of the success of the chicken franchises. Recently, traditionally child-oriented McDonald's has started to market the Arch Deluxe in order to compete with more adult-oriented chains like Burger King, with its Whopper. Various chains are marketing food items like tacos and burritos, products that made the Mexican fast-food chains the fastest growing in the market.

The above is not intended to be an exhaustive list of similarities between the credit-card and fast-food industries, but is suggestive of a wide range of similitudes.[2] With a sense of this range as background, we now turn to the similarities between the two industries in terms of their involvement in the process of McDonaldization.

McDonaldization

While all of the above likenesses are important, the major similarity between fast-food restaurants and credit cards from the point of view of this book is that both can be seen as part of the process of rationalization. Just as

McDonald's rationalized the delivery of prepared food, *the credit card rationalized (or "McDonaldized") the consumer loan business.* Prior to credit cards, the process of obtaining loans was slow, cumbersome and non-rationalized. The modern credit card has made the acquisition of at least one type of loan, the non-collateralized consumer loan, highly rational. It is now a very efficient process, often requiring little more than the filling out of a short questionnaire. With the existence of credit bureaus and computerization, credit records can be checked and applications approved (or disapproved) very rapidly. Further, the unpredictability of whether or not a loan will be approved has been greatly reduced and, in the case of pre-approved credit cards, completely eliminated. The decision as to whether or not to offer a pre-approved card, or to approve an application for a card, is often left to a non-human technology – the computer. Computerized scoring systems (see pp. 102–5) exert control over credit card company employees by, for example, preventing them from approving an application if the score falls below the standard. And these scoring systems are, by definition, calculable, relying on quantitative measures rather than qualitative judgments about things like the applicant's "character." Thus, credit card loans, like fast-food hamburgers, are now being served up in a highly rationalized, assembly-line fashion. As a result, a variety of irrationalities of rationality, especially dehumanization, have come to be associated with both.

It is worth noting that in terms of being an independent force in the process of McDonaldization, the rationalization of credit card loans has played a central role in fostering the rationalization of other types of loan such as automobile and home equity loans. Automobile loans used to take days, but now a loan can be approved, and one can drive off in a new car, in a matter of hours, if not minutes. Similarly, home equity loans are obtained much more quickly and easily than in the past. Such loans utilize many of the same technologies and procedures (e.g. scoring systems: Varney, 1994) that are used in decision making involving credit cards. Just as the process of rationalization is rushing through society as a whole spearheaded by the fast-food industry, it is reverberating across the banking and loan business led by the credit card industry. Furthermore, we can anticipate that over time other types of loan involving larger and larger sums of money (mortgages and business loans, for example) will be increasingly McDonaldized. More generally, virtually every facet of banking and finance will be moving in the same direction.

We can already get a glimpse of the rationalized future of banking at one branch of Huntington Bancshares of Columbus, Ohio (Hansell, 1994). The branch in question is the busiest of the bank's 350 outlets, doing as many home equity loans as 100 typical branches and handling as many new credit cards as 220 of those branches. It is distinguished by the fact that *none* of its business is done in person, it is *all* done by telephone. Of the fear of alienating customers because of the dehumanization associated with this type of banking, the chairman of Huntington says, "'I don't mind offending customers and losing them if it benefits the bank in the long run . . . I'd rather have fewer customers and make an awful lot of money on them than have a lot of customers and lose our shirt'" (Hansell, 1994: D13).

Whatever its impact on customers, the branch is certainly efficient. For example, it is able to approve a loan in ten minutes, even if the request is made by phone in the middle of the night. Here is the way the system works:

> As soon as a "telephone banker" types the first few identifying details of an application onto the computer, the machine automatically finds the records of the customer's previous activity with Huntington and simultaneously orders an electronic version of the applicant's credit bureau file. The phone banker then contacts by pager one of two seasoned loan officers who roam the maze of office cubicles in the telephone center.
>
> With printouts of the banking records, credit file and computer-analysed loan application in hand, a loan officer can generally make a decision in less than a minute. The bank says its credit problems are no greater than for loans from its branches. (Hansell, 1994: D13)

It is interesting to reflect on the so-called "telephone banker" described above in relation to the process of rationalization. This would appear to be the counterpart at the bank to the McDonald's counterperson or the worker at the drive-through window. Telephone bankers are far less skilled than their predecessors. They are reduced to glorified computer operators with the truly important and difficult work (analyses of credit records and loan decisions) being done by the computer technologies and the loan officers. In this way, McDonaldized banking brings with it "deskilling," and more generally the further rationalization of bank work.

It is forecast that about 40 percent of the 100,000 bank branches in the United States are likely to be closed over the next decade (Hansell, 1994). Some of this is due to mergers, but much will be the result of these new, more efficient branches and telephone bankers replacing a number of the conventional branches and traditional bankers. Of course, ATMs (see p. 109) have long played a key role in the decline in bank branches and now there is evidence of similar technologies that, for example, actually grant and dispense small loans (Singletary, 1996).

Let us now turn to a discussion of each of the dimensions of McDonaldization and the ways in which they apply to the credit card business.

Calculability

Calculability is reflected in the fast-food restaurants by, for example, the names they give to their products. These usually emphasize that the products are large in size. Examples include the Big Mac, the Whopper, the Whaler (renamed, not too long ago, Big Fish) and Biggie fries. The emphasis on things that can be quantified is also reflected in products like the Quarter-Pounder, in publicity on how many billions of hamburgers are sold and in how quickly pizzas can be delivered.

The credit card industry also emphasizes various things that are quantified, although this more conservative industry generally shies away from the clever, size-oriented names employed in the fast-food industry. (However, one is led to wonder just how long it will be before we see something like the "Whopper Card.") Among the most visible of the quantified aspects of credit cards are their credit limits, interest rates and annual fees (or lack thereof).

The credit card permits people to maximize the number of things they can buy and optimize the amount of money they can spend on them. After all, by offering instant credit up to a pre-defined, but expandable, limit, credit cards allow people to be able not only to spend all of their available money, but in the case of those who revolve their accounts, to go into debt for perhaps thousands of dollars. In an effort to increase their level of debt, people often seek to maximize their credit limits on each of their cards and to accumulate as many cards as possible, each with its own, hopefully (from their point of view) high, credit limit. In fact, important status symbols in modern society are the number of credit cards one has in one's wallet as well as the collective limit of credit available on those cards. Rather than the amount of savings one has, the modern status symbol is often how much debt one has and, better yet, how much more debt one can incur. In sum, credit cards emphasize a whole series of things that can be quantified – number of cards, magnitude of credit limits, amount of debt and the number of goods and services that can purchased.

Calculability involves not only an emphasis on quantity, but also a comparative lack of interest in quality. In the fast-food restaurant this is manifest in the concern for large portions (Big Mac) and low prices (value meals) and a corresponding lack of interest in taste (there is no "Delicious Mac" for sale at your local McDonald's).

The stress on the quantity of credit card debt permitted also leads to a lessening of interest in the quality of the things that one can acquire while running up that debt. With a finite amount of cash on hand or in the bank, the consumer tends to be more careful, often buying a relatively small number of high-quality goods that promise a long and useful life. But, if things are bought on seemingly ever-expandable credit, there is often less emphasis on quality. Instead, the accent is on buying large numbers of things. There is comparatively little concern that those things are likely to deteriorate swiftly. After all, if things wear out quickly, they can be replaced, often on the basis of a later, and higher, credit limit.

Relatedly, the ready availability of virtually anything and everything on credit leads to a leveling in the value of goods (and services). This reduction of everything to a common denominator causes the cynical attitude discussed by Georg Simmel that everything has its price, that anything can be bought (or sold) on the market. Since anything can be bought at any time, people develop a blasé attitude toward those things. Simmel (1907/1978: 256) describes this as a view of "all things as being of an equally dull and grey hue, as not worth getting excited about." The blasé person has lost completely the ability to make value differentiations among the ultimate objects of purchase. Put slightly differently, the credit card (and before that

money) is the absolute enemy of esthetics, reducing everything to formless-
ness, to purely quantitative phenomena.

Leaving qualitative issues aside, it could be argued that from the point of
view of calculability, high levels of credit card debt make sense, at least in
periods of high inflation. For example, in the late 1970s and early 1980s
when inflation rates in the USA were 10 percent (or more), it made little
sense to put money in the bank at 5.25 percent since at that rate one would
lose on savings each year (Rupkey, 1979). Furthermore, in buying on credit
in inflationary times, one ends up paying back debts at a later time with
cheaper, that is inflated, dollars. Add to this the fact that interest payments
were fully tax deductible in the USA until 1986 and credit card consumption
made even more sense from the point of view of calculability. It was just this
kind of thinking that led to the dramatic rise in credit card debt.

In very different economic times, calculability should lead people to cut
back on credit card purchases. For example, during the recession of the early
1990s consumers tried to reduce their credit card debt and banks were more
restrictive about issuing new cards and canceled some existing cards
(Crenshaw, 1991a). To take another example, in the year following the Tax
Reform Act of 1986, which over a five-year period reduced and ultimately
eliminated deductions for interest on credit card debt, a record number of
people (40 percent, compared to 33 percent in 1986) paid off their balances
in full. When people did the calculations they realized that it made sense to
pay off the debt.

However, while people do try to analyse their situation carefully, the lure
of all those goods and services one can buy with high credit card debt seems
to win out in the long run over the attractiveness of little or no debt and low
or non-existent monthly payments. For example, the rush to pay off credit
card debt after 1986 began to wane quickly and by 1988 only 35 percent of
cardholders were paying off their debt in full (Kantrow, 1989). Today, about
the same proportion of people (between 30 and 40 percent) pay off their
credit card debts in full each month as did in 1986, the last year that interest
on credit card debt was fully tax deductible.

A particularly revealing example of quantification in the credit card
industry, one that we have mentioned above, is the use of "credit scoring" in
determining whether or not an applicant should be issued a credit card (or
receive other kinds of credit). Of course, it should be noted that in the end
the majority of applicants *are* approved by one credit card firm or another.
Most people are approved because of the fact that the profits from the credit
card business are extraordinarily high, largely because interest rates on credit
cards are routinely so much higher than rates on other loans and even higher
than the rates the credit card companies must pay for their money. Given the
high rates and profits, credit card firms can afford to have a small proportion
of cardholders who are delinquent in paying their bills, or who default on
them. Nonetheless, it is obviously in the interest of the card companies to
weed out those who will clearly not be able to pay their bills.

Scoring usually involves a two-step process (Updegrave, 1987). First, the application itself is scored by the credit card company. For example, a homeowner might get more points than a person who rents. Some applicants are weeded out at this stage. Where a sufficient number of points are scored on the application, the lender proceeds to buy a credit report on the applicant from a credit bureau. It is the score on the credit report that is key to the decision on whether or not to issue a card. Said a vice-president of a company in the business of designing scoring models for lenders: "'You can have an application that's good as gold, but if you've got a lousy credit report, you'll get turned down every time'" (Updegrave, 1987: 146). In other words, it is the numbers and not more qualitative factors that are ultimately decisive.

Scoring models vary from one locale to another and are updated to reflect changing conditions. While there is great variation from report to report, the following items usually receive the most weight.

First, 30 percent, or more, of the total points may be earned if the applicant simply already has a number of credit and charge cards. Having too many cards may cost points, but having no cards at all may be an even more serious liability.

Second, 25 percent, or more, of the points are based on the applicant's record of paying off accumulated charges. Being delinquent on a Visa or MasterCard is likely to cost more points than being late on a payment to a department store. The credit card companies have found that even when people are having economic difficulties, they try to stay current on their credit card payment while they might let their department store bill slide. Falling behind, or being delinquent, on credit card bills is a sign of serious financial difficulties. Delinquencies on such accounts of 30 days might not be too costly in terms of points, but delinquencies of 60 days, or more, might well scuttle one's chances of getting another card.

Third are suits, judgments and bankruptcies involving the applicant. Bankruptcies are likely to be especially costly. According to the president of a credit-scoring firm, "'Lenders aren't very forgiving about bankruptcy. . . . They figure a bankrupt ripped off a creditor and got away with it legally'" (Updegrave, 1987: 146).

Fourth are measures of stability such as the applicant's length of tenure on the job and in his or her place of residence. Someone who has lived in the same place for three or more years might get twice as many points as someone who has recently moved.

Fifth, the higher the income of the applicant, the greater the number of points on this dimension.

Sixth, occupation and employer are important. Those in the highest-rated occupations, executives and professionals, are likely to earn a large number of points. Similarly, being in the employ of a stable and profitable firm is likely to garner the applicant many points, whereas employment in a firm on the edge of bankruptcy is likely to be very costly.

Seventh, age is important and generally the older the applicant, the greater the number of points.

Eighth, the possession of savings and checking accounts by the applicant are important. Checking accounts, because by their mere existence they tend to demonstrate more ability to manage finances, generally get twice as many points as savings accounts.

Ninth, being a homeowner is likely to yield 15 percent of the total number of points needed.

Scoring systems such as this one quantify the decision-making process involved in the determination of whether or not to issue a credit card. However, these scoring systems, like most calculable systems in a rationalized society, reduce human qualities to abstract quantities. For example, they reduce the individual quality of creditworthiness to a simple, single number. It is this number that "decides" whether or not an applicant is, in fact, worthy of credit in the eyes of the credit card firm and not the more human judgment of an official of that firm. But as one banking consultant put it, "'The character of an individual is much more important than [a credit score]. You can't decide who to lend to by using a computer'" (Shiver, 1988: 5). However, with a crush of applicants brought on in large part by their own hyperactive recruiting efforts, credit card firms *are* more often relying on such computerized scoring systems.

Scoring systems are not used just to weed out applicants; they are also being employed with existing credit card customers. Said the president of a company with 2 million credit card accounts:

> "the software goes in and looks at attributes of a customer's account and how that account is being handled [by the customer]. And through a statistical methodology . . . [i]t looks at payment patterns, usage patterns. . . . We look at every account automatically and assign a behavior score. That score is, if you will, an odds quote, 100 to 1 or 1,000 to 1.
>
> "It can't predict a specific account. . . . It can look at a lot of accounts and predict that out of that pool of, say, 10,000 accounts that one of them will go delinquent. So we can look at that pool and get a sense of risk from the profile." (Crenshaw, 1991b: H4)

These scoring systems are used on existing credit-card users with a number of different purposes in mind. First, the scoring systems help the credit card firm decide whether or not to increase a current account holder's credit limit. The system will help the computer "decide" whether the account will remain current even with an increase in the limit. Second, the scoring systems are used to help with decisions on whether or not to authorize transactions that are over the credit card's limit. The computer can make such an authorization on its own, or it can pass it on to a human evaluator for a decision. Third, a credit card company might, more generally, develop scores based on its own records, or those of the credit bureaus, to determine whether cardholders are likely to pay their bills. Fourth, scoring systems help decide whether cardholders who have just become delinquent will eventually return to "current" status (that is, no longer be delinquent), or become more seriously delinquent. This helps the bank decide whether or not action is needed and, if action is required, what type (for example, let the account ride, begin a collection effort, cut the account off completely). Fifth, scoring is sometimes used to determine which cardholders are likely to become bankrupt. Finally, accounts are scored to assess which ones are likely to be the most profitable and those that offer little in the way of profits (especially accounts of "convenience users" – those who pay their account balances in full each month, as opposed to the much more profitable "revolvers" who run a balance from month to month) are likely to be dropped or not renewed (Detweiler, 1993).

Efficiency

The second dimension of rationality, *efficiency*, is manifest in the fast-food industry, among many other ways, in the drive-through window which is a far more efficient way of obtaining a meal than parking one's car, walking to the counter, ordering, paying and returning to the car with one's meal-in-a-sack. The latter, of course, was (and is), in turn, a much more efficient method for obtaining a meal than cooking from scratch. To take one other example, finger foods like Chicken McNuggets are far more efficient to eat than chicken parts like wings, legs and breasts with their skin, sinew and bone. Unlike chicken wings, Chicken McNuggets can be eaten by tossing them into one's mouth as one drives on to the next rationally and efficiently organized activity (perhaps obtaining money from the ATM).

The credit card is a highly efficient method for both obtaining and granting loans, as well as for expending loan funds. As pointed out above, applicants need do little more than fill out a brief questionnaire, and in the case of pre-approved credit cards even that requirement is waived. Compared to the traditional loan process, which can be seen as the parallel of "cooking from scratch," this method is clearly more efficient for both the loan agency and the borrower. Most customers are granted a line of credit which is accessed and expended quickly and easily each time the card is used. Assuming a good credit record, as the credit limit is approached it will be raised, thereby increasing the potential total loan amount.

The credit card tends to greatly enhance the efficiency of virtually all kinds of shopping. Instead of carrying around large and unwieldy amounts of cash, all one needs is a thin piece of plastic. No need to plan for purchases by going to the bank and loading up on cash. No need to carry around burdensome checkbooks and the IDs needed to get checks approved. There is no longer even any need to count. With their credit cards, consumers are no longer required to know how to count out the needed amount of currency, or to be able to check to see whether the change is correct. One can buy things wherever and whenever one wants as long as the trusty card is sitting in one's wallet.

Credit (and debit) cards are also more efficient from the merchant's point of view. While the average cash transaction at, for example, a supermarket is still fastest (16–30 seconds), it is closely followed by card payment (20–30 seconds), while a check transaction lags far behind (45–90 seconds). While it might be a tad slower than cash, a card transaction is far more efficient than a cash deal because it requires little from the merchant except the initial electronic transmission of the charge. Cash, however, is, as one supermarket electronic banking services executive points out, "'labor intensive. From the time it leaves the customer's hands to the time it hits the bank, cash may get handled six to eight different times, both at the store and at the bank level'" (*Chain Store Executive*, 1992: 28). All of these steps are eliminated in a charge (and debit) transaction, making it more efficient to the merchant than doing business on a cash basis.

While cards *may* be more efficient than cash, credit cards and debit cards are unquestionably more efficient than checks as far as the merchant is concerned. In fact, debit cards can be thought of as "electronic checks." Their greater efficiency stems from the fact that the amount of the bill is immediately deducted from the customer's account. Eliminated with both credit and debit cards are bounced checks and all of the inefficiencies, and costs, associated with trying to collect on such checks. Furthermore, it is quicker to get a card transaction approved than it is for the customer to write a check and have it approved. "'That's important to the merchant, who wants to move customers through the lines as quickly as possible'" (*Chain Store Executive*, 1992: 28). Other electronic funds transfers (EFTs) such as paying bills via computer or by phone promise even greater efficiencies since they can be utilized in the comfort of one's own home.

Yet despite their greater efficiency in comparison to cash, credit and debit cards have until recently rarely been accepted in that center of efficiency, the fast-food restaurant. The executive vice-president of Visa describes the problem: "'In the fast food arena, we have traditionally had next to no presence for one reason – speed. In a business where fast is beautiful, the card authorization and purchase process has been too slow to make cards attractive'" (Pierce, 1990: 11A). However, we are beginning to see growth in the use of cards in this area. The same Visa executive describes a recent effort to make the charging of fast food more efficient:

> "At the point of sale, the card is passed through a stripe reader and immediately checked against a hot-card file. If a card is good, the amount of the purchase is automatically credited to it. Then the authorization is flashed on a video screen in front of the checker.
> "The entire process is instantaneous: no phone calls, no imprint and signature procedures. Consumers get more convenience and flexibility. And speed-minded merchants get a payment system that's even faster than cash." (Pierce, 1990: 11A)

The highly rationalized Wal-Mart stores have recently installed new technology that makes the process by which card transactions are approved almost instantaneous. According to a spokesman for the company, "'Not too long ago, customers hesitated to use their cards because it took so doggone long to get a transaction processed'" (Strom, 1993: 45). Such hesitation is clearly a thing of the past at Wal-Mart, and at many other highly rationalized settings as well. Indeed, various changes have recently been made to make the highly efficient credit card transaction even more efficient.

Predictability

Predictability is manifest in the fast-food restaurant in the fact that the food, the physical structure and the service are likely to be the same from one time or place to another. Even the demeanor and behavior of the employees is highly predictable. For example, the Roy Rogers hamburger chain used to have its employees dress, after its namesake, like cowboys (and cowgirls). Following the corporate script, employees greeted customers with a friendly "Howdy pardner," and bid them adieu after paying with a hearty "Happy trails."

The credit card has made the process of obtaining a loan quite predictable. Consumers have grown accustomed to a routine series of steps (filling out the questionnaire, for example) leading to the appearance of a new card in the mail. After all, many people have gone through these same steps many times. In the case of pre-approved credit cards, the few remaining un-predictabilities have been eliminated since offer and acceptance arrive in the very same letter.

Credit cards, themselves, are highly predictable. Whatever company issues them, they are likely to be made out of the same materials, to feel the same, to be the same shape, to include similar information in similar places, and to do just about the same things. In fact, it is their similarity in all these ways that prompts the credit card companies to attempt to distinguish their cards from all the others by, for example, their advertisements and by offering an array of enhancements. The fast-food restaurants do much the same thing (e.g. giving away glasses or selling toys or video tapes of movies at bargain prices) because the hamburgers, fried chicken, french fries and soft drinks of one are difficult to differentiate from those of its competitors. As pointed out above, the goal of both the credit card firms and the fast-food restaurants is to manufacture a sense of difference where little or none, in fact, exists.

There is far less human contact in the credit card, than in the fast-food, business (and there is painfully little genuinely human contact in fast-food restaurants). The limited contact that does exist in the credit card business is likely to take place over the phone. It might take the form of unsolicited phone calls made in an effort to recruit new card users. More likely, it would involve calls by card users to their company to inquire about bills, or by employees of the company wondering about why users are late with their payments. However one comes into contact with employees of the credit card firms, those employees will probably behave in highly predictable ways since there is a strong likelihood that much of their interaction will be scripted. Those who solicit us by phone on behalf of the credit card firms are reciting scripts mindlessly. It is even likely that when we call with inquiries or complaints, those on the other end of the phone have been trained to recite scripts and even a wide range of sub-scripts depending on the nature of the inquiry or complaint and the direction taken by the conversation.

Before credit cards, people had to actually slow down, or even stop consuming altogether, at least momentarily, when cash on hand or in the bank dipped too low or disappeared altogether. This unpredictability at the individual level was mirrored at the societal level by general slowdowns in consumption during recessionary periods.

The credit card serves to free the consumer, at least to some degree, from the unpredictabilities associated with cash flow and the absence of cash on hand. It even frees the consumer, at least for a time, from the absence of funds in checking and even savings accounts. Overall, the credit card has a smoothing effect on consumption. We can purchase things or engage in various forms of entertainment even though we have no cash on hand or in the bank. We are now better able to avoid "painful" lulls when we are unable to participate in the economy. Most generally, the credit card even allows people to consume during recessionary periods. The availability of credit cards serves to make the world of the purveyors of goods and services more predictable by helping to ensure a more steady stream of customers during bad as well as good times.

Non-Human for Human Technology

A variety of non-human technologies have come to *control* both customers and employees within the fast-food restaurant – soft-drink machines that shut themselves off when the cups are full, french-fry machines that buzz when the fries are done and even automatically lift the baskets out of the oil, and soon robots rather than real human beings that serve customers. These technologies control employees, deskill jobs and ultimately replace people with machines (see Chapter 5).

The credit card is itself a kind of non-human technology. More importantly, it has given birth to a range of technologies that intervene between buyer and seller and serve to constrain both. Most notable here is the vast computerized system that "decides" whether or not to authorize a new credit card. More frequently, that system determines whether or not to authorize a given purchase. Shopkeeper and customer may both want to consummate a deal, but if the computer system says no (because, for example, the consumer's card is over its credit limit), then there is likely to be no sale. Similarly, an employee of a credit card firm may want to approve a sale, but is loath, and may even be prohibited, to do so if the computer indicates that it should be disapproved. This is part of a general trend within rationalized societies toward taking decision making away from people (customers, shopkeepers and credit card company employees alike) and putting it in the hands of non-human technologies.

With the advent of smart cards (cards with embedded computer chips that enable them to be used in many different ways), the card itself will, in a sense, be a non-human technology that "decides" whether or not a sale is to be consummated. Embedded in the card's computer chip will be things like spending limits and the card itself may trigger the rejection of a purchase that is over the limit.

Not only do aspects of our credit card society take decision making away from human beings, but other of its elements eliminate people altogether. Thus, the smart card may come to eliminate many people who operate a credit card company's computer system. This is clearest today in the case of ATM cards and the ATMs which have been replacing bank tellers. A bank vice-president is quite explicit about the substitution of non-human for human technology in the growth of ATMs: "'This might sound funny, but if we can keep people out of our branches, we don't have to hire staff to handle peak-time booms and the like. That drives down costs . . .'" (*American Banker*, 1991: 22a). A similar point can be made about debit cards which involve a far less labor intensive system than the banking organization that stands behind the checks that they are designed to replace. The growth of debit cards has led to the loss of many bank positions involved in the various steps in the clearing of a check. Furthermore, since credit cards are designed to be used in place of cash, the increasing use of such cards has led to the loss of positions involved in a cash economy (e.g. bank tellers needed to dole out cash).

The next steps in this historical process entail the further development of the so-called "information highway" so that people will no longer need to leave their homes in order to conduct financial transactions. They will be able to use their ATM, debit or credit cards to make electronic funds transfers through their telephones, home computers and television screens (Piskora and Kutler, 1993: 1A). The result will be even more non-human technology and even less contact with other human beings.

A variety of pressures have forced the credit card industry to pursue ever higher levels of rationalization through new and more sophisticated non-human technologies. For example, because both consumer and shopkeeper want quick authorizations of credit card sales this leads to the need for ever more sophisticated computers, as well as for computer programs to make such authorizations possible. Similarly, the credit card companies have a strong interest in seeing charges entered speedily into a customer's account so that the bills are likely to be paid sooner or, better yet, that interest charges can begin accruing sooner on unpaid balances.

We can illustrate this by looking at Visa's computer system, Visanet, which serves as the intermediary between merchant, merchant's bank and the card-issuing bank. This is a huge network encompassing (in 1993) "9 million miles of fiber-optic cable that links about 20,000 banks and other financial institutions and 10 million merchants in 247 countries and territories worldwide" (*Los Angeles Times*, 1993: C1). This system handles an average of 11,000 transactions per minute. Most of them go through two "super centers" in Virginia and England, as well as 1,400 smaller Visa computers. From the swiping of the card through the point-of-sale terminal to approval, the entire process ordinarily takes between six and 20 seconds.

In this time, the system determines whether the card is stolen, whether the credit limit has been exceeded, and whether the purchase is an unusual one which might indicate that the card use is unauthorized by the cardholder.

Similarly, the development of on-line systems like Visa's Internet and MasterCard's Maestro has permitted instantaneous transfer of funds when a debit card is used. These systems are deemed preferable to far less sophisticated off-line systems that take a few days before a transfer of funds is completed.

Another pressure pushing in the direction of technological advancement and control is the need to decide quickly and correctly whether or not to give someone credit and how much credit to extend. As discussed above, the movement is away from leaving this up to human beings to decide on subjective bases and in the direction of developing the computerized credit scoring systems that come up with scores that allow the computer to make these "decisions." In some cases the computer even generates the acceptance or rejection letter. It is likely "that the entire process is handled without anyone looking at your application or file" (Detweiler, 1993: 15).

Perhaps the most visible example, though, in the credit card business of taking control away from humans is the movement away from what in the industry is called "country-club" billing and toward "descriptive billing." In country-club billing, customers receive with their monthly bills copies of the actual charge slips used for each purchase. American Express is one company that continues to provide its customers with such copies (or facsimiles). This is an expensive undertaking for credit card companies so most have moved away from country-club billing and toward descriptive billing.

In descriptive billing the consumer merely gets a list of the charges, dates and amounts. No copies of receipts are sent. The problem with descriptive billing is the loss of control by consumers. With copies of receipts, cardholders can clearly see whether or not they actually made each purchase. After all, copies of the actual receipts contain their authorizing signatures. With only lists, often long lists, attached to the bill, consumers must rely on memory, or on their own record keeping, to verify a purchase. People often throw up their hands and assume the list of charges is correct, thereby surrendering control over this issue to the credit card companies and their computers.

By the way, the consumer's need to keep records and to verify long lists of bills is indicative of another characteristic of a rationalizing society (see Chapter 5) – pushing more and more work on to consumers, who are compelled to do it on an unpaid basis. In the credit card business customers are required to keep the copies and check them against the list provided with their monthly bill. Another example involves errors in one's credit bureau records. As Detweiler puts it:

> Creditors are not responsible for the accuracy of their information. If a creditor or collection error reports wrong data about you to the credit bureaus, it's your

responsibility to catch the error, and then straighten it out. . . . *The system is not user-friendly: you have to do all the work.* (Detweiler, 1993: 39; italics added)

The Irrationality of Rationality

Finally, there is the irrationality of rationality, which takes a variety of forms. At one level, this simply means that what is rational in planning does not work out that way in practice. For example, while the drive-through window in the fast-food restaurant is supposed to be a very efficient way of obtaining a meal, it often ends up being quite inefficient, with customers finding themselves on long lines of cars inching toward the take-out window. Similarly, credit cards sometimes end up being quite inefficient. Take the program undertaken by Discover Card to allow its members access to Sprint's long-distance service. To make a long-distance call with the card, "all you need do is dial Sprint's 11-digit access number. Then 0. Then a 10-digit phone number. Then the 16-digit account number from your Discover Card. Then a four-digit 'Personal Access Code'" (*Consumer Reports*, 1992: 7). That turns out to be a highly inefficient 42 digits that need to be entered just to make one long-distance call.

To take another example, the credit card companies are supposed to function highly predictably. For example, we should be able to expect that our bills will be error-free. However, various types of billing errors *do* find their way into our monthly statements: there may be charges that we did not make, or the amount entered may be incorrect.

At another level, the most notable irrationality of rationality in the fast-food industry is the creation of a dehumanized and dehumanizing setting in which to eat or work. Such an inhuman world is irrational from the point of view of the human beings who must deal with it. Of course, the credit card world is also highly dehumanized since it is one in which people generally interact with non-human technologies, their products such as bills or overdue notices, or with people whose actions or decisions are constrained if not determined by non-human technologies. Horror stories abound of people caught up in the "heavy machinery" of the credit card companies. Pity the poor consumers who are charged for things they didn't buy, or are sent a series of computer letters with escalating threats because the computer erroneously considers them to be delinquent in their payments. Then there are the many complaints of people who are turned down for credit because erroneous information has crept into their credit reports. Trying to get satisfaction from the technologies, or their often robot-like representatives, is perhaps the ultimate in the dehumanization associated with a rationalizing society.

More generally, the irrationality of rationality is a general label for the problems associated with rational systems. For example, credit card companies tend to discriminate against minorities and women. Women have often found themselves in a Catch-22 situation, unable to get credit cards because they do not have a credit history since their credit cards have been in their husbands' names. Full-time homemakers often find it difficult to get credit cards on their own because they lack an independent income. Credit card companies also discriminate against those who in the past resisted credit and preferred to pay for what they bought, often in cash.

There are various irrationalities associated with the rationalization of the process of granting credit card loans. In addition to dehumanization, there is the greater likelihood of delinquency and default than when financial institutions employ more traditional methods. These institutions are willing to accept such risks because of the relatively small amounts involved in credit card loans and the fact that credit cards in general are so profitable that such losses are hardly noticeable.

The largest set of problems is that associated with actions taken by credit card companies to increase revenues and profits. For example, companies have been known to alter their accounting methods so that customers end up paying more in interest than they expect to, or should. Initially, the GM credit card featured a potentially costly "two cycle billing method" which worked in the following way:

> A $500 purchase made Jan. 1 does not have to be paid off until late February under typical grace periods. If only a minimum payment is made, most cards calculate interest for the March billing period on the unpaid charges from the February bill. Under the two-cycle method, a card issuer will go back two cycles and calculate the interest from the time the purchase was made.
>
> This extra charge will be levied only once for people who carry balances from month to month. But for those who constantly switch from paying off to carrying a balance, this two-cycle method can be costly. (Bryant, 1992: 35)

It is interesting to note that GM was forced to drop its two-cycle billing method due to negative publicity and cardholder complaints.[3]

In spite of the successful effort to end GM's billing method, in general few customers are knowledgeable enough to understand the implications of such rational accounting procedures, or even to realize that they have been implemented. The problem, however, is more general than that: "A number of banks took advantage of consumer complaisance by changing annual fees, rates, grace periods, late charges, and other card restrictions without attracting a great deal of consumer attention" (Mandell, 1990: 79). Few consumers have the will or the ability to carefully oversee the activities of their credit card companies.

But perhaps the most persistent and reprehensible activities of the credit card companies involve their efforts to keep interest rates high even during periods when interest rates in general are low and/or declining.

Of course, many other irrationalities of the rationalized credit card industry can be discussed (for more on this, see Ritzer, 1995) – the tendency of companies to engage in practices that lead people to spend recklessly, the secrecy of many aspects of the credit card business, the invasion of the privacy of cardholders, and fraudulent activities engaged in by a number of different players in the credit card world.

In sum, credit cards (and similar instruments), like the fast-food restaurant, can be seen as part of the rationalization process and, as such, are characterized by each of the major dimensions of McDonaldization. The growth of the credit card industry (like the fast-food industry) is a reflection of the increasing McDonaldization of society and it, in turn, is playing its part in furthering the McDonaldization process.

The latter is an extremely important point. Credit cards are not merely key elements of a McDonaldizing society. They are that, but they are also implicated in, and permit the further extension of, many other aspects of that society. Credit cards are crucial to the efficient operation and the continued expansion of the rationalized business world. It is in this way that credit cards are central not only to the future rationalization of society, but also to the emergence of the problems and irrationalities that are such worrisome aspects of such a society.

Personal Troubles, Public Issues and the Rationalization Process

Let us look now more explicitly at the McDonaldization process as it applies to credit cards from the perspective of C. Wright Mills's (1959) twin themes – personal troubles and public issues. Rationalization can be seen as a large-scale social process that is manifesting itself in the credit card industry (among many others) and is creating personal troubles for individuals as well as public issues of concern to society as a whole.

While our focus is on the problems it creates, the McDonaldization process does have a wide array of benefits.[4] In fact, most of the major dimensions of rationalization discussed above may be seen as advantageous. Thus, most of us regard the emphasis on things that can be counted (rather than relying on qualitative judgments), efficient operations, predictable procedures and results, and the advances offered by non-human technologies as highly positive characteristics of a rational society. We will assume these advantages, but our focus will be on private troubles and public issues.

We begin with personal troubles resulting from each of the dimensions of the rationalization process. The emphasis on buying large numbers of easily replaced things leaves us surrounded by poor quality goods that do not function well and that fall apart quickly. Since we can more easily acquire, and reacquire, many of the things that we desire, we are left with a cynical and blasé attitude toward the world. The scoring systems relied upon by credit card firms reduce all of us to a single number. Our fundamental character means little and that contributes to the expansion of a flat, dull, characterless society. Decision making is handed over to the computers that calculate and assess the scores. Consumers are left feeling that they exist in, and are controlled by, cold, inhuman systems. A perfect example is the fact that once the credit bureaus have a file on a person, it is *impossible* for that person to opt out of the system.

The greater efficiency of making purchases with credit cards in comparison to the alternatives, especially cash and checks, contributes to a society in which the emphasis is on speed (Virilio, 1986). Lost in the process is a concern for the quality of the experience and of the goods and services obtained. Overall, something important but indefinable is lost in a world in which the sole emphasis sometimes seems to be on speed and efficiency.

A similar point can be made about the personal troubles associated with predictability. Something vital about life is lost when all of the things we consume, and the experiences we have, are highly predictable. Life becomes routine, dull, boring. The excitement associated with at least some un-predictability – a surprising discovery or an unexpected experience – is lost. When people had to rely on cash on hand, there were likely to be periods of self-denial, but when the cash supply had been replenished there was excitement in being able to afford some object or participate in some experience. The tendency to reduce or eliminate such periods of self-denial eliminates that excitement.

A considerable amount of humanity is lost when people are in the thrall of large-scale systems such as the credit card industry and its computerized systems. Instead of being in control, people are controlled by these systems. This is well illustrated by the switch from country-club to descriptive billing in most of the credit card industry. Similarly, the technologies associated with credit cards tend to reduce or eliminate human interaction. They also eliminate jobs, leaving many people without the income and meaning that work accords.

Thus, each of the major dimensions of the rationalization of the credit card industry can be seen as causing personal troubles for individuals. Many of those troubles relate, more generally, to the irrationality of those rational systems, especially their tendency toward dehumanization. Many of the specific personal troubles discussed in the last several paragraphs are part of, and contribute to, the process of dehumanization. In many ways our lives are less human because of the advances in the credit card industry and the rationalization process of which it is part. When one adds all of the other problems caused by the expansion of the credit card industry to its dehumanizing aspects, it is clear that it is the cause of innumerable personal troubles.

What are the public issues associated with credit cards? At one level, the aggregation of all of these personal troubles can be seen as a public issue (Liska, 1990). At another level, the policies of the credit card industry that cause these problems can also be viewed as a public issue. Fundamentally, the industry is in the business of luring people into debt, indeed into a lifetime of perpetual indebtedness. The companies compete to come up with gimmicks (no annual fees, low introductory interest rates, free gifts) that will lead consumers into accepting yet another credit card. Those prized custom-ers who are unable to pay their debt in full (and most fall into this category) are charged usurious interest rates. The policies of the credit card industry are (or should be) a public issue.

However, the broadest public issue is the threat of totalitarianism posed by the credit card industry in concert with the other major elements of the rationalizing society. Galanoy (1980) called such a totalitarian system Lifebank and saw it as the logical derivative of the credit card society.

Galanoy envisioned Lifebank as a system in which all of our assets will be combined into one account. This account will be controlled by one or more banks or financial institutions and their computers. All of our credit cards will be replaced by a single Lifebank card. Virtually all consumption will be on credit. As our bills come due, they will be automatically deducted from our Lifebank account. We will be granted an allowance for day-to-day expenses. There will, as a result, be little cash and little need for it. Checking accounts as we know them will have largely disappeared. Lifebank's computers will make virtually all of our economic decisions. Our credit ratings will be continually updated. Our Lifebank card will be the key to virtually everything, and those without such a card will not only not have any credit in a society that depends on credit, but will literally have ceased to exist as far as Lifebank's computers are concerned.

While we may some day see a centralized electronic funds transfer system like Lifebank, Galanoy was wrong in his predictions. For example, he argued: "Lifebank could become a reality by 1985, perhaps sooner" (Galanoy, 1980: 20). As I write this over a decade later, it is clear that Lifebank did not occur in 1985 and while we may be somewhat closer, we are still a long way from such an all-encompassing system.

Galanoy (1980: 13) may have been more accurate when he wrote of "the terrifying certainty of an all-controlling system called Lifebank – in our lifetime." But even here his analysis is marred by superheated terms like "terrifying." Or, take the following statement:

> We will have lost control. Even the banks will have lost control. The Lifebank-type system will have its own reasoning, its own standards, its own momentum, its own energy, its own life; and operating without conscience, without soul, without social logic, it will also be out of control by all standards we should still live by today. (Galanoy, 1980: 215)

While such a system has yet to come into existence, many developments and technological advances (e.g. smart cards) have made something like Lifebank possible today, and continued technological advances make it an even greater likelihood in the future.

Lifebank resembles the "iron cage of rationality" that lay at the base of Weber's concern with the rationalization process. Weber feared that the world was moving toward a seamless web of rational systems that would control more and more aspects of our lives. Furthermore, we would be less and less able to escape from the rational society until eventually we would be left with little more than the ability to choose among rational systems.

The credit card industry has become highly rationalized and has taken its place as a key element of our rational society. What is particularly disturbing about the role of the credit card industry is that it involves means rather than ends. The result is that it is one of the preferred means to a wide array of rationalized ends.[5] As a means, it contributes to the further rationalization of the ends to which it provides access. Furthermore, credit cards, seen as meta-means, contribute to the rationalization of various means (for example, in the realm of consumption, shopping and cybermalls). In these ways, the credit card is playing a distinctive and unusually powerful role in the emergence and solidification of the iron cage of rationalization. *That* is the central public issue as far as credit cards are concerned and it is one that subsumes the wide range of more specific issues discussed in this chapter that *should* be of great public concern.

Notes

This is a revised version of Chapter 6 of *Expressing America* (Ritzer, 1995).

1. For a discussion of *Character and Social Structure* in light of an integrative theoretical perspective, see Ritzer (1981: 193–8).

2. There are, of course, differences, as well. For example, the fast-food restaurants are marketing end-products, while the credit card firms are pushing means to that end, and many other ends, as well.

3. Personal communication from Gerri Detweiler, former executive director of Bankcard Holders of America.

4. For a discussion of the advantages of the fast-food restaurant, see Ritzer (1996a: 11–13).

5. However, it should be pointed out that credit cards can also provide access to non-rationalized ends (for example, a one-of-a-kind antique or a trip around the world on one's own). In that sense, they can help to liberate people from rationalization, at least until the bills come due. I would like to thank Meghan S. Lee for making this point.

III

THE NEW MEANS OF CONSUMPTION

9

The "New" Means of Consumption: A Postmodern Analysis

In previous works, as well as throughout much of this book, I have analysed the rise of fast-food restaurants and credit cards largely from a modern point of view. For example, I have associated both with a characteristic – rationality – that most analysts see at the heart of modern society. I have consistently drawn on the work of such modern social theorists as Max Weber, Georg Simmel and C. Wright Mills. Furthermore, I have used a modern epistemology to describe both fast-food restaurants and credit cards in terms of grand narratives – especially McDonaldization, but also globalization and Americanization. While I think that these and related phenomena are usefully analysed from a modern point of view, this chapter is devoted to demonstrating that other insights come to light when they are analysed from a postmodern perspective (Ritzer, 1997).

The objective here is to apply at least some key aspects of postmodern social theory not only to fast-food restaurants and credit cards, but to the broader set of phenomena that I am combining under the heading of the "means of consumption" (e.g. Baudrillard, 1970/1988: 54). Specifically I have in mind a number of relatively new means of consumption that are almost all recent products of American society. Two of these new means are of course the fast-food restaurant and the credit card. Related innovations in the means of consumption include shopping (including mega-) malls, superstores, cybermalls, theme parks, cruise ships, gambling casinos, home shopping via television, infomercials, telemarketing, catalogue shopping, and even the somewhat older supermarkets.

This raises an immediate issue: how can these phenomena be discussed under the heading of postmodernism when at least two of them have already been discussed as modern phenomena? The answer is that in this context I am not adopting the chronological view that postmodernity supplants modernity (in fact, Lyotard (1988/1992: 76) argues that the "idea of linear chronology is itself perfectly 'modern'"), but the view that one can analyse any social phenomena from the point of view of *both* modern *and* post-modern theory.

In fact, it may be far more useful to regard modernism and postmodern-ism, not as epochs that follow one another, but as different "modes" of analysis (Lyotard, 1988/1992: 24). In analysing social phenomena altern-ately from a modern and then a postmodern perspective, one would be following the logic employed by Weinstein and Weinstein (1993: 21) in their postmodern analysis of Simmel:

> To our minds "modernism" and "postmodernism" are not exclusive alternatives but discursive domains bordering each other. . . . We could be working the modernist side of the border (as we have in the past) if we didn't think that the postmodernist side contained more resources for mapping present culture.

The attraction of postmodernism is that it offers new and different resources to look at these phenomena. One is quite safe in doing this kind of analysis since the postmodernists, themselves, have tended to look at phenomena like the fast-food restaurant through the lens of postmodernism. Take, for example, the following description of postmodernism by Lyotard:

> Eclecticism . . . of contemporary general culture: one listens to reggae, watches a western, eats *McDonald's* food for lunch and local cuisine for dinner, wears Paris perfume in Tokyo and "retro" clothes in Hong Kong; knowledge is a matter for TV games. (Lyotard, 1979/1984: 76; italics added)

I (and many others) tend to look at the new means of consumption in a very material (Marxian) sense, but most postmodernists (and poststructural-ists) focus far more on non-material signs associated with such phenomena and their place in the similarly non-material code. However, these two approaches are not mutually exclusive and we will have many things to say about signs and the code in the context of a discussion of these means of consumption.

Postmodern Society as a Consumer Society

The place to begin a postmodern analysis of these means of consumption is with the view that postmodern society is a consumer society (Featherstone, 1991); indeed one often sees the terms used synonymously. Baudrillard's (1968/1988, 1970/1988) early work focused on consumer society and, more recently, Bauman (1992) has viewed postmodernity in these terms. Capital-ist society *has* undergone a shift in focus from production to consumption. In the early days of their economic system, capitalists concentrated almost exclusively on controlling production in general, and production workers in particular. As factories have moved out of advanced capitalist nations, those nations have moved toward controlling consumption in general, especially the thoughts and actions of consumers (Gabriel and Lang, 1995). While producing more and cheaper goods remains important, attention is increas-ingly being devoted to getting people to consume more, and a greater variety of, things.

In the realm of consumption, the focus of thinking and research is usually on marketing and advertising (Ewen, 1976, 1988; Ewen and Ewen, 1982; Fowles, 1996). While these are certainly significant, what I want to examine are the new means of consumption as social structures that constrain both people and signs (and as producers, sponsors, and so on of signs). In doing so, I am following Baudrillard (1970/1988) who discussed such means of consumption in some of his early work. He looked at the distinctively French drugstore as such a (then) new means, but closer to my area of interest he also discussed the shopping mall.

The new means of consumption are just that: means to allow people to consume. Just as the means of production are necessary to, and facilitate, production, means of consumption perform the same roles in the sphere of consumption. All new means of consumption are increasingly necessary to, and facilitate, consumption. This helps us to see that there are important analogies between workers and consumers. In fact, as discussed earlier, consumers now "work" in conjunction with these new means of consumption and, to the constant joy of capitalists (and their profit margins), they perform that work without compensation.

On the surface, means of consumption and their functions seem benign enough, even quite positive (facilitating consumption, for example). But looked at more deeply and more critically, they are means to gently, and not so gently, lead consumers to consume in ways that are most advantageous and most profitable to manufacturers and sellers. This means that at least some of the time they act to the detriment of consumers.[1] For example:

- Fast-food restaurants lead people to eat foods that are detrimental to their health because they are high in cholesterol, sugar, salt and other additives.
- Credit cards induce people to spend more than they should and beyond their available capital.
- Shopping malls (Kowinski, 1985) entice people into buying things they often do not need.
- TV shopping networks and cybermalls permit people to shop 24 hours a day, seven days a week, thereby increasing the likelihood that they will spend more than they should; buy things that they should not.
- Catalogues allow people to purchase products from anywhere in the world; people may be induced into buying unneeded products.
- Casinos lead people to gamble more and lose more money than they can afford.

While these and other new means of consumption *enable* people to do things they could not do before, they also *constrain* them to buy more than they need; to spend more than they should (Giddens, 1984).

I will not dwell on the well-known ways in which people are enabled to obtain more and different goods and services. My focus is on the very material constraints that these new means place on people to consume goods and services that they often do not need or even want. Of course, consumers always possess the capacity to refuse to use the new means of consumption, or to resist consuming when they find themselves in contact with them (see Chapter 13). However, these means are structured in such a way that people are lured into them and, once in them, they find it extremely difficult not to consume. Many people find it hard to resist turning on Home Shopping Network (HSN), going to the mall, or to a gambling casino when in Las Vegas, Atlantic City or Monaco. Once one is watching HSN, it is difficult to go very long without picking up that phone and becoming a participant. Similarly, one could go to the mall and not shop, but it is hard to do. In any case, what's the point of going to the mall if it's not to shop? The same applies to casinos. One could go and just watch, but more likely one's inhibitions will be overcome and one will become a player (and, most likely, a loser).

Malls are physically constructed so that one is led past one alluring shop after another. Window displays, signs advertising sales, and perhaps goods placed in bins outside the store attract the consumer's attention. Many malls have also added small kiosks and pushcarts in the middle of aisles to offer yet more attractions. One can pass all of these by, but the longer one is in the mall, the harder it gets. A similar point could be made about hotel-casinos. The sights and sounds of the casino assault one on entering the hotel. It is possible to stay at the hotel and not gamble, but the lure of the casino is too great for most people. Once in the casino, one walks past a wide range of machines and games, all beckoning with lights flashing and bells ringing (to say nothing of the promise of vast riches) to the potential gambler. One could resist all of these allures, just as one could resist all the mall shops, but both are structured to make that extremely difficult to do. In any case, the die has been cast once one enters a mall or a casino (or the fast-food restaurant or cruise ship); these are not places set up to attract people who are only interested in window shopping or watching others gamble.

The fact is that capitalists need customers to spend more than they should, and often more than they can afford, on consumption in order to keep the economy operating at a high and ever-increasing level. Thus, capitalism is a major force in the invention of these new means of consumption. Furthermore, capitalists need to keep on having them invented so that it can continue to be the kind of economic system (characterized by ever-increasing profits, stock prices and wealth) we know. More attention seems to be devoted these days to inventing new means of consumption than to the more traditional course of creating new means of production.[1] If postmodern society is consumer society, at least in part, then these new means of consumption are key elements of the postmodern world.[2]

An enormous amount of money is spent on advertising the glories of the various new means of consumption and this reflects the growing need for consumption in modern capitalism. While we usually associate labor with production, Baudrillard has made it clear that consumption has become a kind of labor. As we saw earlier (especially in Chapter 5), we perform a variety of work-like tasks as consumers in fast-food restaurants. Similarly, we work during our treks to shopping malls, supermarkets, and even Las Vegas casinos. All of this is work and capitalism must keep us at it in order to keep expanding and to prevent the consuming masses from thinking about anything remotely resembling criticism, let alone revolution.[3] Capitalism *wants* to keep us at it because instead of paying workers, people are willing, even eager, to pay for the privilege of working as consumers. Without ever-increasing consumerism, capitalism would collapse, or at least be transformed dramatically. To take just one example, what would happen to our economy if people had to pay their credit card balances in full each month, if they were no longer permitted to revolve their accounts? Hundreds of billions of dollars of purchases would simply not be made and the economy would suffer accordingly. As a result of the necessity for ever-increasing consumption, the focus of capitalism has shifted from exploiting workers to exploiting consumers.

The new means of consumption also lead to the proliferation of goods and services. Bauman (1992) recognizes this and relates it to Simmel's (1907/1978; Nedelmann, 1991) tragedy of culture. The tragedy is that our capacities do not develop fast or far enough to allow us to deal with the enormous profusion of commodities available to us. In addition to the expected goods and services, in the postmodern world virtually every aspect of culture (art, music, and so on) is for sale. In fact, we have recently seen the development of so-called "museum" and "archeology" chains designed to sell a variety of simulated artifacts. Such cultural products add enormously to the commodities to be sold in the consumer society. In other words, we come to be overwhelmed by objects of consumption, to say nothing of the vast array of means in existence to allow us to obtain these goods and services. Let us turn to a more general postmodern analysis of these phenomena.[4]

A Postmodern Analysis

The new means of consumption are characterized, and to a very high degree, by simulacra (Baudrillard, 1983). For example, instead of "real" human interaction with servers in fast-food restaurants, with clerks in shopping malls and superstores or with telemarketers, we can think of these as simulated interactions. Employees follow scripts, and customers counter with recipied (Schutz, 1932/1967) responses, with the result that no authentic interaction ever takes place. So many of our interactions in these settings (and out) are simulated, and we become so accustomed to them, that in the end all we have are simulated interactions; there are no more "real" interactions. The entire distinction between the simulated and the real is lost; simulated interaction *is* the reality.

The same point applies to objects associated with the new means of consumption. Any given credit card is a simulation of all other cards of the same brand; there was no "original" card from which all others are copied; there is no "real" credit card. Furthermore, credit cards can be seen as simulations of simulations. That is, they simulate currency, but each bill is a simulation, a copy, of every other bill and, again, there was never an original bill from which all others have been copied. But currencies, in turn, can be seen as simulations of material wealth, or of the faith one has in the Treasury, or whatever one imagines to be the "real" basis of wealth. Thus, the credit card shows how we live in a world characterized by a never-ending spiral of simulation built upon simulation.

Credit cards are simulated means that allow people to purchase all of the other simulated goods and services being created in contemporary society and being sold through other new means of consumption – for example shopping malls, theme parks and catalogues.[5] To build on one of Fredric Jameson's (1984, 1991) examples, we could charge a copy (a simulation) of Andy Warhol's (simulated) painting of Campbell soup cans. Or, we could even charge a copy (a simulation) of a second artist's reproduction (another simulation) of Andy Warhol's "original" (yet another simulation). We could even go so far as to charge a "real" can of Campbell's soup (which is, of course, a copy of perhaps billions of other such cans in label, design, physical structure and contents) in the local branch of our supermarket chain (which is undoubtedly a simulation of many other such markets). As credit cards (and other forms of electronic funds transfer – debit, ATM cards, etc.) increase in importance in the coming years, society will be dominated even more by simulations.

Simulations also characterize the fast-food industry. There are the simulated playgrounds that grace the entrances to many fast-food restaurants. Then, there are the foods – the hamburgers, the pizzas, the tacos – which, while they may be very good simulations of others of their genre, are poor copies of their ancestors, bearing only the faintest resemblance to the homemade hamburgers, pizzeria pizzas, and roadside-stand tacos that may still be found here and there. In fact, such "real" food, if it ever existed, has largely disappeared under an avalanche of simulacra. Today, to most Americans under the age of 30 or 40, the McDonald's burger is the "real" burger, or to put it more accurately, there is nothing (or at least hardly anything) but simulated hamburgers. One who wants to unmask these simulacra for what they are runs the risk of discovering that there are no "real" hamburgers, there is no "true" hamburger (or anything else, for that matter).

Then there are the completely invented foods, for example the millions, perhaps billions, of virtually identical (and simulated) Chicken McNuggets, which fit perfectly Baudrillard's (1983) idea of a simulacrum as an identical copy for which no original ever existed. The original, the chicken, had the temerity to be created with bones, skin and gristle. But then chickens themselves, given modern factory farming, are nothing more than simulations which bear little resemblance to the dwindling number of their "free-ranging" brethren.

Then there is the structure and décor of the fast-food restaurant. The Roy Rogers chain is modeled, I suppose, after the movie cowboy's ranch house, a ranch house that never existed, except perhaps in the movies where, of course, it was already a simulation. The whole western atmosphere created by the chain, and its commercials, has much more to do with the movies (simulations) than it does with the "real" old west (whatever that was).[6] Another example that comes to mind is the "Arthur Treacher" chain of restaurants which is a simulated old English fish and chips shop (whatever that may be). For those of you too young to remember, Arthur Treacher was a British actor who was most associated with butler roles in the movies. This simulated British butler is the symbol of this chain of simulated fish and chips shop. A similar point could be made about the fictional Long John Silver (known best to the public from the movie! i.e. simulated) version of *Treasure Island* rather than the original book) chain of seafood restaurants, as well as many other simulated purveyors of simulacra. By the way, these examples reflect the importance that the media (movies, TV) play in the postmodern world. In the above instances they are affecting us indirectly, but they also have a more direct impact on us that has been the concern of many postmodernists.

As simulated worlds selling simulated products, the new means of consumption in general, and the shopping mall in particular, have a hyperreal quality to them; they seem more real than real. A typical mall is cold and sterile; it is not quite of this world; it is not quite real, or rather it is a little bit more real than "real" shopping plazas in large cities or small towns. The malls are outdone by the theme parks (although malls are, as we have seen, coming to look more and more like theme parks) such as Disney World in which Disney products are sold in a world which seems more real than reality. The same sort of thing can be said about Las Vegas casinos and cruise ships which create a hyperreal world in order to separate us from our money without the need to give us any goods at all in return. The products purveyed in glossy catalogues (e.g. the lingerie marketed in the Victoria's Secret catalogue, to say nothing of the women who model the underwear and nighties) and on the home-shopping networks are made to appear far more real than they will be when they find their way into our homes and on to our backs.[7] Obviously, even more hyperreal are the new cybermalls. Can we be far from "virtual shopping?" We already have virtual sex, or "teledildonics," involving a combination of computer programs and body suits that allow the transmission of sensory information to the wearer (Edelman, 1996).[8]

Baudrillard (1986/1989) describes America as a dry and emotionless desert and it is not surprising that fast-food restaurants, perhaps the quintessential American product, are similarly desert-like. Lacking in depth and emotion, every fast-food restaurant seems like every other. Ultimately, the entire terrain seems like some vast desert in which it is difficult to differentiate one superficial landmark from another. Each fast-food restaurant seems like one more meaningless outpost in the desert. People are dashing from one to another, but there is nothing significant about any of the outposts or in the monotonous process of travelling between them. People seem to come from nowhere and to head to nowhere. (Much of what is said in this paragraph describes the shopping mall equally well. It is an even better description of Las Vegas casinos, which not only create such an environment, but are, of course, in the desert.) And America is rapidly exporting this mode of consumption to much of the rest of the world, which eagerly awaits it, or at least the seemingly desirable signs that go with it. From Baudrillard's perspective, the rest of the world is rushing headlong in the direction of creating a similar consumer, and ultimately social, desert.

While they are characterized by this flat, desert-like quality, there is, as Jameson (1984, 1991) points out, a peculiar kind of euphoria ("intensity") associated with these postmodern settings. There is, for example, the sense as one arrives at the fast-food restaurant that one is in for excitement, or at least some fun. Indeed, what fast-food restaurants really sell is not food, but a (simulated) kind of fun (Luxenberg, 1985). Yet the food is of the most prosaic type one can imagine. What could be less exciting to most Americans than eating yet another fast-food hamburger, chicken wing or pizza slice? Yet we seem to be fooled (or to fool ourselves) continually by the peripherals into believing that we are in for some fun when we pass through the portals.

This excitement pales in comparison to the intensity of feeling on the part of the consumers who enter yet another shopping mall with credit card at the ready. Malls promise, and seem to deliver on, excitement, especially those like the Mall of America in Minneapolis with its amusement park. Just as fast-food restaurants are not really peddling food, malls are not really selling goods, or at least they are not selling themselves on the basis of the goods they have to offer, since those same goods can be purchased almost anywhere else. What they are peddling is their version of an enchanted environment in which to buy those goods. And lo and behold, in come the customers and what do they have at the ready? The credit card; the key to the kingdom! What could be more exciting? Here we are in a magical world and we've got the golden key that will unlock every door. Better yet, and even more magical, it appears as if it's all free! Merchants gladly take our plastic, we sign our names, and off we go with as many goods as we can carry (and as our credit limits will allow). Of course, we know that a downer (the credit card bill) awaits us down the road, but who cares? We're too happy to worry about such future consequences. Even if we "max" out on one card, some other bank will admire our profligacy and give us another. We might even be able to take a cash advance on the new card in order to make a minimal payment on an overdue bill from the old card. (All of this pales in comparison to the intensity of feeling associated with tourist destinations like casinos, cruise ships, resort hotels, Club Meds, amusement parks, and the rest – see Chapter 10.)

Related to the idea of intensities is the sense that Bauman (1992) and others (Debord, 1977) convey that postmodern systems are intent on offering "spectacles." Examples include the garishness of fast-food restaurants and their amusement-park qualities such as playgrounds for children, the modern malls that are more entertainment complexes as well as the amusement parks themselves. Cruise ships, casinos, hotels, even supermarkets seek to present themselves as spectacles so that they can elicit that intensity that is otherwise made so difficult to experience by the unemotional and affect-less character of most postmodern systems.

Then there is the fragmented character of life associated with the new means of consumption. Tacos today, burgers yesterday and pizza tomorrow add up to discontinuity. Credit cards are perhaps the ultimate means to a fragmented and discontinuous life. Limited only by the number of cards in our possession and their collective credit limit, we can be anywhere we want, buy anything we wish. We can spend a little time here, and a bit more time there, and we can put it all on the card. We can buy a new leaf blower today, skis tomorrow, and swimsuits the next day. The only continuity is the constant spending and the fact that that inevitable reckoning will be appearing in our mailboxes. The package tour is another wonderful example of this as vacationers whirl through a series of sites often so quickly that they hardly know where they are, let alone the significance of what they are seeing.

Baudrillard (1983/1990) describes much of this experience as "ecstasy." Each and every fast-food restaurant can be seen as but one of a series of empty forms which endlessly differentiate themselves from one another (even though they are all essentially alike). They are constantly reinventing the same products (other empty forms) over and over again, with only slight variations. Fast-food restaurants and their products are hypertelic, that is, increasing at astronomical rates without any reason (save new or greater sources of profit) for their increase; there is an ecstasy associated with this pure movement (Baudrillard, 1983/1990). Involved in this is a kind of empty inflation. As a result, we find ourselves asea in an ecstatic system in which fast-food restaurants (or shopping malls, supermarkets, superstores) and their endlessly different, yet surprisingly similar, products whirl about us. The massive proliferation and differentiation of signs ultimately end up being an incoherent blur. We are lost in a world of relentless and mean-ingless, expansion. Customers, fast-food restaurants, their products and the resulting signs are all madly and meaninglessly spinning about in this hyperreal world. There is too much meaning (we actually know the meaning of "Chicken McNuggets" and "Egg McMuffin"), much of it superfluous (do we really need to know the difference between a Whopper and a Big Mac?). We are left with a feeling of vertiginousness. Things in the world of fast food go round and round at a dizzying pace, but there is no essential meaning to the process.

As significant and highly visible sponsors, the fast-food restaurants play a key role in the proliferation of signs by the media, perhaps the main source of sign overload in contemporary society. Through the media, the fast-food restaurants not only bombard us with all of their own signs, by their sponsorship they help support a media system that produces a daily avalanche of signs. In so doing, they contribute to the perception that everything is available for communication, signification, banalization, commercialization and consumption.

Of course, all of this is much more true of credit cards and the world of shopping it has helped spawn – communication, signification, banalization, commercialization and consumption are all very apt terms to describe that world (McAllister, 1996). As means to means, credit cards have contributed to the hypertelic expansion of all of the other means of consumption.[9] Shopping malls, casinos, cruise ships, package tours and the like have exploded because, at least in part, credit cards have permitted people to use them more quickly and easily and, more importantly (at least sociologically), they have permitted people to spend far beyond their cash on hand. An interesting case in point is the coming growth in cybermalls. At the moment, the use of cybermalls is limited by the fact that there are questions about the reliability of the means to protect people's credit card numbers when they are used to charge things over the Internet. However, the major credit card companies have promised that they will soon have the capacity to offer such protection. Once people feel safe in using their credit card numbers on the Internet, we can expect to see a hypertelic proliferation of such malls, the businesses that participate in them, the goods sold through them, and the consumers who buy through them.

There is a new type of technology associated with postmodern society and the new means of consumption. Instead of productive technologies like the automobile assembly line that are associated with modernism, we have the dominance of *re*productive technologies, especially electronic media like the television set and the computer. Rather than the exciting, explosive technology of the industrial revolution, we have flattening, implosive technologies. The technologies of the postmodern era give birth to very different cultural products, and a very different way of life, than the expanding technologies of the modern era.

All of the new means of consumption can be seen as implosive: they are not technologies that produce anything new (at least directly). Rather, they better permit us to get what is already in existence and that entrepreneurs want us to purchase. In the vast array of fast-food restaurants, the range of foods available to us implodes into a black hole of hard-to-differentiate salty-sweet foods. Subtlety of taste is not the strong suit of fast-food restaurants. Similarly, in the mad race to acquire as many goods as we can with our credit cards, the products implode into a mass of largely indistinguishable stuff. Stuff that we don't really want, don't need, and will likely replace as soon as our credit card limits will allow. Again, there is no explosive production of goods with credit cards, but an implosive consumption of wares.[10] Much the same can be said about virtually all, if not all, of the new means of consumption.

While they may be implosive technologies, they are undergoing explosive growth; that is, there is enormous expansion of all of the new means of consumption in postmodern society. One could say, following Baudrillard (1983/1990), that, like cancer, they are metastasizing throughout American society and around the rest of the world.

To some postmodern social theorists, especially Jameson (1984, 1991), the multinational capitalistic system is a key element of the postmodern world. In fact, it can be seen as lying at the base of the development and expansion of all of the new means of consumption. With his focus on the economy, Jameson, unlike many other postmodernists, does not accord central importance to technologies, but sees them as a means by which we can begin to grasp the postmodern capitalistic world.

The credit card fits well into this aspect of Jameson's approach: it is a central aspect of contemporary capitalist society. Much like the Treasury, credit cards create money. Of course, Visa doesn't actually print currency, but it does imprint credit cards with varying limits. With these cards, people can spend all the currency in their possession printed by the Treasury and then they can spend the additional "money" available in the collective credit limits of their cards. This additional money has been created by the credit card companies (not the Treasury) and it allows capitalism to operate at a far higher level than it could if it was limited to extracting all of the consumer's available cash.

Most of the other new means of consumption assist the capitalist system. Take the example of mega-stores like Price Club. The whole idea behind these stores is to get people to buy things they do not need and in far larger quantities than they ordinarily would, sometimes in larger quantities than they could ever use. Multiples of a given item are packaged together so that instead of one, several must be purchased. Similarly, enormous containers, jars, bottles, and so on are used so that people buy far larger quantities. People go to outlets like Price Club to save money. While the unit prices are ordinarily lower, people often end up spending more money than they otherwise would. Going to Price Club is a sign that one is a wise shopper, but that sign conceals the fact that one is buying and spending more than one would in other settings.

Today, credit card firms (and most of the other new means of consumption) are concentrating on international expansion. This will mean greater profits for them. It will also allow more and more people around the world to do what Americans are doing – spend far beyond their available cash resources. Consuming more like Americans, they will inevitably consume more American goods as well as the goods of other capitalist nations. The result will be a more active capitalist system and greater profits to the capitalist firms.

Jameson is an atypical postmodernist in viewing postmodernism as continuous with capitalism and therefore modernity. In contrast, for example, Baudrillard (1976/1993, 1983) sees us as having moved from the industrial era in which there is serial production of simulacra by the industrial system to an era in which the code predominates and in which simulacra are reproduced by the code. The era of the code brings with it a possibility of control that far exceeds that of the industrial-capitalist system. Furthermore, while the industrial-capitalist era is marked by production, the era of the code is one of reproduction (see p. 126).

The new means of consumption reproduce the same settings and products over and over and, more generally, they reproduce the code and the system. For example, while the fast-food restaurant exerts control through more modern industrial-capitalist mechanisms and contributes to capitalistic expansion, it is also a significant contributor to, and part of, the code and it is through that code that it also manifests control. We can, following Baudrillard (1968/1988), think of the code as a "code of signification," that is, the code is a set of signs that exerts control over people. In the postmodern world, objects and commodities are signs; in using or consuming them we are using or consuming signs. Thus, in using or consuming fast-food restaurants and their products we are making statements about ourselves. Of course, those statements are controlled and kept in a narrow range by the code. It is much like the referenda to which Baudrillard (1983) devotes so much attention. In a referendum, our ostensibly free choices are defined for us in advance; our free choices are tightly constrained. Similarly, our ostensibly free choice of food is constrained by the fact that fast-food restaurants are driving the alternatives out of business. The differences they appear to offer turn out to be, at best, superficial. Following Baudrillard's notion of the referendum, when we "vote" on which fast food to eat in a given day, that choice can hardly be deemed to be a free one.

The fast-food restaurant and the other new means of consumption constrain us, limit our choices, in many other ways. Thus as the various fast-food restaurants drive local cafés and diners out of business,[11] our choice is progressively reduced to which chain we are going to patronize on a given day. Let me use one new means of consumption to further illustrate this point – Wal Mart, a discount department store focusing at least initially on small towns eschewed by other large retailers. Typically, when a Wal Mart arrives in a small town it drives out many of the competing "downtown" businesses. In a sense, it becomes virtually the only game in town. When people choose to shop at Wal Mart it is because, in many instances, it has helped create a situation in which there are few if any alternatives to it.

Jameson (1991) argues that these postmodern settings exemplify hyperspace (also characteristic of multinational capitalism) where modern conceptions of space are useless in helping us to orient ourselves. While the interiors of fast-food restaurants do not have this characteristic, the typical "strip" on which a vast array of fast-food restaurants, and other McDonaldized systems, is found, does. It is difficult to get one's bearings when one is adrift in such a seemingly endless sea (or desert). The strips are characterized by things Jameson associates with postmodernism – an "existential messiness," and the feeling of a "bad trip" (Jameson, 1991: 117). Even better examples of hyperspace are to be found in modern hotels (see Jameson's discussion of the Hotel Bonaventure in Los Angeles, for example) and shopping malls, especially the mega-malls. Las Vegas, as well as many of the enormous new casinos (MGM Grand, for example), is also characterized by hyperspace. The new and increasingly huge cruise ships would have this feel as well (Fox and Radin, 1996).

In addition to material constraints and characteristics, and of far greater importance to most postmodernists, is the fact that the new means of consumption are busy fabricating and manipulating signs and it is those signs that are controlling our behavior. For example, fast-food restaurants clearly signify "fast." To the degree that the sign "fast" has become part of the code, we are led in the direction of doing many things, not just eating, quickly and efficiently; conversely, we are led away from slow, cumbersome processes in most, if not all, settings. Concretely, this means that we will be drawn to fast-food restaurants and away from traditional restaurants where it might take an hour or two to dine.

Another sign associated with fast-food restaurants is "fun." Again, with fun food part of the contemporary code we are going to gravitate toward the fast-food restaurants and away from the "old-fashioned" restaurants that offer only good food in staid surroundings. More generally, we are led to look for fun in most, if not all, other means of consumption. In Neil Postman's (1985) terms, we are intent on "amusing ourselves to death." Thus, one of the cruise lines is the *Carnival* line; we are not just getting a cruise, but a carnival – and what could be more fun than that? Today's Las Vegas seems, at least on the surface, to be more about fun than gambling. At the minimum, there is more and more fun available to some family members while others are freed to devote their time and money to gambling.

The code, and the fact that we all implicitly understand it, enables us to understand what people are saying about themselves when they utilize one of the new means of consumption. In eating in one fast-food chain rather than another, or in eating one type of food rather than another, we are saying, at least implicitly, that we are like some people and different from others (Bourdieu, 1984b). In other words, our eating habits constitute a text that it is possible to read. "Reading McDonald's" might involve such things as understanding what some people are saying when they consume "value meals" and what others are saying by eschewing such meals. Those who are regulars at Taco Bell are telling us something about themselves and how they differ from those who are habitués of Burger King, Kentucky Fried Chicken or Popeye's. Those who eschew McDonald's for higher-status McDonaldized chains like Red Lobster are communicating a message and that message is even stronger from those who avoid all fast-food restaurants of any type and frequent only traditional, up-scale restaurants where meals are cooked from scratch with fine ingredients by culinary experts. Because it is all coded, there is no end to our ability to read the signs associated with people's eating habits.

There are also the signs associated with different credit cards. Use of American Express, Diners Club and Carte Blanche communicates that one is of higher status than those who use the more prosaic and widely available Visa and MasterCard. Using a gold or platinum card, rather than one of the basic cards (and colors), communicates the same message. (There are even reports of a mysterious black American Express card for really big spenders: Lewis, 1995.) Then there is the need to read the significance of using cash rather than a credit card. A rich person using cash may be saying one thing, while a poor person who pays in cash is saying something quite different. One can read credit card use (or its absence) just as one can read fast-food preferences; indeed, utilization of all of the new means of consumption is coded and therefore can be, and is, read.

From the perspective of signs and the code, eating, shopping and vacationing have little or nothing to do with "needs" as they are conceptualized conventionally. We do not eat in fast-food restaurants because we "need" to eat there (as opposed, for example, to at home). More to the point, we do not eat Chicken McNuggets (as opposed to any other food) because we "need" them, and only them. The desire to eat Chicken McNuggets has been manufactured, like all other needs, by the code (and the economic system). The human race survived quite nicely for the eon before the Chicken McNugget was "invented." We do not eat what we need, but what the code tells us we should eat; the code produces our needs (if they can still be called needs when they are manufactured externally). In general, we eat to express our similarities and differences with other humans and not to satisfy our need for food and, more generally, to survive. When we eat a Big Mac we may think that we are consuming a glorified hamburger, but in fact we are eating an object-sign. In eating that object-sign and not others we are expressing much about our position within the system.

One tangential point worth mentioning briefly relates to the focus of postmodernists (and poststructuralists) on expressing differences in the signs we consume. While there is certainly much truth in this, it is *also* the case that we use signs to express our commonalities with others. The consumption of signs associated with fast-food restaurants is clearly much more an expression of commonality than difference. Indeed, with the massification of signs, people are being led in the direction of "needing" to express far more commonality and far less difference in sign consumption. There will always be signs of difference, but they are now dwarfed by signs of commonality – McDonald's golden arches and Nike's "swoosh" logo.

Many of the same kinds of things said about fast-food restaurants can be said about the other means of consumption. When we whip out our credit cards at the mall we are saying, among other things, that we are "players" in the postmodern economy. A similar sign is communicated when we take a cruise or gamble in a Vegas casino (many cruise ships offer casinos). Here we are demonstrating that we are not merely players, but "high rollers" (when, of course, most of us are not and will need to spend months or years paying off the trip and/or the gambling debt), but there are also times when we demonstrate that we are knowledgeable and cautious consumers. A trip to Price Club might be designed (although not consciously) to demonstrate that fact, even though we often spend more money and buy more goods than we intended or should have. Then, there is making a purchase via a cybermall, which is a sign that we are among the most progressive of consumers utilizing the latest technological advances.

In the preceding pages we have been dealing, in the main, with a stage in which the code is dominant, but Baudrillard (1990/1993) has recently added a later, fractal stage. Here we are talking about endless proliferation, the end of difference, the interpenetration of everything. All negativity has been eliminated and all we are left with is a vacuous positivity: the "Hell of the same." Fast-food restaurants, shopping malls, Las Vegas casinos, cruise ships, TV shopping networks are all characterized by their efforts to remove all negativity; to create at least the illusion of total positivity. While many other things could be discussed under the heading of the fractal order, perhaps the most important relates to the end of differences. For example, while there are many different kinds of fast food, they all end up being pretty much the same; a vast "black hole" of fast food.

An even better and broader example is the erosion of the distinction between shopping and non-shopping areas. More and more places are taking on the characteristics of a shopping mall. We have already discussed how this is happening to amusement parks. Then there are college student unions, airport and train terminals and the like which are also looking increasingly like shopping malls. With the arrival of TV home shopping networks, our living rooms and dens have become outposts of the malls. Soon our studies and offices will be extensions of the cybermalls. There used to be many areas where one could escape from, be free of, shopping. Those areas are being drastically reduced as more and more of them become malls, or at least extensions of them. Following Baudrillard, we could say we are in the era of "transconsumerism."

At one level, most of this section has been devoted to a discussion of the new means of consumption from the perspective of postmodern social theory. At another level, there is a great deal of, perhaps even a pervasive, critique of those means of consumption and of the postmodern world of which they are part. This raises several issues. For example, if, as they do, postmodernists see no hope of ever finding the "truth," how can they be critical of things like these means of consumption? Following Jameson, we can respond that the inability to discover truth does not inhibit the critique of that which is false. Thus, much of the critique of the means of consumption can be categorized under the heading of the critique of the falseness (e.g. simulacra) associated with them.

However, this begs the question, at least in part. Without a fundamental sense of what is true, without such an Archimedean point, how do we determine what is, or is not, false? This is a serious, perhaps even a fatal, problem for postmodern social theory, especially if we accept the post-modern argument that the real is disappearing, or has already disappeared, in a sea of simulacra. If all we have are simulations, what basis do we have to critique some rather than others?

Even if we are willing to concede the obviously highly dubious point that postmodernists might be able to critique that which is false, they cannot, following Bauman (1992) and others, come up with an alternative sense of truth. Thus, we cannot await the emanation of a new grand narrative of what is true from the practitioners of postmodern social theory. As a result, we are doomed to perpetual ambivalence as well as to the need to find individual ways of coping with postmodern society. (This is linked to Foucault's (1979) idea that since power exists at the micro level, resistance must also take place at the micro level.) While ambivalence and such a lonely search for ways of coping may be problems, they are preferable, in Bauman's (and others') view, to the terrorism of the single grand truth. We are largely on our own in the postmodern social world in general, and in our relationships with the new means of consumption in particular.

It is worth bearing in mind that however critical the postmodernists may be of contemporary society, few if any would seek a return, if one can call it that, to modern society. To many postmodern theorists, modernity conjures up images of Auschwitz: in comparison, life adrift in the hyperspace of a postmodern shopping mall is preferable.

Conclusion

The purpose of this chapter has been to explore fast-food restaurants, credit cards, and many other new means of consumption from the perspective of postmodern theory. This chapter is a supplement to previous interpretations by the author of fast-food restaurants and credit cards from a modern perspective. The new means of consumption can be analysed just as easily and effectively from a postmodern perspective. Furthermore, a postmodern perspective leads to a different set of insights into the new means of consumption. They are not better, or poorer, insights than those derived from modern theory; they are simply different insights. The analysis of the new means of consumption clearly indicates the utility of *both* modern and postmodern theory; indeed it demonstrates the great strength of using both approaches *simultaneously*.

The new means of consumption are not modern or postmodern phenomena. They are social phenomena that can usefully be analysed from both perspectives. There is not much utility in worrying about whether or not we have moved from a modern to a postmodern society. Indeed, such thinking is often counterproductive, leading to endless wrangling over whether or not we have undergone some sort of epochal change. However, the body of postmodern theory, especially the thinking of people like Baudrillard, Lyotard, Jameson and Bauman, is, as is demonstrated in this chapter, of great utility in thinking about contemporary social developments. Good theory is good theory, whether it carries a modern or a postmodern label. We need to spend less time worrying about labels, and more time developing and using strong, useful theoretical perspectives.

From the point of view of the sociology of consumption, the goal here has been to highlight the importance of a number of the new means of consumption. Much attention is devoted to what we consume, and what causes us to consume what we do (e.g. advertising, marketing), but not enough attention is devoted to the means that allow us (or lead us) to consume. Yet such means are of great importance. We are living in a epoch in which the United States is witnessing the generation of a wide range of new means of consumption. These new means are not only revolutionizing consumption in the United States, but they are being exported to a large portion of the rest of the world where they are leading people to consume more like Americans. This not only brings great economic gains to the United States, but it is an important new mechanism for cultural imperialism.

Notes

Versions of this chapter appeared in *Sociale Wetenschappen*, December 1996, and were presented as an Invited Plenary Address at the Popular Studies Conference in Tampere, Finland in July 1996 and at the annual meetings of the American Sociological Association, New York City, August 1996.

1. This is clearly in line with the view that one way to think of consumers is as victims (Gabriel and Lang, 1995).
2. There are many others, of course, including advertising.
3. In this view, and many others expressed in this chapter, I am taking a position close to that adopted by supporters of critical theory.
4. Since postmodernism is not a coherent theory, indeed it generally denies the possibility of such a theory, in the following section we will present a "pastiche" of postmodern ideas and their applicability to an analysis of the new means of consumption.
5. Theoretically, credit cards could be used to purchase "originals," but in postmodern society all we have are simulations.
6. The real old West has been filtered for so long through the simulations of movies and TV shows that is difficult to even have a glimmer of what it "really" was.
7. For example, the myriad weight-loss machines advertised on television always appear more usable and more effective than they turn out to be when they end up in our dens.
8. I would like to thank Martin Barron for bringing this to my attention.
9. Fast-food restaurants were slow to incorporate the use of credit cards because, at least in part, of the small amount of money associated with any given purchase, but that is now changing.
10. The increased consumption leads to increased production. However, much of that production does not occur in the United States. Furthermore, an increasing amount of what is consumed is services, not goods, and that does not lead to explosive new production.
11. Or in some cases, create simulated cafés and diners.

10

"McDisneyization" and "Post-Tourism:" Complementary Perspectives on Contemporary Tourism

Tourism, like much else in the social world, is undergoing a dramatic transformation. One way to look at these changes is to argue that they help constitute a stage that is continuous with modernity; they are part of advanced modernity (Giddens, 1990; Beck, 1992). The most obvious problem with such a view is that the new world of tourism seems so different that it appears to lack much, if any, immediate connection with its modern ancestor. Hence, the second way of thinking about this change is that it is both part, and a reflection, of the movement from a modern to a totally new and discontinuous postmodern society. While there is much merit in this second mode of thought, one is led to wonder whether the changes are dramatic enough to qualify as an entirely new social form. Furthermore, such a view tends toward the kind of periodization attacked by postmodernists. Worse, it involves the kind of grand narrative that, as we have seen before, is the *bête noire* of postmodern social theorists, especially Lyotard (1979/1984).

It seems of limited utility, if not totally pointless, to pursue questions like: have the social changes associated with tourism been continuous enough with recent realities to allow us to retain the modern appellation or dramatically different enough to require a new postmodern label? Rather than looking at modernity and postmodernity as epochs, it is once again far more useful to view them as alternative perspectives to be brought to bear on the analysis of changing social phenomena (Lyotard, 1979/1984; Weinstein and Weinstein, 1993). Specifically, we will look at tourism as one domain (of many) characterized by substantial social change. We will look at those changes first from a modern point of view and then from a postmodern perspective. Our objective is not to ascertain whether or not we have, within this domain, left the modern age or entered a postmodern world. Nor is it to determine whether one of these perspectives is better than another. Rather, our goal is to use both perspectives in order to see what new light we can cast on the changing nature of tourism and, perhaps, on the social world more generally.

A Modern Approach to Tourism

There is no shortage of theories of modernity among the classic sociological theorists (Marx, Weber, Durkheim and Simmel), or among their contemporary offspring – Giddens (1990, 1991, 1992), Beck (1992), Bauman (1989, 1991), Wagner (1994), Touraine (1995), and many others.[1] In this section we will employ another modern perspective – the McDonaldization thesis. This perspective, strongly influenced by Weber's theory of rationalization, is clearly interpretable as a modern grand narrative. However, while most grand narratives (e.g. that of Marx) offer a utopian view of the future, this one, following Weber, has a more dystopian view emphasizing not the advantages of the process (efficiency, predictability, calculability, control), but the increasing irrationality of rationality.

The logic of this perspective leads to the view that tourism is growing increasingly McDonaldized. The highly popular Disney theme parks can be seen as paradigms of this process (Fjellman, 1992; Rojek, 1993; Bryman, 1995). Indeed, these parks are discussed at various points in *The McDonaldization of Society* in order to illustrate the reach of McDonaldization. Furthermore, Bryman has examined the Disney parks from the point of view of McDonaldization and has found them to be largely congruent.

Disney World (to take a specific Disney park) is efficient in many ways, especially in the way it processes the large numbers of people that would easily overwhelm a less rationalized theme park. The set prices for a daily or weekly pass, as well as the abundant signs indicating how long a wait one can expect at a given attraction, illustrate calculability.[2] Disney World is highly predictable – there are no "con men" to "rip off" the visitor; there are teams of workers who, among their other cleaning chores, follow the nightly parades cleaning up debris – including animal droppings – so that visitors are not unpleasantly surprised when they take an errant step. Disney theme parks work hard to be sure that visitors experience no surprises at all. And Disney World is a triumph of non-human over human technology. This is not only true of the numerous mechanical and electronic attractions, but even the human employees whose performances (through lip-synching, for example) and work (following scripts) are controlled by non-human technologies. Finally, there is no lack of irrationalities of rationality at Disney World – for example, long lines and long waits make for great inefficiency; costs (for food, the unending hawking of Disney products, both in and out of the parks) mount up, become incalculable, and often make what is supposed to be an inexpensive vacation highly costly. What is supposed to be a human vacation turns for at least some into a non-human or even a dehumanizing experience.

Disney's theme parks came of age in the same era as McDonald's. The original Disneyland and the first outlet of the McDonald's chain both opened in the *same year* – 1955. They are based on and manifest many of the same principles (King, 1983b). In fact, the two corporations have recently agreed to, and embarked on, a series of joint ventures. McDonald's has arguably been the more powerful symbol and force in our age, if for no other reason than because its 20,000 or so outlets worldwide (Gibson, 1996a – and an objective of 30,000 outlets by the year 2000: McDonald's, 1996) are more ubiquitous than the few Disney theme parks.[3] But if McDonald's has been the paradigm of rationality for society as a whole, Disney has certainly been such an exemplar for the tourist industry (Bryman, 1995: 179). To the chagrin of professional gamblers Las Vegas hotels, and the city in general, are coming to exemplify the Disney model. Las Vegas, both in the downtown area and the "strip," looks more and more like a huge theme park and many of its large hotels are, at least in part, theme parks. This is a trend that was begun several decades ago by Circus Circus and is epitomized, at least until it too is surpassed, by the MGM Grand. According to one expert on gambling, "Las Vegas *is* [already] gambling's Disney World" (Grochowski, 1995; italics added). While McDonald's itself has not been without influence in the tourist industry, it is Disney and its phenomenal success that has been most responsible for bringing the principles of McDonaldization (or of rationalization, if you prefer) to the tourist industry. Combining the two, perhaps we can talk – if the reader will excuse the creation of another, even uglier, neologism than McDonaldization – of the "McDisneyization" of the tourist industry.

Whatever its source, the tourist industry in general, and virtually every theme and amusement park in particular, has been McDisneyized, at least to some extent. Cruise ships are taking on the appearance increasingly of floating theme parks. (Disney has its own cruise ship, the Big Red Boat, to take tourists to Disney World, and the new Disney Cruise Line will begin operations in 1998.) Beyond cruise ships, theme parks and casinos, shopping malls have been McDisneyized, coming to look more and more like amusement parks. One could extend this list much further, but the point is that through the influence of the Disney theme parks, many aspects of the tourist world have been McDonaldized. Not only do these tourist attractions look more and more like a Disney theme park, but they come to embrace the four basic principles of McDisneyization (McDonaldization) *and* tend toward generating irrationalities of rationality.

We have not even mentioned the package tours that receive much attention in the *McDonaldization of Society*. Yet while these tours are undoubtedly highly McDonaldized, we are faced with a problem here since Urry (1990a) argues that such tours, or at least the most standardized of them, have passed their heyday and are in decline. They represent the application of Fordism to the tourist industry, but in Urry's view we have moved into a post-Fordist era in tourism (and elsewhere). However, the McDonaldization thesis builds upon and has much in common with Fordism; indeed I argue that McDonaldization runs counter to the view that we have moved from a Fordist to a post-Fordist society (Ritzer, 1996a). Urry's argument on the decline of standardized tours appears to stand in direct contradiction to the McDonaldization thesis, at least in that sector of society.

Urry is undoubtedly right that the rigidly standardized tours he describes have been in decline for some time, but the package tour remains alive and well. Today's tours may be more flexible than their forerunners described by Urry, but they are still highly McDonaldized.

But the key argument to be made here is that today's tours are less McDonaldized than their predecessors *because*, at least in part, of the success of McDonaldization. That is, it is *because* so much of the larger society has been McDonaldized that there is less need to McDonaldize the package tour itself. Take standardized meals, for example. In the past, one of the reasons that tour operators had to offer standardized meals was that the food available at a given tourist site would probably prove too unusual and unpredictable and therefore unpalatable for many tourists. However, now tourists can be safely left on their own at most locales since those who want standardized meals will almost undoubtedly find them readily available at a local McDonald's, or an outlet of some other international chain of fast-food restaurants. Failing that, the modern tourist is even likely to feel comfortable at indigenous fast-food chains like Nirula's in India which specializes in mutton burgers. Similar chains, or indigenous spinoffs, in many other sectors (e.g. Benetton in clothing, the Body Shop in cosmetics) make most tourist sites quite familiar and comfortable for the majority of tourists. As society itself grows more and more McDonaldized, there is less and less need to rigidly standardize the package tour.

More generally, in *The Tourist Gaze* Urry (1990a) argues that there are nine social practices associated with what we normally call tourism. In relation to the package tour, Urry was implicitly questioning the McDonaldization thesis, while that thesis casts doubt on his iteration of touristic practices. Among other things, Urry (1990a: 2–3) argues that tourism is the "opposite" of "regular and organised work," that tourism often involves the movement of people to a "new place or places," that tourist sites are "outside the normal places of residence and work" and there is "a clear intention to return 'home'," that tourist sites are of "a different scale or involving different sense," and that they are separate from everyday experience and "out of the ordinary". There is a sense that tourism is separate from our day-to-day lives; we tour in order to see and experience something different. In fact, Urry (1992) later argues that tourists do not want to "gaze" on and frequent that which is ordinary; that which is not visually distinct.

While all of this is certainly true to some extent, and true of some people more than of others, the McDonaldization thesis leads to the view that people often travel to other locales in order to experience much of what they experience in their day-to-day lives. That is, they want their tourist experiences to be about as McDonaldized as their day-to-day lives. (They may even delight in finding and frequenting a McDonald's in some far-off locale.) Accustomed to a McDonaldized lifeworld, many people want the following:

Highly predictable vacations   They may not want to be in step with fellow tourists, but many want few, if any, surprises.[4] Perhaps as our everyday life grows more and more predictable, we have less and less tolerance for, and ability to handle, unpredictable events. The last thing most of today's tourists want to experience is an unpalatable meal, a wild animal or a rat-infested hotel room. Said a Hawaiian hotel official, "The kids are safe here; there's low crime, you can drink the water and you can speak the language" (*Travel Weekly*, 1995). In addition to avoiding the unfamiliar associated with a different culture, many tourists want the things they are familiar with. For example the cruise ship *Norway* features a television in each cabin offering, among many other things, another key element of McDonaldization – CNN (Carpenter, 1994).

Highly efficient vacations   The same point applies here. Accustomed to efficiency in their everyday lives, many people tend to have little tolerance for inefficient vacations. They want the most vacation for the money (hence the popularity of cruises and package tours) and to see and do as much as possible in the time allotted. One tourist was pleased to find that a huge cruise ship that carried about 2,000 passengers, as well as nearly 1,000 crew members, had no queues (Carpenter, 1994). Maiden voyages on cruise ships are often avoided by knowledgeable tourists because the inefficiencies have yet to be eliminated.

Highly calculable vacations   Many people want to know in advance how much a vacation is going to cost, and they abhor cost overruns. They also want to have itineraries that define precisely where they will be at a given time and for how long. Cruises, for one, typically have all of these characteristics and this goes a long way toward explaining their booming popularity.

Highly controlled vacations   This can take various forms. For example, there is a preference for dealing with people whose behavior is tightly controlled by scripts (just as with McDonald's employees: Leidner, 1993) rather than with those who are free to behave as they wish. (Disney parks are infamous for the tight control they exercise not only over how their employees behave, but over how they dress, how long their hair and nails can be, what kinds of jewelry they may wear, and so on.) Then there are the routines on cruises ("bingo and 'Dicey Horse Racing' to line-dance lessons and napkin folding to 'pool olympics' and aerobics classes": Newbern and Fletcher, 1995) that give order to many vacationers' days. Sites housing advanced technologies (modern airplanes, cruise ships, hotels, amusement parks) are preferred both in their own right as well as for the control they exercise over both tourists and employees.

Of course, this all brings with it the same kinds of irrationalities that come with the McDonaldization of all other sectors of our lives. In addition to its dehumanizing character, tourism often does grave danger to the eco-system.[5]

However, we tend to accept the irrationalities, just as we accept them in our daily lives, as a modest cost to pay for the gains from McDonaldization. The central point in this context is that McDonaldized tourism stands in opposition to all of the points made above by Urry about tourism: it is less and less likely to offer the kinds of difference outlined by him. Our vacations are becoming more and more like the rest of our lives.

To put this in its most extreme form: McDonaldization is undermining the main reason for tourism. That is, if people have in the past toured to experience something new and different, and if tourism itself, as well as the locales to which one journeys, are McDonaldized, then there is little or no reason to tour. Could it be that the McDonaldization of tourism will eventually mean its demise? (See p. 140 for a discussion of touring via the Internet and virtual touring.)

Probably not. Tourism will undoubtedly continue to flourish. Increasing affluence, at least in some segments of society, will continue to fuel tourism. Culturally, tourism offers people a number of hard-to-resist symbols of success and sophistication. Those who rebel against McDonaldized tourism will unquestionably force some tour operators and tourist sites to de-McDonaldize, but I think there will continue to be a market for McDonaldized vacations. Raised in McDonaldized systems, accustomed to a daily life in those systems, most people not only accept, but embrace, them. Instead of being put off by McDonaldized vacations, many will gravitate toward them. I could even envision a world tour of McDonald's restaurants (or Disney theme parks). In addition to mandatory visits to McDonald's in Moscow and Beijing, who wouldn't want to visit Norway and eat McLaks, the Netherlands and devour a groenteburger, Uruguay and feast on McHuevos and McQuesos and Japan and devour a Chicken Tatsuta sandwich (Sullivan, 1995)? This itinerary is presented with a sense of irony, but on second thought my guess is that some clever tour operator could earn a bundle by adopting it.

While many welcome highly McDonaldized tours, there are certainly others who are willing, even eager, to take risks when they tour. However, for many of those who desire to see the extraordinary, there is also a desire to have McDonaldized stops along the way, and to retreat to at the end of the day. The ideal in this case is the right combination of non-McDonaldized and McDonaldized elements.

Then there are those tourists who want nothing to with anything McDonaldized. While it is still possible to experience something approaching totally non-McDonaldized travel, it is growing harder to find. The main reason is that those who profit from such activities rapidly McDonaldize any escape route from rationalization discovered by a significant number of people. This has been underscored by Heywood (1994) in his work on mountain climbing. He sees this, and recreation in general, as an effort to escape the increasingly rationalized lifeworld. He contrasts sport climbing, which has already been rationalized to some degree, with adventure climbing which is more of a pure sport. However, even in the latter, Heywood concludes, "attempts to *evade* or *resist rationalization* are becoming increasingly rationalized *from* within" (Heywood, 1994: 179). The same point can be applied to tourism in general and such a development constitutes a grave threat to those who want to completely avoid rationalized settings when they travel.

All of this rationalization flies in the face of the idea that tourism is growing more diverse; "tourism is growing into a series of 'tourisms'" (Parrinello, 1993: 239). McDonaldization implies homogenization, not diversity. Surely things like "lethal" tours (say, of the world's nuclear waste dumps) or "deviant" tours (pornographic film-making around the world, for example) (Rojek, 1995) must be able to evade McDonaldization? I think not. There are already tours of this type and there will be more of them as soon as enterprising agents find that there are enough people interested to make the effort profitable. The growing diversity of travel represents only a momentary barrier to McDonaldization. More generally, the future of McDonaldization lies in being able to apply its principles to smaller and smaller market niches.[6]

Whatever happens, tourism will continue to flourish, but the McDonaldization thesis leads us to believe that, at least for some, anticipatory technologies (Parrinello, 1993) such as videos, the Internet (Loving, 1996; Faiola, 1996a), and especially "virtual (or techno-) touring" will not only prepare people to travel, but replace journeys to far off locales.[7] As the technology of virtual reality improves, some people will find that it is far more efficient to "visit" Thailand in the comfort of their living rooms than to actually journey there. They will also find a virtual visit more predictable than a "real" one; there are no surprises on a virtual tour. Virtual tours will be highly calculable: one will know precisely how long one's "trip" will take and what it will cost. Non-human technology reigns supreme in virtual touring and it exerts great control over the tourist while it controls others (especially those pesky "natives") completely out of existence. Of course, there are those vexing irrationalities. A virtual tour can hardly promise the same kind of human experience afforded by a "real" tour. The issue of reality, or rather its absence, brings us to a discussion of postmodernism.

Postmodernism and Tourism

Postmodernism is often and easily applied to tourism. The problem with most such analyses, indeed with most applications of postmodern social theory, is their reliance on a general characterization of that theory. The fact is that there are profound differences among the major practitioners of postmodern social theory – Baudrillard, Foucault, Lyotard, Jameson, Virilio, and so on (Ritzer, 1997). There are even significant differences within the bodies of works of many of these thinkers. Thus, one must always be wary of general statements about postmodern social theory.

The place to begin this discussion is with the more specific and concrete idea of the "post-tourist." Feifer (1985) is most often linked to this idea and its major elements. First, the post-tourist finds it less and less necessary to leave home; the technologies discussed previously – television, videos, CD-Rom, the Internet and virtual reality – allow people to "gaze" on tourist sites without leaving home. Second, tourism has become highly eclectic, a pastiche of different interests – visits to sacred, informative, broadening, beautiful, uplifting, or simply different sites. The postmodern tourist simply has a lot more choices: for example, one can take a pleasure voyage on one of the huge cruise ships or choose a much smaller, but still comfortable, ship and make an expedition to more remote locales (Houser, 1994). Then, there is the growth of eco-tourism (Hill, 1995) as well as lifestyle cruises (and other kinds of vacation) like those for seniors, as well as for gays and lesbians (Tazzioli, 1995). Third, post-tourists play at and with touring; they recognize that there is no "authentic" tourist experience (MacCannell, 1976).

Rojek (1993) has also analysed post-tourism in terms of three basic characteristics. First, the post-tourist accepts the commodification of tourism: it and the products hawked along the way are all manifestations of consumerism. Second, tourism is seen as an end in itself, and not a means to some loftier goal. Third, post-tourists are drawn to the signs, especially the more spectacular signs, associated with tourism.[8]

Bryman sees Disney as fitting reasonably well with the idea of the post-tourist, indeed it "may well have played a prominent role in stimulating the attitude of the post-tourist" (Bryman, 1995: 177). Bryman adds additional weight to the idea of post-tourism by, for example, discussing the simulacra, the fakes that are more real than real, associated with post-tourism in general, and more specifically with Disney.

The obvious questions seem to be: are we in fact in the age of the post-tourist? Have we left the era of the modern tourist? These may be the obvious questions, but once again they are really the wrong questions. As before, they imply the kind of periodization and grand narrative rejected by most postmodernists. The real question is: do these postmodern ideas cast new and interesting light on tourism?[9]

The idea that there is a close linkage between commodification, consumerism and tourism is worth exploring (Baudrillard, 1968/1988, 1970/1988; Featherstone, 1991). Clearly, tourism has become a commodity to be advertised, marketed and sold much like every other commodity (Urry, 1990a). However, what is not emphasized enough is the degree to which tourism can become little more than a means to sell lots of other commodities. Again, Disney offers a wonderful example of this. A trip to Disney World is a desirable goal in itself as far as the Disney Corporation is concerned, but perhaps more importantly it is the gateway to the sale of other Disney products. The process begins on entering the theme park which can be viewed as a thinly disguised shopping mall set up primarily to sell a wide array of Disney products. It ends with the Disney Village Marketplace which is open late for those who still have the desire (and the money) to shop after they have visited the park. Indeed, it is becoming difficult to differentiate between shopping malls like Mall of America and theme parks like Disney World (Fjellman, 1992; Barber, 1995). The former is a mall with an amusement park, the latter an amusement park with a mall. (I will have more to say about this kind of "implosion" below, but other examples are the way Las Vegas is currently being transformed into "the world's largest theme park" (Grochowski, 1995); the "Las Vegasization" (Weeks and Roberts, 1996) of shopping malls and cruise ships (Fox and Radin, 1996); and the coming of Segaworld, the world's first interactive entertainment theme park, to London, combining the theme park with virtual reality (May, 1995).)[10] The only real difference between the contemporary mega-mall and today's amusement park is in the relative mix of shops and amusements.[11]

The growing popularity of outlet malls, often adjacent to resorts, also reflects this kind of implosion of shopping and amusement. According to one industry insider, "Shopping has more and more become recreation. . . . You can combine your vacation or weekend away with outlet shopping" (McEnery, 1995). Some outlet malls, like Potomac Mills outside Washington, DC, have become tourist destinations in their own right. Similarly, more Canadian package tours now go to the West Edmonton Mall than to Niagara Falls (Davidson, 1995). Timothy and Butler (1994: 17) examined cross-border shopping between the United States and Canada and concluded: "There are strong indications that under some conditions shopping is the primary motive, if not the only significant one, in the decision to make such a trip." Says a woman who plans travel programs for shopping malls, "Tourism is California's No. 1 business and shopping is the No. 1 thing tourists want to do" (*Seattle Times*, 1994). A large proportion of the time and money devoted to vacations is spent on shopping while on vacation. And some, as we have seen, have taken this to its logical extreme – shopping has *become* the vacation.

Returning to our main example, Disney World is selling Disney products, and visitors may easily spend far more on overpriced Disney goods (leading to incalculability) than on the visit to the park itself. But that is just the beginning. Visits to the parks help to fuel interest in shopping at the Disney store in the local mall (which, in turn, had probably played a role in creating an interest in visiting the park). Visits to the parks and mall shops stoke up interest in Disney movies, the Disney Channel (both of which, of course, helped create the interest in visiting the theme park and the shops), Disney books, Disney recordings, and so on. Here we have a synergistic system to sell and keep selling Disney products. Yes, Disney World is itself a commodity and part of the consumer society, but it also plays its designated role in this highly integrated system.

Barber (1995: 97) has recently summed up (and extended) much of what is being said above with his concept of "McWorld:"

> McWorld *is* an entertainment shopping experience that brings together malls, multiplex movie theaters, theme parks, spectator sports arenas, fast-food chains (with their endless movie tie-ins), and television (with its burgeoning shopping

networks) into a single vast enterprise that, on the way to maximizing its profits, transforms human beings.

The various components of McWorld give us, as tourists (and more generally), a choice of goods and services to consume (although they are goods and services of a very limited type); what they seek to limit, if not eliminate, is our ability *not* to consume.

As the postmodernists suggest, signs are central to contemporary tourism; in touring, people are consuming a wide array of signs. It is important that we understand the nature and significance of those signs and the ways in which they relate to other signs. McDonald's and Disney are important signs in themselves and within each is a wide array of key signifiers. Much the same could be said for all of the major icons of tourism – Las Vegas in general, as well as each of its major hotels; the major cruise lines (e.g. Carnival, Princess); Paris and the Eiffel Tower; India and the Taj Mahal, and on and on.

However, while signs are crucial, an undue emphasis on them leads one to ignore the more material aspects of tourism. Bauman (1992: 155) is one who makes this argument in a more general critique of postmodern social theory:

> To many people . . . reality remains what it always used to be: tough, solid, resistant and harsh. They need to sink their teeth into some quite real bread before they abandon themselves to munching images [on a visit to Disney World or in front of the TV].

The idea of the new "means of tourism" allows us to get at the more material aspects of tourism, without losing sight of the significance of signs. This idea is obviously derived from the broader concept of the new "means of consumption" (see Chapter 9), which are not unrelated to tourism.[12] Obviously, fast-food restaurants and other chains have, as pointed out above, permitted package tours to become less standardized. Malls, especially the mega-malls, have become tourist attractions in their own right. Furthermore, since much of tourism is about selling things, it has been profoundly affected by the coming of age of the mall. Disney World, too, is in a sense a mall; Las Vegas hotels, cruise ships and many tourist destinations have taken on characteristics of a mall. And the tourist ships turn at least some of their destinations into malls:

> While shopping is good on either side, cruise ships usually dock off Philipsburg [St Martin], the capital on the Dutch side, and its Front Street is very popular. With as many as eight cruise ships and countless smaller vessels in port at once, the three main streets can be a mass of congestion with pedestrian and motor traffic competing for the same street space. (Newbern and Fletcher, 1995)

Above all, modern tourism would simply be impossible without the credit card: as a meta-means of tourism (and consumption), it permits one to make full use of all the new means of tourism. A trip to Euro Disney or a world cruise would be virtually unthinkable without a credit card. Returning to the theme of implosion in this context, many cruise ships issue passengers their own cruise cards to make shopping and gambling easier while at sea.

Beyond all of this, we must consider the new means of tourism themselves. The Disney theme park, the cruise ship and the modern Las Vegas
hotel, among many others, are all such means. They are of great symbolic
importance, but they are also carefully designed structures that lead people
not only to come, but also to behave the way the designers want them to. As
we saw above, the Disney theme park forces people to make at least two
treks through Main Street and to distribute themselves in a certain way
throughout the park. The Las Vegas hotel makes it easy for visitors to get in,
but harder to get out and visit other hotels. In any case, the hotels and
casinos are so vast ("hyperspace") that one has little need or desire to go
anywhere else. (The absence of clocks and windows also serves to keep
people in a given casino and at the gaming tables.)[13] The hotels are
structured to lead people to spend money and to lose money at the gaming
tables and slot machines. The new "megaship," Carnival Line's *Destiny*, the
world's largest cruise ship, also has the quality of hyperspace being 893 feet
long and 116 feet wide, and having 12 decks, 1,321 cabins, several
restaurants, a two-level health spa, a nine-story central atrium, four swim-
ming pools, a number of entertainment centers including a 1,500-seat show
lounge and a casino (Fox and Radin, 1996). All of these are designed to lure
people to the ship and the ship is structured to extract their money once they
are on board.

We are in the midst of the development of revolutionary new means of
tourism. We will undoubtedly see the increasing spread and utilization of
techniques that are being pioneered in places like Disney World, the MGM
Grand and the Carnival Cruise Line. These developments have given far
more people the opportunity to do far more things; large numbers of tourists
are able to do things today that would have been unimaginable not too long
ago. While this constitutes greater freedom in one sense, in another sense
these new means of tourism are highly constraining.

In fact, the major examples used here – Disney World, the Las Vegas
hotel and the cruise ship – have many of the characteristics of Erving
Goffman's "total institution," which he defines as places "of residence and
work where a large number of like situated individuals, cut off from the
wider society for an appreciable period of time, together lead an enclosed,
formally administered round of life" (Goffman, 1961: xiii). A Disney theme
park, a Las Vegas hotel and a cruise ship fit perfectly under this definition;
they *are* total institutions. However, there are differences between these and
Goffman's prisons or mental hospitals. Stays are much shorter and the
control that is exerted is not nearly as blatant and brutal. It is the more
postmodern gentle, subtle, "soft," rather than the modern "hard," form of
control. No one accompanies the visitors to Disney World and insists that
they go through Main Street at least twice, or that they disperse themselves
throughout the park. They do so because the park is structured to lead (even
force) them to do so. But, as Foucault (1979) showed in his work on the
Panopticon, gentle and subtle control can be far more troubling than the
blatant and brutal forms. People do not know how they are being controlled,

or even that they are being constrained. Without such knowledge, it is difficult, if not impossible, to question and rebel against the control. Not all of the new means of tourism exert such a high level of control, but the above are models that many in the tourist industry will seek to emulate as much as possible in the future.

Perhaps the ultimate in a tourist site as a total institution (as well as of the fact that virtually *anything* can be turned into such a site) is the planned "Ossi Park" in what was East Germany (the German Democratic Republic: GDR).[14] Here:

> One-day visitors will be *required* to leave by midnight, as they were in the GDR; guards will patrol the border; attempts to escape will lead to hour(s)-long *imprisonment*. All visitors will be *required* to exchange a minimum of hard currency for eastern marks. . . . [The whole park will be surrounded by *barbed wire* and a *wall* and will] include badly stocked stores, snooping state *secret police* . . . and scratchy toilet paper known as "Stalin's Revenge," whose texture, according to an old GDR joke, ensured that "every last ass is red." (cited in Barber, 1995: 133; italics added)

How do we account for the rise of the new means of tourism? Obviously, many factors are involved. Ultimately, however, they are being created and pushed by material interests. There are vast sums of money to be made by creating these new tourist "machines" designed to ensnare tourists and wring every possible dollar from them. That these are figuratively and sometimes even literally machines makes it clear that they are quite material forms. Postmodernists must not lose sight of this in their rush to focus on the signs associated with them. People are consuming signs, but at least in part that is because they are being coerced into doing so by these new structures. We need to understand the intimate relationship between signs and structures in the contemporary world of tourism (and in many other contexts as well).

The issue of authenticity is central to the literature on tourism (MacCannell, 1976). Authenticity (or the lack of it) is also of concern to postmodernism in general, and post-tourism in particular, specifically under the heading of simulacra. Baudrillard's simulated world (1983) is nowhere more true than in the realm of tourism. MacCannell argues that tourists are searching, not always successfully, for authenticity. The logic of post-modernism, with a society increasingly dominated by simulations, would lead us to believe that, if we assume that MacCannell is correct, tourists are doomed to failure in their search.

I have already offered an overview of Ossi Park, the planned simulation of life in the old German Democratic Republic. Among the other examples are "Fort Clatsop," in Astoria, Oregon, where tourists can find a "full-scale replica of [explorers] Lewis and Clark's winter camp" (Houser, 1994). Baudrillard cites the caves of Lescaux. A tourist who journeys to the authentic site will find that the caves have been closed and an exact replica, a simulation, has been opened to the public. While these are extreme cases, most "authentic" tourist destinations have been turned into simulations, at least in part.[15] By the way, the coming of virtual reality will mean a vast increase in the scope of simulations. There is already a virtual tour of the tomb of the Egyptian queen Nefertari (Stille, 1995). And this says nothing about the totally simulated, tourist destinations like Disney World.

But I would like to make a different argument here. That is, rather than seeking authenticity as MacCannell suggests, people raised and living in a postmodern lifeworld dominated by simulations come to want, nay to insist on, simulations when they tour. For one thing, it is growing difficult to differentiate between the simulated and the real; indeed Baudrillard argues that the real has already disappeared, imploding into the world of simulations. In such a world, the tourist would not know an "authentic" experience even if one could be found. For another, living on a day-to-day basis with simulations leads to a desire for them when one becomes a tourist. Accustomed to the simulated dining experience at McDonald's, the tourist is generally not apt to want to scrabble for food at the campfire, or to survive on nuts and berries picked on a walk through the woods. The latter may be "authentic," but they are awfully difficult, uncomfortable and unpredictable in comparison to a meal at a local fast-food restaurant or in the dining room of a hotel that is part of an international chain. Most inhabitants of a postmodern world might be willing to eat at the campfire, as long as it is a simulated one on the lawn of the hotel.

I would like to put forth the thesis, in contrast to MacCannell, that many tourists today are in search of *in*authenticity. The enormous popularity of the tourist destinations focused on in this chapter speaks to the relentless search for inauthenticity. Blissfully content with our simulated lives, why should we search for anything but inauthenticity in our leisure-time activities?

Baudrillard (1983: 23) makes this point about Disneyland, "a perfect model of all the entangled orders of simulation." Take, for example, the simulated submarine ride to which people flock in order to see simulated undersea life. Strikingly, many go there rather than to the more "genuine" aquarium (itself, however, a simulation of the sea) just down the road. How many actually go to the sea to view (say by snorkeling) undersea life? And for those few who do, hasn't the sea itself been altered (simulated) to accommodate the tourist? It has, at least in one setting:

> For the snorkeling enthusiast, the place to head is Folkestone National Marine Reserve, Park and Marine Museum at Holetown [Barbados]. A taxi there costs about $12 from the ship. The government has built an area where the novice can swim and follow a series of underwater markers that picture what fish are likely to be seen. (Newbern and Fletcher, 1995)[16]

Perhaps the best examples of this simulation of a tourist experience are the tropical islands *owned* and completely controlled by the cruise lines (Carey, 1996). Only passengers of the cruise line are allowed on shore. There are about ten such islands already, with more sure to come. In fact, Disney is said to be in the market for one for its soon-to-be-in-existence cruise line, and the existing islands are described as "reassuringly Disney-esque" (Carey, 1996: B1). On these islands the tourist finds no hawkers, no overbuilding, nothing (except perhaps the uncooperative storm) to mar the "perfect vacation." No cash is needed; everything can be charged to one's ship bill. "Real" Caribbean islands pale in comparison. According to one tourist, "St Maarten wasn't a very attractive island. . . . It was dirty. The shops were kind of junky." Said another, "Jamaica was pretty run down to us" (Carey, 1996: B1).

The islands have a strong flavor of Disney-like simulation. The bathrooms are squeaky clean. Food and drink are brought on shore from the ship and the service is provided by the ship's crew. There is even an ersatz market; natives of a nearby island sail over to staff it. On one of the islands, "a *replica* of a 16th century ship [was purposely] sunk in the harbor to give snorkelers a thrill" (Carey, 1996: B1; italics added). More recently, a plane was submerged to give added thrills. Not surprisingly, some killjoy academic (an anthropologist) described a visit to such an island as a "virtual experience" and complained that tourists "don't want to see any of the consequences of colonialism – the poverty, the sex trade" (Carey, 1996: B5).[17]

Certainly, there are those tourists who continue to search out authentic settings and they can still find a few. However, visits to them tend to be more expensive than to inauthentic locales. More importantly, they are likely to grow more difficult to find. Authentic tourist sites are likely to go the way of the caves at Lescaux: they will be shut down and exact replicas will be built nearby. Failing that, they are likely to be so altered by the demands of catering to large numbers of tourists that they will become simulated versions of their original pristine forms.

Let us use another example from Baudrillard's work. Suppose we wanted to spend our vacation among the people of a primitive tribe, the Tasaday. Sounds like an authentic experience. However, Baudrillard regards the Tasaday, at least as it exists today, as a simulation since the tribe has been "frozen, cryogenized, sterilized, protected *to death*" (Baudrillard, 1983: 15). It may at one time have been a "real" primitive tribe, but today what exists is nothing more than a simulation of what the tribe once was. And now we are beginning to see simulations of simulations. For example, the new Sega theme park in London will offer simulated (via virtual reality) rides of an already simulated ride in, say, Disney World (May, 1995). We move ever more deeply into Baudrillardian "hyperreality." Even if we accepted the idea that people know the difference between a simulacrum and the authentic, and we assume that at least some people set out in search of the authentic, Baudrillard would argue that their efforts will be thwarted by the fact that nothing exists but simulacra.

This section has been devoted to postmodern ideas that have previously been applied to tourism. We close with the mention of a concept, "ecstasy," that as far as I can tell has yet to be applied to tourism. As we saw in Chapter 9, by ecstasy Baudrillard (1983/1990) means unconditional metamorphosis, escalation for escalation's sake, a continuing process of spinning out of control until all senses are lost. Ultimately, this out-of-control system reveals its emptiness and meaninglessness; it "shines forth in its pure and empty form" (Baudrillard, 1983/1990: 9).

It could be argued that tourism is becoming such an ecstatic form. Given the implosion discussed above, the de-differentiation that is affecting tourism in many different ways (Urry, 1994), anything and everything is coming to be defined as tourism. This is well illustrated by bus tours to shopping centers and even better by the proposed Ossi Park. With everything defined as tourism, it becomes a meaningless form. Yet, tourism is escalating dramatically. Baudrillard uses fashion to illustrate the ecstasy of the (post-) modern world, but tourism is becoming just as good an illustration. It is increasingly obese and cancerous, that is, it is growing hypertelic. There is no end to tourism other than limitless increase. There is no end for the tourist than to visit as many sites as possible, if only on the Internet. This is obviously not intended as an exhaustive application of the idea of ecstasy, but to illustrate that there are many more conceptual resources within postmodern social theory that the student of tourism might find useful.

Conclusions

This chapter has sought to demonstrate the utility of bringing both modern and postmodern theory to bear on contemporary phenomena, in this case in the realm of tourism. The use of the two perspectives yields far more and deeper insights than would be derived from employing one or the other.

From a modern viewpoint, we have demonstrated the applicability of the "McDonaldization thesis" to tourism. We have also extended it to the idea of "McDisneyization" in order to be able to argue that Disney World not only reflects the principles of McDonaldization, but has itself become a model for the extension of these principles, as well as some of its own, to the rest of the tourist industry. In contrast to the extant view of tourism as motivated by the desire to see something different, McDonaldization and McDisneyization lead to the view that many people are touring to see pretty much what they see on an everyday basis. For those who still tour in order to see and do something unusual, that is growing progressively difficult as such activities and settings become McDonaldized. While there are more diverse options available to the contemporary tourist, those options have themselves grown rationalized. It is counterintuitive ideas like these that indicate the continuing utility of a modern perspective.

However, the fact that modern perspectives continue to be useful does not preclude the fact that postmodern perspectives might also be of utility. The postmodern interest in the consumer society leads us to underscore the increasing interpenetration of the tourist experience and the sale of commodities. Tourist sites like Disney World have become shopping malls, and for their part, shopping malls have not only become amusement parks, but destinations for tourists. While the signs associated with tourism are important, we must not lose sight of the more material new means of tourism – Disney World, Las Vegas casinos, cruise ships, and so on. These can be seen as "total institutions" locking people in tourist sites designed to sell them goods and services. Further, the postmodern perspective leads to the view that instead of searching for authenticity, the contemporary tourist is looking forward to, and increasingly will find, simulated experiences. Tourism, like consumption, is characterized by an ecstatic, hypertelic and meaningless expansion.

There are no grand conclusions to be drawn here. Indeed, if the postmodern perspective has done nothing else, it has alerted us to the dangers, even the terrorism, associated with grand narratives offering grand conclusions about the past, present and future. What we can say is that social theory, in its modern and postmodern forms, has much to offer the analysts of the changing world of tourism. There is no "truth" to be uncovered about the contemporary world of tourism. Both the McDisneyized tourist and the post-tourist exist, but neither gets at *the* truth of tourism. What exist are concepts that allow us to understand things about tourism that we might not have understood before. We are left with a pastiche of insights, some from a modern, and others from a postmodern, perspective. They exist side by side without any grand overarching theory with which to integrate them. That is a relatively modest accomplishment, but as postmodernists have shown, social theorists have good reason to be modest about their conclusions about tourism, or anything else for that matter.

Notes

This chapter was co-authored by Allan Liska. It is to appear in Chris Rojek and John Urry (eds), *Touring Cultures: Transformations in Travel and Theory*. London: Routledge, 1997.

1. Indeed, such theories are what define sociology's classical thinkers.
2. Although, as we will see, Disney World is also in a sense a shopping mall oriented to getting people to spend far more than they do on their daily pass.
3. Of course, it could be argued that Disney's movies, television programs and products make it even more omnipresent than McDonald's.
4. For those who do, there are the unpredictabilities of "adventure travel" (Hill, 1995). Of such adventure travel (or eco-tourism), one writer says, "Ideally, it offers enriching alternatives to the contrived 'big playpen' resorts in which packaged Americanized comforts are simply grafted onto exotic backdrops" (Belleville, 1995: G1).
5. Hence the growth of interest in "sustainable tourism" (Burr, 1995).
6. And to make them "seem" less and less McDonaldized – "McDonaldization without seeming to be McDonaldized." A good example is the movement of groups of chain stores to "village centers," usually in affluent suburbs. While described by one chain store executive as the "de-malling of America," it is in fact the bringing of the mall concept to smaller locales and making them seem less mall-like, less McDonaldized (Pacelle, 1996: B1). According to one real-estate investor, "You have to be careful not to make it look like a shopping center. You can't make it look too uniform" (Pacelle, 1996: B3). Another way of making malls seem less McDonaldized is seen in the trend toward transforming shops in malls so that they look more like city shops (Ahrens, 1996).
7. Faiola feels that it is extremely unlikely that people will travel via the Internet rather than in person. But Faiola is discussing the Internet and not virtual touring. In any case, he may be a bit too optimistic for our McDonaldized age.

8. Munt (1994) discusses "other" middle-class post-tourists who seek to distance themselves from crasser post-tourists.

9. Bryman makes the point that what Disney has to offer in this realm is not so new; its precursors had characteristics that could be described as postmodern.

10. There is a broader kind of implosion taking place involving various corporate purchases and mergers (e.g. of Disney and broadcasting giant Capital Cities/ABC). These are designed to increase the horizontal and vertical integration of organizations involved in consumption in general, as well as in tourism in particular.

Some shopping malls are being transformed, at least in part, into what Weeks and Roberts (1996) call "amusement malls." These are malls which are defined in large part by their amusement centers and not by their shops and department stores. Among the most notable of these amusement centers are the Discovery Zone playgrounds for children and Dave and Buster's, a chain that specializes in adult entertainment.

11. Barber (1995: 128) describes not only malls, but commercial strips and chain eateries as theme parks. More specifically,

> There is a sense in which McDonald's is a theme park: a food chain featuring its own Mickey Mouse (Ronald McDonald), its miniature nonmechanical rides in the "playlands" outside, its commercial tie-ins with celebrities . . . and with hit films . . . and its pervasive claim on American lifestyle.

While McDonald's might not be the kind of tourist destination that malls have become, they are an integral part of such malls and many other tourist sites.

12. In fact, some of them (e.g. cruise ships) are means of consuming tourist goods and services.

13. Dave and Buster's also lacks clocks and windows. Says a general manager (again reflective of implosion), "'It's like Las Vegas. . . . We don't want you to know what time it is'" (Weeks and Roberts, 1996: C5).

14. "Ossi" was the Easterners' slang term for the Cold War.

15. Not all such efforts are successful. A notable failed attempt was Disney's plan for a Civil War theme park outside Washington, DC "'with fake Indian villages, a replica farm, mock Civil War battles and a faux fair'." As with the caves of Lescaux, this simulation was to be constructed "'within hailing distance of real Indian trails, actual farms, a county fairgrounds and a town that was sacked and burned by Union troops'" (cited in Barber, 1995: 135).

16. All is not lost: the McDonald's built on the island was forced to close after six months.

17. They probably would if it was simulated.

11

McUniversity in the Postmodern Consumer Society

Universities, like most other social structures, rarely change as rapidly or as much as prognosticators anticipate. Thus, in the near term, the university is going to have many characteristics in common with today's university. However, accompanying the many continuities will be a variety of dramatic changes, many of which are already in their early stages. There are different ways of conceptualizing these changes, but one approach is to begin by thinking about the retention of the viable elements of today's university and then adding elements derived from a range of everyday experiences with the new means of consumption (including tourism).[1]

On the surface, this seems a startling assertion. What does the university have to do with fast-food restaurants, ATMs, Disney, MTV, Las Vegas and the like? The answer, at least in the near future, is plenty! My view is that universities will be borrowing liberally from all of these; indeed they will come to be a pastiche of diverse elements derived from them (and from many others, of course) and combined with elements that are holdovers from its past (our present). In fact, this combination of traditional and more contemporary elements will make the university of the near future even more postmodern than it is today.[2]

When thought about in these terms, the university can be conceived of as a means of educational consumption, one that allows students to consume educational services and eventually to obtain important "goods" – degrees and credentials.[3] Thus, the university is squarely within the realm of a focal concern of the postmodernists – the consumer society. This chapter looks at changes (current and on the horizon) in the system of higher education, as well as responses to them, from the vantage point of the consumer society and the postmodern theory that privileges it.

A major problem facing today's university is that, at least in comparison to many of the modern means of consumption, it is a decrepit mode of consumption. As a result, it is coming under pressure, at least in part, because there is a growing sense that it does not do a very good job of allowing students to consume education. It also looks awfully dated, boring and cumbersome in comparison to other cutting-edge, exciting and efficient means of consumption such as ATMs,[4] fast-food restaurants, mega-malls, superstores, theme parks and cybermalls.

Students (and often, more importantly, their parents) are increasingly approaching the university as consumers; the university is fast becoming little more than another component of the consumer society. Long before they enter the university, students are quite expert about the world of consumption, and how to find their way about in it. Parents are, if anything, likely to be even more adept as consumers than their children and because of the burgeoning cost of higher education more apt to bring a consumerist mentality to it. The increasing number of adult students, often returning to school after a hiatus, are even more likely than other kinds of students to adopt a consumerist orientation to higher education, in part because they have more experience at it and in part because they are usually spending their own money.

Supporting this contention is the view of many school officials, including one who said: "Research data is telling us that students are consumers, and they are looking at cost, quality and convenience when choosing a school. . . . In a sense, students want to get the best product for their money" (Sulski, 1995). Educators are being compelled to recognize this new reality:

> While we may not be ready to think of students as customers, or even as purchasers of services, they may well behave that way, exercising choices that seem unusual to faculty who are used to prescribing student behaviors. Many students at public universities already walk away from courses, forfeiting tuition, to protect their time; in the future, they may expect refunds for inadequate or inaccurately advertised courses. Faculty will soon find themselves changing their ways of teaching and interacting, giving priority to meeting specified learning objectives instead of managing classroom meetings. (Plater, 1995)

Educators are coming to recognize that universities are going to need to adapt to these new realities:

> we can begin to think of education as a product. Whether we feel comfortable with such terminology or not, we need to recognize that virtually every other sector of American society has gone (or is going) through a transformation that makes funding contingent on the delivery of valued outcomes. The public we serve sees us, and our work, through that new lens; it will not much longer fund us as a self-evident good. What we do with our time, then, will be reordered by a recognition that we are becoming a constituent-based service industry or profession. (Plater, 1995)

A recent study of undergraduates at 30 campuses in the United States revealed the following about today's students:

- Higher education is *not* the center of most students' lives; it isn't necessarily even their most important activity. Going to school, like going to McDonald's, Disney World or the mall, is just one part of a student's life.
- Students generally want their universities to operate like their banks and fast-food restaurants:

> They want education to be nearby and to operate during convenient hours – preferably around the clock. They want to avoid traffic jams, to have easy, accessible and low cost parking, short lines, and polite and efficient personnel and services. They also want high-quality products but are eager for low costs. They are willing to comparison shop – placing a premium on time and money. (Levine, 1993: 4)

- Students generally do not want frills and extras; they want the equivalent of a McDonald's "value meal" or a discounted "passport" good for a week-long visit to Disney World. According to Levine:

  > They are seeking a stripped-down version of college without student affairs, extracurricular activities, residence life, varsity sports, campus chaplains, Greek life [fraternity and sorority], the proliferation of specialty courses faculty like to teach, the research apparatus, museums, the panoply of auxiliary enterprises, and the expansive physical plant that constitute a college today. (1993: 4)

- In sum, "All they want of higher education is simple procedures, good service, quality courses, and low costs. . . . They are bringing to higher education exactly the same consumer expectations that they have for every other commercial enterprise with which they deal" (Levine, 1993: 4).

Assuming the reader accepts my basic premises – the university is a means of educational consumption, it is increasingly being seen in that way, and students are adopting a consumerist orientation to it – what is the university to do in the face of these new and emerging realities? Of course, one option is to do little or nothing and in fact some, especially the highest-status, most prestigious universities (Harvard, Oxford, and so on), may be able to do just that and survive very nicely.[5] However, most other colleges and universities will not be able to take the high road and will need to adapt to these new realities. While they can fabricate wholly new responses, it is more likely that universities will cast about for ready-made solutions that can be adapted to their needs. They will find such answers at, among other places, the ATMs, fast-food restaurant, mega-mall, cybermall, home shopping network, and so on. Here are a set of means that have clearly been enormously successful in attracting consumers and in satisfying their demands. Similar fortune appears to await the universities that successfully adapt and utilize the innovations pioneered by these new means of consumption.

It is not unusual for universities to turn to business for answers (Damrosch, 1995; Seymour, 1995). Plater (1995), for example, says:

> While we should never turn blindly to business for answers to our organizational problems, we can at least observe how large corporations have struggled to remake themselves into decentralized operations that flatten the administrative hierarchy and place more resources and greater authority for decision-making closest to the customer and the deliverers of the product or service.

However, it is one thing to turn to prestigious industrial giants like IBM or GM; it is quite another to look to the seemingly far humbler McDonald's or Disney. Universities continue to look to industry for innovations (e.g. TQM – total quality management), but the contemporary university is *not* primarily a means of production and therefore has more in common with, and to learn from, the new means of consumption.[6]

In addition to the demands of consumerist parents and students, the pressure on colleges and universities to change is fueled by economic factors, especially the relative decline in the funding of higher education. With outside funding being reduced, the university responds by cutting costs and by attempting to attract and keep more new (and paying) "customers." The new means of consumption are attractive models because they excel not only at attracting customers, but also at reducing costs. For example, banks have found that ATMs both attract customers because of their efficiency, and are a much less expensive way to dispense cash than human tellers. Similarly, the fast-food restaurant can be seen as not only a magnet to customers, but also as a highly cost-efficient machine for the dispensing of hamburgers and similar finger foods. Universities will seek to emulate settings like fast-food restaurants not only because they attract hordes of customers, but also because they save large sums of money (at least relative to the inefficient operation of the comparatively dilapidated university).

There is still a third reason that will lead university administrators to become students of the new means of consumption – technology. Many of the new means (ATMs, cybermalls) are deeply implicated in the latest technologies and others are much further ahead than the university in the utilization, even creation, of those technologies. The lure of new technologies is closely related to the other factors. Student consumers are far more likely to be attracted to a university that appears to be "high tech." Furthermore, those technologies promise to lower the university's cost of carrying out its educational business.

What might a university of the future (a not too distant future at that) that draws on these new means of consumption look like? Immediately relevant models for tomorrow's university are today's McDonald's Hamburger University or Disney University. These "universities" already represent the kind of pastiche discussed above, and unlike traditional universities they are increasingly popular and offer to their graduates virtually guaranteed jobs and careers in thriving industries.

Here is a description of McDonald's Hamburger University (where one can earn a very useful and marketable BH, bachelor of hamburgerology):

> Hamburger university today has a campus many conventional colleges would envy: a secluded enclave [on 80 acres] featuring a 130,000-square-foot, state-of-the-art learning facility and a 200-room hotel, the Lodge, operated by Hyatt Hotels as a high-class, high-tech dormitory.
>
> The learning complex includes six amphitheater-style classrooms rigged for everything from interactive testing to simultaneous translations; four "team rooms" where attendees practice role plays under the electronic eyes of a bank of video cameras; 17 break-out rooms; four fully functioning equipment labs for mastering the gear of the modern burger business; an auditorium; a library; and the faculty offices of 30 full-time instructors recruited from field operations. (Schaaf, 1994: 19)

In addition to its central campus, Hamburger University has smaller "campuses" in England, Germany and Japan, ten other training facilities, as well as a satellite link to Australia.

Another direct model of the future of higher education was dedicated in early 1996 in, where else, Orlando, Florida (Bannon, 1996). The new Disney

Institute offers 60 adult-education programs including cooking, topiary creations and "relationships."[7] There are no cartoon characters walking the grounds, no rides, and the gift shop offers things like dried porcini mushrooms. Modeled loosely after the high-brow Chautauqua Institution in upstate New York, the "campus" is designed to look like "Anytown, USA." In fact the creation of the Institute was set in motion after the Disney chairman visited Chautauqua and decided to create a similar setting "to enhance and improve quality of life *in the Disney fashion*" (Bannon, 1996: C5; italics added). Included under the heading of the "Disney fashion" are "breathtaking cleanliness, manicured grounds and an unflappably perky staff: After receiving a wake-up call request at midnight, one operator couldn't help but gush, 'Have a nice day!'" (Bannon, 1996: C5). Unlike the workers at other Disney theme parks, the instructors and other staff members are not considered "cast members." However, like cast members, their hair must be cut short and kept neat, they are not permitted facial hair, and they must wear a Disney uniform. Said one teacher, "You would think that people want to see what a real photographer or filmmaker actually looks like, not a Pirates of the Caribbean character" (Bannon, 1996: C5). The Institute will contain a liberal mix of entertainment and information; in other words, it will be yet another form of highly rationalized infotainment.

The officials of more traditional universities can learn much from Hamburger University and the Disney Institute about how their institutions can better meet the desires of tomorrow's students. But there is a range of other lessons to be learned from the means of consumption themselves. In the following pages we discuss a variety of changes one can expect in a university that seeks to learn from the new means of consumption. Following the work of Parker and Jary (1995; see also Prichard and Willmott, 1996), which is in turn based on my work on McDonaldization, we can for obvious reasons call our forward-thinking, but hypothetical, institution "McUniversity."

To start with, McUniversity will continue to have a central campus, but it is likely to be more compact and run by a meaner, leaner organization (McDonald's is famous for running its far-flung operations with a minuscule staff). Downsizing will be the norm on campuses like that of McUniversity as it is these days in the business world and in government.

However, downsizing is not enough. Controlling costs is only part of the answer; another major component is attracting and keeping students and the revenue they represent. To attract large numbers of "paying" students, most campuses will need to become more like shopping malls or theme parks. They are going to have to offer at least some excitement, color and fun if they are to be able to draw students away from their home computers or classes at more convenient satellite locations (see p. 156). Many student unions are already being transformed into mini-malls with the inclusion of ATMs, video games and fast-food outlets. The future of the university may be found, at least in part, in its current student unions.

Making themselves more like shopping malls is a positive step that universities can take. However, in order to attract and please their student-consumers, universities will also need to eliminate as much negativity as possible. After all, shopping malls have few, if any, negatives; the emphasis is on the positives. Thus, we can expect universities to continue the trend toward "grade inflation" by limiting poor grades even further than they do now. Similarly, steps will be taken to reduce the number of students who drop out or flunk out. Overall, the objective will be to eliminate as many barriers as possible to obtaining degrees. In fact, this is already occurring in a process Simon (1996) has labeled "the dumbing down of higher education." This focus on positivity will produce an educational world that, in Baudrillard's (1990/1993: 45) words, resembles "the smile of a corpse in a funeral home."

The goal of the university will also be to make it far easier for students to obtain the various educational services it offers. Among other things, this means that it will go to the students rather than waiting for students to come to it.[8] As a result of such developments, higher education will be decentered; the heart of education will be less and less likely to be found on the college campus or even in a college building. This is exemplified by the spread of small educational satellites. (Not surprisingly, an important growth area for fast-food restaurants themselves is the construction of small satellites – some of them *in* universities – rather than "full-service" outlets.) While it might have a central campus and a number of smaller satellites, McUniversity is more likely to be nothing more than an expanding "chain" of such satellites. "One solution post-secondary institutions have found is to make like a retail store and franchise. These 'chains' are called satellite campuses, and they are springing up all over . . . the nation" (Howard, 1996). Satellites are likely to be found in pre-existing sites (community colleges, high schools, work places, and even in the Mall of America: Winerip, 1994), but if they are newly constructed, they are likely to be in or near shopping malls and to take the form of small office buildings or large fast-food restaurants. Students will "drop by" for a course or two. Parking lots will be adjacent to McUniversity's satellites (as they are to fast-food restaurants) to make access easy.

The University of Northern Arizona is one of the pioneers of such a satellite system and in the view of its president:

> The challenge is not how we produce mini-versions of the university all over Arizona, but how we invent new models of interactions between students and the institution, and how we invent new communities of learning that are different from the traditional campus, but no less valuable to the students. (Monaghan, 1996: A25)

Said an official at one satellite school: "We are designed around the concept of convenience for the students. . . . If 20 students at one company want to take the class right after work, then that's what we'll offer" (Howard, 1996). Universities will not only make it easier for students to take courses, but also to transfer credits to and from other educational institutions.

Advanced technology will make it unnecessary for students even to go to the satellites. They will be able to access virtually all of the course-related materials from their home computers or via video-conferencing. "Distance-education" is already with us and virtual education is not far behind; education will become national and even international in scope. In other words, as in most other aspects of postmodern society, the nature of the time and space associated with education will be altered dramatically (Harvey, 1989). Students will be able to access much of their educational material at any time of the day or night. And education will take place in many different locales, most of them great distances from the source of the educational transmission.

The University of Northern Arizona currently delivers over 50 courses to about 1,000 students a semester (an estimated 2,000 more students watch the classes on cable TV and they can enrol for credit) at 12 satellites (plans are afoot to expand that to 21 sites) via a microwave based two-way-television system (Monaghan, 1996). In addition, the school employs computer-based teaching via the Internet. These methods are very cost-effective – some satellites do not even have instructors present. Said a state education official: "they take a multimillion-dollar structure and make it available at sites statewide" (Monaghan, 1996: A24). Not surprisingly, traditional faculty members are less than happy with the development: "'A lot of us feel it's unfortunate that many students won't, can't, don't have the experience of a university campus'" (Monaghan, 1996: A25).

We can expect that the nature of higher education will grow even more class-linked. That is, upper- and many middle-class students will still get most of their education on campus (especially in the elite schools like Harvard and Oxford), but some middle-class and most lower-class students will spend little or no time on traditional campuses: instead they will receive the bulk of their education at satellite locations or in their own homes.

In their associations with the new means of education, it will be increasingly clear that students are not only receiving educational signs but are also purchasing signs and that those signs serve to differentiate them from students who purchase other signs. For example, those who purchase a set of signs from a satellite of McUniversity are differentiating themselves from those who obtain a degree from Hamburger University. Similarly, those few who can still afford to attend McUniversity's main campus are buying signs that differentiate them from those who are only able to attend one of McUniversity's satellite locations. Of course, all of us will come to know the "code" that allows us to "read" the differences between degrees from McUniversity main campus, a McUniversity satellite, and Hamburger University.

Advanced technology will abound at McUniversity and courses and course-related materials will be available on TV, video tape, via computer, and so on (Barker, 1994–5). According to Green and Gilbert (1995): "Midway through the '90s . . . colleges and universities confront a second major phase of [the computer] 'revolution' – a shift in emphasis from the computer as a desktop tool to the computer as the communications gateway to colleagues and 'content' (databases, image and text libraries, video, and more) made increasingly accessible via computer networks." These technologies and others will reduce both the need for instructors and the cost of education. Courses can be beamed from a central studio, some other university, or even some other country to satellite locations. This further reduces the need for a satellite to have a faculty of its own. Libraries will be international multi-media centers with students able to access most material from home computers.

As a result of such advanced technologies, McUniversity will be hyperreal, more real than its contemporary predecessors. For example, instead of taking a course in person with a professor who bases her lecture on the work of an eminent colleague at a far-off university, the student can take a telecourse with that eminent professor, watch a videotape of a long-dead scholar of great renown, or even one featuring a computer-generated virtual "professor." Or, instead of taking a book from the college library, a student can access a CD-Rom which includes the book, live action shots and comments by the perhaps deceased author.

Those who teach in McUniversity and its satellites are highly unlikely to be full-time, tenured faculty members (Howard, 1996). Most will be parttimers brought in to teach a course or two. Their pay, like that of employees of fast-food restaurants, will be low and their benefits few, if any. Also as in the case of fast-food restaurants, rules, regulations, system-wide syllabuses and constraints of all types will abound. The latter make it possible for courses (like hamburgers and our interaction with counterpeople) to be much the same from one satellite to another (Howard, 1996). Efforts will be made to script "professors" (like counterpeople) as much as possible through the use of uniform lectures and ancillary materials. The existence of many satellites leads administrators to seek some uniformity in what is taught. They will want to be sure that instructors say much the same thing from one time or place to another. In other words, teaching positions at McUniversity will look increasingly like McJobs (Chapter 5).

Because of the nature of its faculty, as well as of the constraints it places on them, McUniversity will be far more concerned with reproducing existing knowledge than producing new knowledge. Those who staff satellite "campuses" (and university television studios or computer labs) will have little time, few inducements, and little in the way of facilities to engage in original scholarship and research. With traditional universities and scholars in decline the issue becomes: who will produce the new knowledge to be taught in the new means of education?

The knowledge transmitted in universities will be less and less foundational. Satellite, tele- and computer-mediated campuses will increasingly offer students what they say they need and want, not what is part of some canon. Universities will be less insular; they will be more physically embedded in, and intellectually intertwined with, the community. Another way of saying this is that education will become more local.

We have yet to mention the universities (for example the California Institute of Integral Studies, the Teacher's University, the National Universities Degree Consortium and the Mind Extension University) that exist *entirely* in cyberspace. One leading example is Virtual Online University's Athena University with over 350 courses in eight "schools." As a result of these virtual universities, as well as the kinds of things that are taking place in traditional universities like Northern Arizona, higher education, like much else in society, will be dominated by computerized, televised images. These images will be circulating in hyperspace side by side with similar images from many other sources (MTV, CNN, the Disney Channel, the Home Shopping Network); it will grow difficult to distinguish the university's images from all the rest. Relevant here is Baudrillard's (1976/1993: 9) description of a generalized brothel of signs, but "a brothel not for prostitution, but for substitution and commutation." Not only will all signs, educational or not, be substitutable and commutatable, but we will also find it hard to distinguish the university's satellites from those of the fast-food industry; in fact many of the latter will be found in the former.

As the differences between universities and commercial purveyors of images implode, the latter will come to be important competitors of McUniversity (CNN's Ted Turner has proposed an electronic university; MTV is already publishing books). Said one observer:

> Mathematics, science, writing, public speaking, and critical thinking are already packaged and commercially available, often employing as consultants faculty from our own institutions. As cable, movie, telephone, and other communication companies merge, they are lured by the enormous education market, including the possibility of *making education entertaining*. Rudimentary as the audio and video cassettes of The Teaching Company may be, they signal the beginning of a "home university staffed with the most brilliant classroom lecturers in America," to cite the company's own publicity for one of its products, the "Greatest Lectures by America's Superstar Teachers." (The Teaching Company is one of the more active proprietary learning organizations using home technologies and represents over 30 professors from some of the nation's most prestigious universities.) (Plater, 1995; italics added)

Traditional universities may go out and hire "superstar" professors at other institutions to teach distance courses for them, but it is just as likely that

> an independent distributor such as a telephone company, a cable television system, or an electronic publisher might hire a faculty member to produce a "personal enhancement package" – still a course by another name. (Plater, 1995)

Perhaps no term captures the nature of the universities of the future better than "implosion." Today's universities will be imploding into the locations of their satellites, the media (especially television), the computer and cyberspace, entertainment, consumption, and so on. In fact, they are imploding into so many things and so extensively that one is left to wonder: what, if anything, will be left? The image that comes to mind is a Baudrillardian black hole where it is hard to distinguish the university from everything else.

Furthering this implosion is the fact that in an effort to be competitive in the world of images, officials of McUniversity will come to emphasize many of the same kinds of production values that one sees on MTV and CNN; officials might even hire their former employees. The result will be a simulated world of education very similar to such obvious simulations as Hamburger University (which, in addition, already relies on simulations to teach students) and Disney Institute.

As a result of implosion a simulated higher education will, like everything else, enter Baudrillard's fractal stage where everything interpenetrates; we will be in the era of what might be called the "transeducational." Since education will be everywhere, since everything will be educational, in a sense nothing will be educational.

Universities will be competing with many other organizations for students. They will be at a disadvantage not only *vis-à-vis* many of their far more technologically advanced competitors, but also in comparison with many of the students who, having been raised in a world of cyberspace, will be far better at negotiating their way about in it than most of the faculty. As a result of their high-tech upbringing and work experiences, students will be tough judges of the university:

> Students will have expectations for production quality that are beyond the present capacity of most institutions and low tolerance for instructional deficiencies. Yet we have no choice but to compete for their time and attention. (Plater, 1995)

The coming of all of the new players and technologies will radically alter the nature of teaching:

> Technology will change forever the dominant model of synchronous, time-linked interaction that has made teaching and learning complementary and interdependent. Learning will no longer depend on a faculty member's teaching. Although the centuries-old model of teacher-student-classroom will not disappear, it will no longer dominate. (Plater, 1995)

Many of the new approaches involve a one-way flow of information, with the result that there is no give-and-take; no possibility of Baudrillard's (1976/1993) symbolic exchange between those who teach and those who learn. Such interactions will be more and more characterized by the predominance of exchange values over symbolic exchange. In much work on the computer, students will, in effect, interact only with themselves and the technology. Even in two-way televised courses, it is impossible to engage in truly human interaction with televised or computerized images.

Like all of Baudrillard's other "ecstatic" systems, educational systems will become hypertelic, expanding in innumerable ways in a mindless effort to survive even if that means surrendering everything that has made education distinctive.

To improve efficiency of operations, more and more students will be issued "smart cards" (essentially credit cards with embedded microchips) which they can use to pay for courses, fees, books, food, and so on (see Chapter 8). McUniversity will come close to being cashless and checkless and thereby come to use increasingly simulated means of payment. In addition, such cards can be used to gain entry to school buildings, to identify the student, to store student records and to check out library books (or better, CD-Roms).[9] With such cards, students will be able to do much of their business with the university impersonally through ATM-like machines.

Like their brethren who transact business at the local ATMs (as well as at fast-food restaurants and in interaction with cybermalls), students will be forced to do more of the labor within the new means of education; they will educate themselves more and more on their own in interaction with images emanating from their computer and television screens. Like much else, this development will be driven by cost considerations. Students do this work for free and as a result universities are able to do without the many highly paid employees previously needed to help and instruct them.

Many more things could be said about ongoing and coming changes in higher education from this point of view, but this should give the reader the flavor of the kinds of change to be expected when one looks at the university from a postmodern perspective as a means of consuming educational services and goods.

Conclusion

In closing, I should make it clear that I do *not* expect tomorrow's university to look exactly like a shopping mall or a chain of fast-food restaurants. However, I do expect it to integrate applicable elements of these and other new means of consumption (and tourism) into the existing structure of the university. I also expect the university to borrow liberally from many other sectors of society as well as to retain many of its traditional components. I emphasize the new means of consumption in this chapter in part because, counterintuitively, I think they will be an important model for future universities. This emphasis is designed to provoke a dialogue about how far we wish to move in that direction, and even whether that is really the direction in which we wish to move.

Notes

This chapter is the text of the plenary address to the Dilemmas of Mass Higher Education conference, at Staffordshire University, Staffordshire, England in April 1996. It was published as: "McUniversity in the Postmodern Consumer Culture," *Quality in Higher Education*, 2, 1996: 185–99.

1. For the purposes of this chapter, I subsume means of tourism under the heading of the means of consumption.

2. Thus, I disagree with Bloland's (1995) contention that the university is necessarily the quintessential modern institution.

3. Similarly, the hospital can be seen as a means of consuming medical services and as such will undergo many of the same changes as the university. For a discussion of one example, see Sharpe's (1996: A1) discussion of HealthSouth Corp. which is striving to become a kind of "Holiday Inns or McDonald's of health care."

Students are not the only consumers of the university's services; government and private granting agencies of all sorts are also consumers and they seem to be contributing to the university's problems by "buying" less these days. On the other hand, business seems to be an increasing consumer of the university's products and employer, at least as consultants, of many of its best professors.

4. ATMs are actually better thought of as meta-means.

5. However, it is more likely that even those institutions will change, perhaps dramatically.

6. The university can be seen as a means of producing new knowledge, but that issue, while of great importance, is beyond the scope of this chapter.

7. The Disney Institute is not to be confused with Disney University which is for Disney employees and functions in a manner similar to Hamburger University.

As long as they attract paying customers, there is nothing to stop Disney Institute from offering courses in postmodern social theory or even theoretical physics in the future.

8. Interestingly, companies on the Internet are beginning to do the same thing. Instead of waiting for "surfing" customers to find them, they are broadcasting their messages to the consumer's video screen through companies like the PointCast Network (Bank, 1996: A1, A8).

9. In other words, it will be much like the "Lifebank" card discussed in Chapter 8.

12

Dealing with the New Means of Consumption

While I have paid a great deal of attention in this book to describing fast-food restaurants, credit cards, and other new means of consumption and tourism, one of my continuing concerns is the issue of how to respond to, or cope with, them. A chapter in *The McDonaldization of Society* is devoted to coping with McDonaldized systems, while a discussion of handling the various problems associated with credit cards is scattered throughout *Expressing America*. Those are very modern works, adopting modern grand narratives (McDonaldization, Americanization, and so on), and offering very modern solutions to what are perceived as modern problems. However, as this book has evolved, and the focus has shifted to the new means of consumption in general, the analysis has moved in the direction of postmodern social theory. Since the problems associated with these new means have been described in postmodern terms, it is necessary to discuss methods of coping with them in similar terms.

This chapter has three objectives. The first is a brief review of some of the modern methods of dealing with fast-food restaurants and credit cards, as well as how well such methods apply to the other new means of consumption. The second is to examine what some postmodern responses to these means might be. Finally, in order to be more specific and concrete, we will zero in on McUniversity and discuss more specific methods of coping with it from both a modern and a postmodern perspective.

Modern Coping Methods

Adopting a modern approach to the analysis of fast-food restaurants and credit cards leads to a modern sense of how to cope with them and the problems associated with them. For one thing, the responses tend to be highly rational responses to what are largely seen as problems that are traceable to the rational operation of these systems. For another, there is the very rational tendency to deconstruct the sources of the problems by levels of analysis and therefore to suggest responses that are specific to each level. There are micro (the individual), meso (the group, organization, industry) and macro (the society) dimensions to the problems and coping mechanisms are suggested for each level. Finally, there is a sense that in the end many of these problems are irresolvable and that they must persist. After all, my early thinking on the fast-food restaurant, and a portion of that on credit cards, is animated by Weber's modern grand narrative of the inexorable progression toward the iron cage of rationality. Like Weber, one is led by this to the view that it is important to respond, but that realistically responses are not going to materially alter the situation or the eventual outcome.

Briefly, at the macro level, coping with McDonaldization involves efforts to alter the larger culture and economic system that is supportive of the process. At a more meso level, group pressure can be brought to bear against McDonaldized systems and groups of people can create and support non-McDonaldized alternative systems. At the micro level, individuals relate to McDonaldization differently, so will respond in different ways. Those who regard McDonaldization as a "velvet cage" will do nothing but welcome its forward progress.[1] Those who see it as a "rubber cage" will, in the main, want to take actions that permit them to get out of the cage when they so desire and allow them to be sure that there are non-McDonaldized alternatives available to them when they want them. Finally, those who see McDonaldization as an "iron cage" can respond in various ways. For example, they can seek to carve out non-rationalized niches for themselves in otherwise McDonaldized systems. And there is a wide range of actions, both big and little, that they can take to subvert the system. However, ultimately this perspective tends to lead to a feeling of resignation: one feels destined to a life that will be lived more and more within the confines of the iron cage.

Turning to credit cards, to the degree that McDonaldization is the source of the problems associated with them, the same kinds of response apply. However, a series of other problems – excessive indebtedness, fraud and invasion of privacy – is the focus of attention in *Expressing America* and specific coping mechanisms are suggested for each problem. Again, since the problems are multi-level, the responses to them are determined by level of analysis. For example, in terms of the problem of excessive debt, individuals can become better aware of the danger signals, can better understand the advantages of paying their bills in full each month, and can seek outside help if they find themselves overwhelmed by debt. At the meso level, the credit card industry could, although it is not likely to, stop doing what it focuses on and excels at – drawing people into credit card use and credit card debt. At the macro level, the government could take a variety of actions to stem the worst excesses of the credit card companies (examples include restraints on mail solicitations or even putting warning labels, like those on cigarette packs, on credit cards). Finally, efforts could be made to alter the norms and values of a culture that encourages rampant consumerism and debt.

There is obviously no end to the number of rational responses that could be conceived to deal with the transformations in higher education detailed in Chapter 11. Some faculty members and administrators might choose to resist by developing rational strategies designed to thwart the development of McUniversity. Others might see the trend as inevitable and develop similarly rational strategies to adapt to the transformation. Still others might see much good in the changes and try to determine ways of expediting their development.

Assuming that the changes are inevitable, the rational faculty member (or someone aspiring to such a position) might take certain steps in preparation for them, including becoming well versed in computer technology in general and computer learning techniques in particular; becoming adept at teaching televised courses; reconciling him/herself to the likelihood of teaching at a satellite school rather than a central campus, to the likelihood of academic life without tenure and to an academic life of teaching with little or no time for research. One could go on with such a list, but the steps are fairly obvious. In any case, these are quite modern steps for dealing with what is perceived as a modern problem.

This kind of modern thinking could be applied to the other new means of consumption (including tourism). We could come up with a long list of modern ways of responding to the problems created by amusement parks, mega-malls, cybermalls and cruise lines (among others). Such a list would undoubtedly include sets of macro-, meso- and micro-level responses. While certainly useful, such an effort is not likely to be much of a conceptual advance over what has been discussed above and in my previous work. Instead, since these new means of consumption have been analysed from a postmodern perspective, let us look at what postmodern social theory leads us to say about methods of responding to them.

Postmodern Responses

Postmodern theorists identify, although often only implicitly, a number of ways of responding to the problems associated with postmodernism and many of them can be applied to the new means of consumption. Jean Baudrillard's work is particularly rich in such responses. This is somewhat ironic since Baudrillard, as well as postmodernism more generally, is often seen as nihilistic. But, given the great diversity of work that exists under the heading of postmodern social theory, it is virtually impossible to make such a generalization (or almost any generalization for that matter) about it. In any case, that generalization certainly does not apply to Baudrillard.

While Baudrillard's work is rich in explicit and implicit responses, it should be pointed out that in his view, it was far easier to respond to the modern capitalist system where the proletariat had a clear adversary (the capitalist) than it is to cope with the postmodern code since there is no obvious antagonist associated with it. Furthermore, capitalist hegemony was largely restricted to the economy, while the code is everywhere; it is omnipresent. Therefore, it is difficult to figure out ways of combating the code and even if one is successful in one domain, problems are likely to persist in many other areas. Given these caveats, let us look at several of the responses in postmodern theory and their application to the new means of consumption.

Like many other postmodernists (and not a few modernists), Baudrillard sees the contemporary world as plagued with disenchantment. In various ways he seeks to re-enchant the world and re-enchantment constitutes a way of dealing with the excesses of contemporary society. For example, one of the problems with exchanges between customers and employees in super-stores is that they have lost their symbolic qualities. This is not only true of the economic exchange of money for commodities, but also of the social exchanges between customers and employees in these settings which have taken on a mechanical, non-human quality. To put this another way, a world of simulation (including simulated human relationships) has replaced symbolic exchanges between humans. This implies that one way of responding to this, and more generally to the disenchantment in settings like the superstore, is by re-establishing symbolic exchange among and between workers and customers. Involved in such symbolic relationships is a continual cycle of giving and receiving rather than the self-limiting exchanges that characterize such settings. A wide range of things would need to be exchanged, rather than the highly specific and very limited types of exchange found in superstores. Not just money and goods would be exchanged, but also a range of things like emotions, feelings, experiences, knowledge and insight. Work in such settings would involve unlimited giving and receiving. To customers, employees in superstores are like the dead discussed by Baudrillard (1976/1993): they are physically separated from customers and prevented (by such things as scripts, rules and counters) from engaging in symbolic exchange with customers. In engaging in symbolic exchange with employees, customers would be striking a blow against the powerful, but fragile, code that serves to keep both in their place.

Similarly, Baudrillard (1976/1993) suggests that we respond to the system, in this case the new means of consumption, by offering it "gifts" which it is constitutionally unable to reciprocate. This suggestion comes from his belief that all systems are based on symbolic exchange and that systems which defy such a system of exchange have a fatal flaw that will ultimately prove to be their downfall. In the contemporary world, systems are set up to give, but not receive, or to engage in a highly circumscribed round of giving and receiving (e.g. products for money). The death of the system (which, in Baudrillard's view, is its fate) is hastened if consumers offer it gifts it is incapable of returning. Thus, I suppose, in the case of the fast-food restaurant, we might take to overpaying for our food, performing unpaid and unexpected services for those restaurants, or literally bringing them gifts on anniversaries and openings. This would make their inability to engage in symbolic exchange even more glaring and hasten their downfall. How this downfall might occur is left unclear by Baudrillard, but even Marx was more than a little vague on the details of the communist revolution and the overthrow of capitalism. Unless one buys into Baudrillard's argument fully, it does seem to strain credulity to believe that such acts as overpaying for a Big Mac would jeopardize the current system.

The ability of such minor actions to make a difference, let alone bring down the system, is based on Baudrillard's (1976/1993) belief that while it appears to be omnipotent, it has in fact grown progressively unstable. Such mundane actions do, in fact, have the capacity, at least in Baudrillard's view, to topple the hegemony of fast-food restaurants, the system and the code. Of course, these actions cannot occur only in fast-food restaurants, or even just in the new means of consumption, but must take place at every site in which the code is represented and recreated (which, of course, is close to all, if not all, social sites).

Paying extra for food at McDonald's is related to another of Baudrillard's (1976/1993) suggestions – reckless expenditure. Squandering money on a series of useless expenditures (a cynic might say that this is already what most consumers do in the postmodern society and culture, especially through their abuse of credit cards) is, in a sense, making gifts to the code and the system that they do not know what to make of, and to which they are unable to respond. Baudrillard believes that this, like more specific gifts to entities like the fast-food restaurant, will help set the system on a course to self-destruction.

Jameson's (Stephanson, 1989) ideas on homeopathic remedies can be applied to the issue of dealing with the new means of consumption. Instead of responding with things postmodern systems cannot produce or respond to (like symbolic exchange), homeopathic remedies involve responding to postmodern systems in the same way that they deal with us; using the elements of that world to push it to its limits and beyond. In fast-food restaurants, this might involve formally rational responses to the formally rational system. For example, customers might adhere strictly to all of the rules, formal and informal, that govern the fast-food restaurant. Such adherence would be time-consuming and demanding of the system and its staff; it might well cause the system to slow to a crawl, thereby giving the lie to the label "fast food."

Alternatively, the response to the ecstatic "acceleration of networks" characteristic of McUniversity (and many other new means of consumption), may not be to try to be "faster" than them, but to turn instead to the tortoise-like mass of students characterized by "insoluble immobility, the slower than slow: inertia and silence, inertia insoluble by effort, silence insoluble by dialogue" (Baudrillard, 1983/1990: 8). The masses, including students, are always underestimated, but their "deep instinct remains the symbolic murder of the political class" (Baudrillard, 1983/1990: 94). One of the ways in which the mass of students does this is by challenging the subject and pushing "it back upon its own impossible position" (Baudrillard, 1983/1990: 113). The mass of students can be seen as a mirror, "that which returns the subject to its mortal transparency" (Baudrillard, 1983/1990: 113).

The world of fast-food restaurants and many other new means of consumption (Price Club would be another excellent example) may be viewed, in Baudrillard's terms (in Gane, 1993), as an obscene world in which seemingly everything is visible, indeed hypervisible. Note, for example, the visibility of the food-preparation area in contrast to the traditional restaurant where the kitchen is almost always hidden from view; or the obvious and abundant trash receptacles. To Baudrillard (1983/1990), the traditional restaurant is a "scene" where some things are hidden; where some mystery (e.g. just how the food is prepared; how trash is disposed of) continues. Fast-food restaurants are obscene because almost nothing is hidden; everything is visible. A solution proposed by Baudrillard is the return of some invisibility, some mystery; in other words the return, to use another of his terms, of seduction. Instead of hypervisible fast-food restaurants, we need restaurants which retain some, even a great deal of, mystery. Instead of fast-food restaurants that bludgeon customers into submission, we need restaurants which retain the ability to seduce, rather than overwhelm, customers.

Take the issue of the taste of the food. Fast food tends to overwhelm our taste buds with strong and obvious tastes, especially very sweet and highly salty. Our taste buds are not seduced by a wide variety of subtle flavors, but overwhelmed by a few strong tastes. In contrast, of course, a gourmet restaurant (or a sophisticated home-cooked meal) is oriented to seducing our taste buds. Even the décor of such restaurants is seductive, in contrast to the bright, loud and powerful colors and decorations of the typical fast-food restaurant. The logic of Baudrillard's argument leads us to see the creation and patronage of seductive restaurants as a way of coping with the contemporary world.

This, of course, easily lends itself to the accusation that the postmodern perspective is elitist. After all, such restaurants are costly to build and such meals usually cost the diner a great deal of money. However, one wonders whether one could combine low cost and seductiveness in a restaurant? More generally, are there affordable but more seductive alternatives to the various new means of consumption? Is there a necessary contradiction between cost and seductiveness? The answer is no. One could prepare a seductive meal at home for less than it would cost to dine at a fast-food restaurant. One could also imagine quite a seductive restaurant being built for far less than the cost of the average fast-food restaurant.

Could one go a step further and envision a chain of franchised, but still genuinely seductive, restaurants? The answer is undoubtedly no. Once one moves beyond a single restaurant, to a chain, one is immediately in the realm of simulacra. Simulation is not a characteristic that Baudrillard would associate with the process of seduction. As one tries to institutionalize and replicate seduction from one site to another, it loses its seductive qualities. Yet the time will undoubtedly come when we will see a chain of restaurants that offers simulated seduction. The creators of such chains will recognize that some segment of the population that frequents fast-food restaurants is tiring of being bludgeoned into culinary submission and there is money to be made in offering them simulated seduction, both in the food and in the setting.

Seduction is related in Baudrillard's (1983/1990) work on the fatality of the objects, for example those – the customers – who frequent fast-food restaurants (or utilize the other means of consumption). Instead of customers being constrained by these restaurants, Baudrillard suggests that it is possible that it is the restaurants that are being led on (seduced) by the customers (objects). For example, the seemingly ever-increasing parade of customers is leading the fast-food chains into endless rounds of expansion and proliferation, a game that will ultimately prove fatal as fast-food restaurants eventually proliferate beyond their ability to survive economically. The same process, of course, affects all of the other new means of consumption. To take another example, millions and millions of people can be seen as leading the credit card companies on by accepting offer after offer of new credit cards and overture after overture to increase their spending limit once the old limit has been exceeded. The result is that the banks and credit card firms are extending hundreds of billions of dollars in unsecured credit. This could eventually cause this vast "house of cards" (literally) to collapse when it becomes clear that there is no way that the masses will be able to repay much of this debt, or even the interest on it.

Similarly, students can be seen as engaging in a fatal strategy by seeming to accept all the changes the postmodern educational system throws at them. While we usually think power resides with the educational systems, it could be argued that it is the mass of students who have the power. One can even view them as snobs delegating the annoying and burdensome tasks of learning material and teaching it to others; the elites in charge of education (and other systems) can be seen as relieving the mass of students of the tiresome process of needing to learn on their own.[2] Furthermore, the mass of students have "the ironic power of withdrawal, of non-desire, non-knowledge, silence, absorption then expulsion of all powers, wills, of all enlightenment and depths of meaning" (Baudrillard, 1983/1990: 99). Instead of looking at the mass of, for example, students as alienated, unconscious and repressed, Baudrillard argues that we can see them "as possessing a delusive, illusive, allusive strategy, corresponding to an unconscious that is finally ironic, joyous and seductive" (1983/1990: 99).

The silence of the mass of students can be seen not as a sign of their alienation but of their power: "the silence was a massive reply through withdrawal, that the silence was a strategy . . . they [the mass of students in this case] *nullify* meaning. And this is truly a power. . . . Basically they absorb all systems and they refract them in emptiness" (Baudrillard, in Gane, 1993: 87–8). In other words, the mass of students is another "black hole" in the social world. They are silent because they are overwhelmed with information and there is no way of reversing the flow of that information. (In fact, we are not to think of the mass of students as a social phenomenon (after all, to Baudrillard, the social is dead) involving millions of people, but as an inertial "form" created by the overwhelming flood of information.) Thus the strategy of silence, of inertia. The silence of the mass of students is fatal. It is one of their fatal strategies, strategies that indicate that the "object is more subtle, more ingenious, than the subject" (Gane, 1991: 174). Ultimately, these fatal strategies lead the world of higher education in the direction of a "downward spiral of the worst outcomes into catastrophic outcomes" (Gane, 1991: 207). The victory of the student masses will not be a dazzling revolution, "but obscure and ironic; It won't be dialectical, it will be fatal" (Baudrillard, 1983/1990: 96). It will not be revolution, "but . . . a massive *devolution* . . . a massive delegation of power and responsibility. . . . Massive *de-volition* and withdrawal of the will" (Baudrillard, 1983/1990: 97).

Baudrillard believes that such fatal strategies will lead the world into an ever-spiraling downward trajectory that will end only in catastrophe for the system and the code. The fatal strategies of the "evil genies," the masses, will not lead to revolution in the traditional, grand-narrative sense of the term, but to a gradual devolution as the code, and the system on which it is built and which sustains it, gradually unravels.

As to looking for agents (the masses, as objects, cannot be seen as agents) to respond to the new means of consumption, one can point to those who have avoided their pervasive presence and influence.[3] The problem is that in the United States, and in many other parts of the world, it is difficult to identify very many who have been able to avoid their effects. The young, those most likely in most conditions to form the base of a revolutionary movement, are the most profoundly affected by the influence of the new means of consumption. The working class, the traditional revolutionary subject, would be similarly affected and, in any case, would have no obvious material reason to be in the vanguard of such a revolution. One can only hope that isolated pockets of people relatively immune to the influence of the new means of consumption (say, the Amish) can provide the base for a social movement whose objective is at least to limit their impact.

Baudrillard seems to hold out hope in speech as contrasted to discourse which is controlled by the code. Those excluded by the code, such as the mass of students, can rebel through their use of speech. But, he is not arguing for some ultimate massive outpouring of students (or others) against the code. We ought not to wait for such a future: "Each man is totally there at each instant. . . . The utopia is here in all the energies that are raised against political economy. . . . Utopia . . . wants only the spoken word; and it wants to lose itself in it" (Baudrillard, 1973/1975: 166–7).

More promising is the postmodern idea that the revolution is not the grand product of a group of revolutionary agents, but that such a revolution is possible, even necessary, here and now in the everyday practices of individuals. In postmodern terms, especially in the work of Derrida (1978), everyone, all of the time, has the capacity to "write," that is, to create innovative responses to the code and more specific oppressive structures. By, for example, demanding things of fast-food restaurants that they do not want to deliver (a rare hamburger; extra-brown french fries) people are engaging in a form of writing that can alter the nature of the fast-food restaurant and perhaps ultimately the code. Clearly, we are talking here of millions of very specific behaviors repeated over and over again; in Foucauldian terms, we are talking about innumerable micro-lines of resistance.

The revolt of the masses in general, and the mass of students in particular, will be much like the victory of cancer cells (another object) over the body. Both can be seen as uncontrollable, undisciplined, non-dialectical and subliminal. Both cancer and the student masses are hypertelic. In their mindless, limitless increase the student masses will destroy the educational system in the same way that cancer cells destroy the physical body.

While Baudrillard sees hope in the mass, he rejects the grand narrative of the Marxists (and others) who envisioned a grand culmination in the overthrow of the capitalist system. Baudrillard (1983/1990: 24) concludes, "we are no longer in the age of grandiose collapses and resurrections, of games of death and eternity, but of little fractal events, smooth annihilations and gradual slides." Thus, for example, McUniversity will not be destroyed with a bang, but in a series of whimpers.

A related set of actions would involve scrambling the signs associated with the code. Baudrillard (1986/1989) sees graffiti artists as playing this role within the city, but what form might it take in a setting like the fast-food restaurant? Graffiti on the walls of the local McDonald's would certainly represent an assault on its fetish for cleanliness and, more generally, on it as a system. Another example might involve a deliberate misreading of the signs that dominate the fast-food restaurant. People might come in and sit down and wait for service rather than following the code and waiting in line to order their own food. Or people might do the latter but then leave their food on the counter indicating an expectation that the food be delivered to them. Taking one's time while deciding what to order, or slowly wending one's way through and out of the drive-through, would be highly effective devices. These efforts to scramble the code (Deleuze and Guattari (1972/1983) also seek this goal through schizoanalysis and the schizophrenic process) at the fast-food restaurant might serve to destabilize what, as we've seen, Baudrillard regards as an already fragile system.

Ultimately, Baudrillard favors any sort of indeterminacy as a way of responding to the determinacy of the code with its reproduction and endless repetition. Death, not as a final event, but as a model of indeterminacy, is Baudrillard's (1976/1993) paradigm for responding to the system. This, of course, does not mean that people should take to dying in droves in shopping malls or on cruise ships, but it does mean that any sort of indeterminacy would disrupt the smooth operation of the system and the code. More specifically, Baudrillard recommends that we inject some risk, some small measure of death, into otherwise meticulously regulated systems like fast-food restaurants. This suggests a range of actions anywhere from taking the chance and ordering a Big Mac without special sauce to actually eschewing fast-food restaurants and taking the plunge and preparing a meal from scratch at home. Once again, we are in the realm of "infinitesimal lines of escape" (Deleuze and Guattari, 1972/1983), but they are all that is available in an epoch when the great revolutions are deemed no longer possible or desirable.

Deleuze and Guattari's ideas on freeing desire and the desiring machine would fit here. That is, the mega-mall, and the revolution in the means of consumption of which it is part, would be seen as constraining such desire in a Weberian iron cage. Weakening, destabilizing and ultimately destroying this process and such settings would help free desire. Liberated desire would wreak havoc on the code.

Many of the responses discussed thus far may be combined under the heading of the "strength of the weak" (Genosko, 1994). That is, most of the actors and actions covered here are quite weak, especially given the power of the code and more generally postmodern society. However, customers, the masses, graffiti artists, even children derive strength from their weakness. In the main, they are able to absorb everything the system throws at them, thereby luring the system into riskier and more desperate forays. Eventually, the system grows so reckless and overextended that the slightest disruption would cause it to collapse. There is no better example of this than the hundreds of billions of dollars of uncollateralized credit extended to the masses by the credit card companies. The masses accept every new card, and every increase in the credit limit, offered to them. Money is being thrown at them and they do not need to put up any collateral. While their credit card debt rises, there is no parallel increase in their ability to repay the debt. In the interim, the masses will have used all of the credit offered them.

As for intellectuals, they need to adopt an ironic stance toward McUniversity. This means that they should "embrace contradictions . . . exercise irony . . . take the opposite tack . . . exploit rifts and reversibility, even . . . fly in the face of the lawful and the factual" (Baudrillard, 1990/1993: 39). The latter is related to pataphysics, or the use of science fiction to turn the educational system against itself. Obviously there is no concrete revolutionary strategy here; theoretical rather than practical violence is involved. There is no actual impact – but could we expect any in a postmodern educational world dominated by images and signs?

While the majority of the responses discussed in this section are non-rational or irrational, there are more rational responses to be found in postmodern social theory. One example is Jameson's (1989) suggestion that what we need are new cognitive maps. Adrift in the hyperspace of postmodernity, we need new kinds of guides to help us find our way. This clearly applies to such new means of consumption as hotel-casinos, cruise ships and mega-malls. The need for new maps also means that we need, and need to do, new kinds of social analyses and critiques of the world of the new means of consumption. In addition, we need maps that will help us find the increasingly scarce alternatives to those things.

A more rational task, mainly for scholars and intellectuals, would be to engage in Jameson's (1991; Best, 1989) transcoding. That is, a scholar can examine what one can say, think and do in, for example, the fast-food restaurant and compare and contrast that to the possibilities in other systems (say, the kitchen of a traditional French restaurant). Such a contrast might point up the problems in the fast-food restaurant as well as some alternatives to it.

In sum, the postmodern perspective does not lead us to a clear and coherent set of procedures for dealing with the new means of consumption. Rather, we are offered a number of theoretically informed hints about responses to these systems. In the main, the sense one has is that these responses will occur not because conscious agents determine that they should occur, but rather because they are fated to occur. While a post-modernist might be satisfied with this, a modernist might want to explore this set of ideas for insights to be used in the mobilization of agents against the excesses of the new means of consumption.

Notes

This chapter is derived from several sources – an essay in *Social Wetenschappen*; an Invited Plenary Address to the Popular Studies Conference, Tampere, Finland in July 1996; a presentation at the annual meetings of the American Sociological Association, New York City in August 1996; and a plenary address at the Dilemmas of Mass Higher Education conference, Staffordshire University, Staffordshire, England in April 1996.

 1. For more on the three views of these cages, see Ritzer (1996a: 177–9).

 2. Even though, as we have seen, McUniversity forces students to do more and more on their own. Nonetheless, much of what they do has been pre-planned by educators.

 3. Most postmodern social theorists would reject the idea of an agent, let alone a search for one.

IV

McDONALDIZATION REDUX

13

Some Concluding Thoughts on the McDonaldization Thesis

While this book began with a series of chapters dealing with the McDonald-ization thesis, and more than half of it has been devoted to explicit explorations and extensions of that thesis, in the last several chapters we have moved progressively away from a focus on McDonaldization *per se* and in the direction of an analysis of the new means of consumption. While the fast-food restaurant (and other McDonaldized systems) has been of continuing interest (as one of those new means of consumption), the McDonaldization thesis, that is the idea that (as Weber predicted) society and the world are growing progressively rationalized and characterized by the predominance of efficiency, calculability, predictability, and control by non-human technologies (as well as the various irrationalities of rationality), has tended to recede into the background. In this final chapter I would like to bring that thesis to the foreground once again and explore a range of issues related to it.

The De-McDonaldization of Society?

Perhaps no idea would seem more extreme, at least from the perspective of the McDonaldization thesis, than the notion that we are already beginning to see signs of de-McDonaldization. (An even more heretical argument would, of course, be that the process never occurred in the first place. However, the social world has certainly changed and one of the ways of conceptualizing at least some of those changes is in terms of increasing rationalization. Furthermore, such a view would mean a rejection of one of the strongest and most durable social theories; one that has not only endured but grown through the work of such venerable social thinkers as Weber and Mannheim as well as that of many contemporary social analysts.) If this is, in fact, the case, then McDonaldization would seem to be a concept that may have made some sense at a particular time (and place), but that seems to be in the process of being superseded by recent developments. If McDonaldization has already passed its peak, then its worth and utility as a fundamental sociological concept are severely, perhaps fatally, undermined.[1] What evidence can be marshalled in support of the idea that we are seeing signs of de-McDonaldization?

The first is the fact that McDonald's itself, while still the star of the fast-food industry and continuing to grow rapidly, is experiencing some difficulties and does not quite have the luster it once did. If McDonald's is having problems, that may call into question the concept which bears its name and its imprint. The strongest evidence on these difficulties is the increasing challenge to McDonald's in the highly competitive American market. Indeed, the competition has grown so keen that McDonald's focus in terms of profits and future expansion has shifted overseas, where it remains an unparalleled success. Reflective of McDonald's problems in the United States is the recent and much ballyhooed introduction of the Arch Deluxe (Richman, 1996). A great deal of McDonald's past success, especially in the United States, has been based on its appeal to children through its clowns, playgrounds, promotions and food. However, in recent years McDonald's has become convinced that in order to protect its pre-eminent position in the American market it has to become more adult-oriented and to offer more adult foods. Hence the Arch Deluxe – bigger than a Big Mac, lettuce pieces rather than shreds, tangier Dijon-style mustard, and so on. Whether or not McDonald's succeeds with the Arch Deluxe (and the early indications are not promising), or any other new product or promotion, the fact is that McDonald's recognizes, and is trying to deal with, problems on its home field. And, if McDonald's continues to lose market share and hegemony within the American market, can trouble in other markets around the world be far behind?

A second worrisome trend to McDonald's, and potential threat to McDonaldization, is the fact that McDonald's is becoming a negative symbol to a number of social movements throughout the world. Those groups that are struggling to deal with ecological hazards, dietary dangers, the evils of capitalism and the dangers posed by Americanization (and, as we will see below, many other problems) often take McDonald's as a symbol of these problems, especially since it can easily be related to all of them. Furthermore, these groups can mount a variety of attacks on the company as a whole (e.g. national and international boycotts of McDonald's products), as well as the 20,000 (as of this writing) or so McDonald's outlets around the world. Such outlets make easy, attractive and readily available targets for all sorts of dissident groups.

Much of the hostility towards McDonald's has crystallized in recent years around the so-called "McLibel" trial in London. McDonald's sued five people associated with London Greenpeace for distributing a pamphlet, "What's Wrong with McDonald's? Everything They Don't Want You to Know." Three of the five members apologized rather than face potential ruin, but two others, David Morris and Helen Steel, decided to contest the suit. The case, the longest-running libel trial in the history of Great Britain, ended ambiguously in June 1997 with the judge finding for McDonald's on most issues, but substantiating some of the claims against the company.

Among other things, the pamphlet attacked McDonald's (and America) for economic imperialism, misuse of resources by causing the inefficient use of large amounts of grain in the creation of a far smaller quantity of beef, contributing to deforestation, pushing an unhealthy diet on consumers, seducing children into being McDonald's habitués, being responsible for cruelty to animals, providing poorly paid dead-end jobs, and so on. The pamphlet (and the libel case dealing with it) has become something of a *cause célèbre*. There is a worldwide web site which keeps interested parties apprised of the case. More importantly, it keeps a wide variety of people and groups around the world informed about actions by, and against, McDonald's and the other fast-food restaurants. In addition, many other related issues (e.g. environmental, health) are the subject of communiqués through the web site.

As a result, at least in part, of the McLibel trial, McDonald's has become the symbolic enemy for many groups including environmentalists, animal rights organizations, anti-capitalists, anti-Americans, supporters of the Third World, those concerned about nutritional issues, those interested in defending children, the labor movement, and many more. If all of these groups can continue to see many of the problems of concern to them combined within McDonald's, then there is a real long-term danger here to McDonald's. This problem would be greatly exacerbated if some or all of these groups were to come together and jointly oppose McDonald's. Once, and perhaps still, the model (in a positive sense) corporation in the eyes of many, McDonald's is now in danger of becoming the paradigm for all that is bad in the world in the eyes of many others.

Yet another threat to McDonald's stems from the difficulty any corporation has in staying on top indefinitely. McDonald's may well survive the two threats discussed above, but sooner or later internal problems (e.g. declining profits and/or stock prices), external competition, or some combination of the two, will set McDonald's on a downward course which will end in it becoming a pale imitation of the present powerhouse. While far less likely, it is also possible that these factors will even lead to its complete disappearance.

However, we must not confuse threats to McDonald's with dangers to the process of McDonaldization. McDonald's could disappear tomorrow with few if any serious implications for the continuation of McDonaldization. McDonald's will almost undoubtedly disappear at some point in the future, but by then the McDonaldization process will likely be even more deeply entrenched in American society and throughout much of the world. In the eventuality that McDonald's should some day be down or even out, we may need to find a new paradigm and even a new name for the process, but that process (generically, the rationalization process) will continue, almost certainly at an accelerating rate.

But isn't there a variety of counter-trends that seem to add up to more than a threat to McDonald's? to a threat to the process of McDonaldization itself? Several such trends are worth discussing.

For one thing, there is the apparent rise of small, non-McDonaldized businesses. The major example in my area, the suburbs of Washington, DC, is the opening of many small, high-quality bakeries. There seems to be a reasonably large number of people who are willing to travel some distance and to pay relatively high prices for quality breads made by highly skilled bakers. And there seems to be money to be made by such enterprising bakers. Of course bakeries are not the only example (various health-conscious food emporiums would be another); there are many non-McDonaldized small businesses to be found throughout society.

Such enterprises have always existed; indeed they were far more commonplace before the recent explosive growth of McDonaldized systems. Under pressure from McDonaldized competitors, they seemed to have all but disappeared in many sectors, only to reappear, at least in part as a counter-reaction to McDonaldization. While they exist, and may even be growing, it is difficult to see these alternatives as a serious threat to McDonaldization. The likelihood is that they will succeed in the interstices of an otherwise highly McDonaldized society. If any one of them shows signs of being of more than marginal importance, it will quickly be taken over and efforts will be made to McDonaldize it. It is difficult to envision any other scenario.

Recently, it has been argued that a "New Regionalism" has developed in the United States and that it constitutes a "quiet rebellion" against McDonaldization (Myerson, 1996). Identified here is a series of distinctive regional trends, fashions and products that are affecting the nation and ultimately the world. One example offered by Myerson is a salsa originating in San Antonio, Texas and manufactured by Pace Foods. While certainly a non-McDonaldized, regional product, at least at first, the salsa, in fact the company, was purchased by Campbell Soup Company in 1995 for just over $1 billion. Over time, it will surely become just another McDonaldized product marketed by Campbell Soup. It will probably suffer the fate of Colonel Sanders's original Kentucky Fried Chicken and many other products that at first were highly original and distinctive but over time were turned into pale, McDonaldized imitations of what they once were.

Another example offered by Myerson is Elk Mountain Red Lager and Elk Mountain Amber Ale. These sound like, and reflect the growing importance of, the products of local micro-breweries, but in fact they are produced by the massive Anheuser-Busch company. Furthermore, they are made from the same hops as Budweiser and Michelob. Anheuser-Busch is, of course, trying to capitalize on the success of local and regional micro-breweries. What they are, in fact, doing is McDonaldizing micro-brewery beer.

Myerson cites the preservation of cities like Savannah, Georgia as yet another example of the new regionalism, but he quickly moves on to the development of "Disneyesque" simulacra like the Atlanta restaurant, Pittypat's Porch, which is named after Scarlett O'Hara's aunt in the book and movie, *Gone With the Wind*. He also mentions the "movie-set" New York that is currently emerging in the resuscitation of Times Square (and in which Disney has a stake). Such examples seem far more supportive of the McDonaldization thesis (as well as of a postmodernist perspective, especially the emphasis on simulacra) than any counter-thesis.

Myerson is correct in arguing that many of America's innovations flow from outlying regions. He takes this as evidence of a trend that runs counter to the ideas of homogenization and McDonaldization. However, he ignores the fact that regional creations that show any sign of success are quickly McDonaldized (examples include spicy New Orleans style cooking (Popeye's); southwestern Tacos (Taco Bell)). McDonaldized systems do not excel at innovation: they are at their best in implementing and rationalizing ideas stemming from other sources. Thus, innovations are always highly likely to emerge outside of McDonaldized systems. This represents one of the dangers of McDonaldization. As we move closer and closer to the iron cage, where are the innovations of the future to come from?

McDonald's itself has developed a system for coping with its lack of innovativeness. After all, the creations that have generally flowed from the central office (for example McDonald's Hula Burger – a bun with two slices of cheese surrounding a slice of grilled pineapple) have not been notably successful. It is the ideas that have stemmed from the franchisees in the field (the Filet-O-Fish at McDonald's, for example) that have been the most important innovations.

Another counter-trend worth noting is the rise of McDonaldized systems that are able to produce high-quality products. The major example is the large and fast-growing chain of Starbucks coffee shops (Witchel, 1994). Until recently, virtually all successful McDonaldized systems have been noted for characteristics like low price and high speed, but not for the high quality of the goods and services that they offer. McDonaldization has heretofore been largely synonymous with mediocrity in these areas. Starbucks has shown that it is possible to create a McDonaldized system that dispenses quality products; on the surface, this poses a profound challenge to McDonaldization and, more generally, to the McDonaldization thesis.

However, Starbucks is, in many ways, an atypical chain. For one thing, it sells variations on what is essentially one simple product – coffee. For another, it is relatively easy, especially with advanced systems and technologies, to consistently produce a good cup of coffee. Third, the patrons of Starbucks are willing to pay a relatively large sum of money for a good cup of coffee. In fact, it may well cost as much to get a cup of "designer coffee" at Starbucks as to have lunch at McDonald's. Thus, Starbucks indicates that it *is* possible to McDonaldize quality when we are dealing with one (or perhaps a few) simple products, when there are technologies that ensure high and consistent quality, and when enough patrons are willing to pay relatively large amounts of money for the product. Clearly, most chains are *not* able to meet these conditions, with the result that they are likely to remain both McDonaldized and mediocre. It is also important to remember that even with the kinds of differences discussed above, especially in quality, Starbucks continues to be McDonaldized in many ways (the different types of cups of coffee are predictable from one time or place to another). However, this is not to say that there are not more chains that will meet the conditions enumerated above and follow Starbucks's model. We already see this in the first steps toward the creation of high-quality restaurant chains.

A variety of moderately priced restaurant chains based on the McDonald's model have long since sprung up, including Sizzler, Bonanza, Olive Garden, TGIFriday's and Red Lobster. In fact, such chains now control 35 percent of what is called the moderately priced casual market (Bulkeley, 1996). In contrast, chains account for 77 percent of low-priced restaurant meals. Far behind, with only 1 percent of the market, are chains (actually, at this level they prefer to be called "restaurant groups") involved in the high-priced "linen tablecloth" business where the average patron's bills are in excess of $25. Notable examples include high-end steakhouse chains like Morton's of Chicago (33 restaurants) and Ruth's Chris Steak House (50 restaurants). The challenge in the future is to open high-end chains of restaurants that do not specialize in relatively easy to prepare steaks. Lured by the possibility of large profits, several groups are trying. For example, Wolfgang Puck, noted for his gourmet Spago restaurant in Los Angeles, has opened branch restaurants in San Francisco and Las Vegas (in the highly McDonaldized MGM Grand Hotel) and plans another for Chicago. The problem is that such restaurants depend on a creative chef and it is not immediately clear that one can McDonaldize creativity; indeed the two appear to be antithetical. Said one restaurateur, "The question is, can . . . [one] take a chef-driven concept to a city without a chef?" (Bulkeley, 1996: B1). The editor of *Gourmet Magazine* raises another issue about such chains; one that goes to the heart of McDonaldization and its limitations:

> It's the homogenization of cuisine. Even something as good as Morton's steak-house is, nevertheless, still going to be the same meal in Chicago as it would be in Washington. There are some people who value that – the fact that you'll always get a good meal. But there are others who will miss the individuality, the wonderful surprise of discovering a new, great place to eat. (Faiola, 1996b: 13)

In the context of high-end restaurant chains, it is useful to discuss an analogy between Ford and Fordism and McDonald's and McDonaldization. In the early days of the mass production of cars, people had little or no choice; there was virtually no variation in the number and quality of cars. Over the years, of course, and especially today in the era of post-Fordism, people have acquired a great deal of choice as far as their automobiles are concerned. There are many kinds of choice to be made, but one is certainly high-quality cars (Mercedes Benz or BMW) versus standard-quality (Ford Escort or Plymouth Neon) cars. However, they are all made using standard-ized parts and assembly-line techniques. That is, high-quality cars can be produced using Fordist techniques.

A parallel point can be made about McDonald's and McDonaldization. In its early years, the focus of fast-food restaurants was on the most mundane, standardized products. While various fast-food chains competed for business, they all offered the same relatively low-quality, standardized product. Today, however, people are demanding more choices in foods, including higher quality foods that do not cause them to sacrifice the advantages of McDonaldization. Just as we can produce a Mercedes Benz using Fordist principles, we can offer high-quality quiche using the tenets of McDonaldization. The only thing that stands in the way of a chain of restaurants that offers a range of high-quality quiches is the likelihood that there is insufficient demand for such a product.

As discussed in the case of Starbucks, it is possible to McDonaldize any product, even the highest-quality products, at least to some degree. The secret is to offer one product, or at most a limited number and range of products. What seems to defy McDonaldization is the essence of a fine restaurant – a range of well-prepared dishes changing from day to day on the basis of the availability of high-quality ingredients and/or the whims of the skilled chef. This kind of creativity and variability continues to resist McDonaldization.

The move into high-quality products leads us to question one of the basic tenets of McDonaldization – calculability, or the emphasis on quantity often to the detriment of quality. This is certainly true of virtually all McDonaldized systems that we have known, but it is not necessarily true of Starbucks, or of similar undertakings that we are likely to see in the future. We will see businesses where large amounts of high-quality quiche (to take one possibility) will be purveyed. Don't get me wrong here: I think that most McDonaldized systems will continue to forfeit quality in the pursuit of quantity (high speed, low cost, low price). However, McDonaldization, like Fordism, is changing and we will see more systems that are capable of combining quantity and quality.

Does this mean that just as we have moved into a post-Fordist era, we will soon be entering an epoch of post-McDonaldization? To some degree we will, but just as I think that the argument for post-Fordism is overblown, I would not push the post-McDonaldization thesis too far. Just as today's post-Fordist systems are heavily affected by Fordism, tomorrow's post-McDonaldized systems will continue to be powerfully affected by McDonaldization.

Starbucks (and the fledgling high-quality restaurant chains) deviates from other McDonaldized systems largely on one dimension (calculability, or the emphasis on quantity rather than quality), but what of the other dimensions? Can we conceive of successful chains that deviate from the model in other ways? For example, could one build a chain on the basis of inefficiency? (In fact, as I write this, Chili's is running a nationwide television ad campaign claiming that it is *not* an assembly-line operation; that it is a monument to inefficiency.) Or unpredictability? Or on the use of human rather than non-human technology? All of these seem unlikely. But, there might come a time when most systems are so highly McDonaldized that a large market emerges among those who crave a respite. A chain of inefficient, labor-intensive outlets offering unpredictable goods and services might be able to carve out a niche for itself under such circumstances. However, if such a chain was successful, it would quickly come under pressure to McDonaldize. The paradoxical challenge would be to McDonaldize things like inefficiency and unpredictability. Ironically, it could be done – a chain that efficiently manifests inefficiency, one which is predictably unpredictable, uniformly different, and so on. I even have a name for this proposed chain – "Miss Hap's." (Miss Hap's would be a burger and fries chain, but there could also be a steakhouse twin – "Miss Steak's.")

Imagine, for example, a chain of restaurants that rationalizes inefficiency; in postmodern terms one that produces a simulated inefficiency. A series of procedures to handle inefficiency would be created; procedures designed to attract customers fed up with efficient systems. These procedures would be broken down into a series of routine steps which would then be codified and made part of the company manual. New employees would be taught the steps needed to perform inefficiently. In the end, we would have a restaurant chain that has rationalized inefficiency. On cue, for example, a counter-person at Miss Hap's would effortlessly spill an order of (perhaps fake) fries on the counter. Leaving aside the whimsical example, it is clearly possible to rationalize the seemingly irrational and to produce a system that might well have a ready-made market in a highly McDonaldized society. It would offer more "fun," more spectacle, than the run-of-the-mill fast-food restaurant. And spectacle is often seen as a key element of the postmodern world (Debord, 1977; Featherstone, 1991). It is certainly in tune with trends like "Las Vegasization" and "McDisneyization."

Miss Hap's would also offer a range of products that were, or at least seemed, unpredictable. The shape of the hamburgers (Miss Hap's would certainly need to offer hamburgers) would be uniformly different. Instead of being perfectly round (or, in the case of Wendy's, square), the burgers would be irregularly shaped. The shape would *not* be left to chance. A variety of molds would be used to mass-produce several different types of burger with slightly different shapes (this is the "sneakerization" principle to be dis-cussed below). While the burgers would look different, the differences would not be great enough to affect the ease with which they could be cooked and served: it would still be possible to produce and sell such burgers within the context of a McDonaldized system. For example, all burgers would fit within the same-shaped bun. While the bun might remain uniformly round, it could be made uniformly irregular in other ways (for example, in the hills and crevices on the top of the bun). Similar irregu-larities could be built into the shakes (which could vary in texture), fries and chicken nuggets (which could vary in length without affecting a uniform frying time), and so on.

Another potential threat to McDonaldization lies in the area of custom-ization, or what has been called "sneakerization" (Goldman et al., 1994). There is considerable evidence that we have entered a post-industrial era in which the movement is away from the kinds of standardized, "one-size-fits-all" products, that are at the heart of McDonaldized systems. Instead, what we see is much more customization. True customization (e.g. made-to-measure suits) is not easily amenable to McDonaldization, but that is not what is usually meant by customization in this context. Rather, it is more niche marketing, of which "sneakerization" is an excellent example. That is, instead of one or a few styles of sneakers or trainers, we now have hundreds of different styles produced for various niches in the market (runners, walkers, aerobic exercisers, and so on). This, of course, is not true customization; sneakers are not being made to measure for a specific user.

The central point is that sneakerization does *not* reflect a trend toward de-McDonaldization. Large companies like Nike produce hundreds of thousands or even millions of each type of sneaker with the result that each is amenable to a McDonaldized production (as well as marketing, distribution and sales) system. In fact, one future direction for McDonaldization involves its application to products and services that are sold in smaller and smaller quantities. There is undoubtedly some absolute lower limit below which it is not profitable to McDonaldize (at least to a high degree), but it is difficult to specify what that limit might be with any precision. In any case, that limit will become lower and lower with further technological advances. That is, we will be able to apply economies of scale to increasingly small production runs. More and different sneakers, more sneakerization, do not represent significant threats to McDonaldization.

A similar argument can be made about what has been termed "mass customization" (Pine, 1993). Take the case of Custom Foot of Westport, Connecticut (McHugh, 1996). There, a customer puts a foot into an electronic scanner that measures it on 14 different dimensions. Then a configuration is completed on a computer screen with the aid of a salesperson. It is during this phase that the customer chooses things like style of shoe, type and grade of leather, color, lining, and so on. Computer software then translates all of this into a set of specifications that are transmitted to subcontractors in several cities in Italy. The shoes are cobbled and sent to the USA within two to three weeks. The cost ranges from $99 to $250, about the same price as ready-to-wear shoes for sale in good New York shoe stores. In contrast, traditional custom-made shoes might cost $1200 and take several months to arrive. In short, Custom Foot is McDonaldizing the process of making and selling truly customized shoes.

Now clearly this is less McDonaldized than the mass production of thousands, or even millions, of the same shoe. Mass production is more efficient, it permits greater predictability, more of it is amenable to quantification, and it relies more on non-human technologies than the customized production of shoes, even the way Custom Shoe does it. However, the procedures at Custom Shoe are far more McDonaldized than the traditional methods of producing customized shoes. We are talking here, as is usually the case, about degrees of McDonaldization. Custom Shoe has applied the principles of McDonaldization to the production and sale of custom shoes. The nature of its product, especially in comparison to the mass production of identical shoes, limits the degree to which it can McDonaldize, but it does not affect the fact that it is being McDonaldized.

Thus two of the directions in the future of McDonaldization are the production and sale of goods and services in increasingly small quantities and of goods that are higher in quality. While these are new directions, they do not represent de-McDonaldization. However, several other developments discussed in this chapter could be taken as indicative of such a trend.

The Case *for* McDonaldization

While I readily acknowledge the advantages of McDonaldization (Ritzer, 1996a: 11–13), what I have emphasized are the problems associated with this process. In this section, I want to turn the argument around, at least briefly, and make at least some of the case *for* McDonaldization.

The strongest point to be made is that McDonaldization has brought an array of goods and services to large numbers of people who otherwise would not have been able to get them, or would have had a great deal of trouble in doing so. This is true of those in many small towns and rural areas in the United States and it is especially true of those who dwell in many regions outside the United States. While the great dangers associated with McDonaldization are homogeneity and uniformity, it could be argued that many people have experienced greater diversity as a result of McDonaldization. For example, an inhabitant of a small American town might now have easy access, perhaps for the first time, to pizza or tacos. Similarly, a resident of Beijing, while still having a wide range of indigenous foods to choose from, is now also able to eat McDonald's hamburgers, pizza from Pizza Hut and the fare offered at Kentucky Fried Chicken.

McDonaldization has also led to the creation of an enormous number of new jobs. Furthermore, McDonaldized systems often provide career ladders to those who otherwise might not have much, if any, career mobility. One might start out as a counterperson, or a hamburger maker, but one can hope to move up the hierarchy and become an assistant manager, a manager, and ultimately even a franchise owner. Franchises have been particularly good at providing jobs and upward mobility for minority group members.

It could also be argued that McDonaldization fosters democratization, since McDonaldized goods and services have tended, at least thus far, to be relatively inexpensive. We will have more to say about this later in this chapter.

Another argument in favor of McDonaldization is that it constitutes no threat to indigenous culture. China, for example, is not going to see its culture radically altered by the invasion of McDonaldized systems. More likely, it will force these systems to adapt to Chinese culture, to become more local. It will also generate its own McDonaldized systems, undoubtedly bearing a strong Chinese imprint.

It is also possible to see McDonaldized systems not as iron cages but as liberating forces. For example, they have liberated many from the tyranny of marketing for, and cooking, family meals. They have helped to free many mothers so that they can enter, or remain in, the work world. They have given retirees a place to go and meet with friends. They have liberated teenagers from dependency on the family meal. Many would say that people have, in the main, been set free, not enslaved, by McDonaldization.

The basic dimensions of McDonaldization – efficiency, predictability, calculability and the substitution of non-human for human technology – can (and should) be seen as advantages of McDonaldized systems. Virtually everyone has been frustrated by inefficient systems and most would, in general, prefer efficiency to inefficiency. Unpredictability can be fun, but there are times when all of us would prefer to be sure that what we want is in fact available. Calculability has many aspects, but to select one, as a general rule we would prefer to be able to get a lot of something at relatively little cost. Finally, all of us have been advantaged by a wide array of non-human technologies. There are certainly powerful reasons behind the phenomenal growth and spread of McDonaldization; behind why so many systems have sought to become McDonaldized.

Obviously, many more things could be said on behalf of McDonaldization. Acknowledging such positive factors, I continue to believe that it is my responsibility as a social scientist to emphasize the problems associated with McDonaldization. This is partly traceable to a belief that good sociology is inevitably aimed at "debunking" social myths (Berger, 1963; Elias, 1978). More practically, it is animated by a need to counter the pro-McDonaldization propaganda emanating from these systems.

McDonaldization and Consumerism

The case has been made in this book that McDonald's, and the fast-food restaurant more generally, is one of the new means of consumption. Thus, the growth of McDonaldization is important not only in itself, but also for the role it is playing in the increasing consumerism not only of American society (McAllister, 1996), but of societies throughout the world. Much of the attention of those concerned with consumerism has been focused on advertising (Ewen, 1976; Fowles, 1996; Jacobson and Mazur, 1995; McAllister, 1996). While such a focus is certainly justified, there are other aspects of consumerism that are worthy of analysis and critique. One of those is the new means of consumption and the role played by McDonaldization in their growth and spread.

McDonald's, fast-food restaurants, and all the other new means of consumption are certainly important advertisers. Along with most of those who study consumerism, I recognize that advertising plays an important role in this domain. Let us look at a few of the ways in which McDonald's (along with the other chains of fast-food restaurants) advertising contributes to consumerism and the problems associated with it.

For starters, McDonald's, of course, spends an enormous amount of money advertising its wares. This is made necessary by, among other things, the fact that its products (hamburgers, french fries, fried chicken, soft drinks) are virtually indistinguishable from those of its competitors. By the sheer volume of its advertisements, as well as the fact that they lead its competitors to advertise at a similar level, McDonald's contributes significantly to consumerism.

Beyond this broad conclusion is the fact that many of the problems associated with excessive consumerism can also be linked to McDonald's and McDonaldization. For example, commercial organizations are often demonized for aiming their advertisements at children and for turning children into our "littlest consumers" (Jacobson and Mazur, 1995: 21). Certainly, no commercial organization is more guilty of this than McDonald's. McDonald's advertisements are a powerful presence on Saturday morning cartoon shows. More generally, McDonald's has historically been defined by its efforts to cater to children with a clown (Ronald McDonald) as its dominant symbol, its playgrounds, its carnival-like atmosphere, its child-oriented foods, and its promotional tie-ins with many movies (e.g. *Batman Returns*) and toys (e.g. Mattel's Happy Meal Snack Maker Set and Barbie dolls; in 1983 one of the Barbie doll outfits was a McDonald's waitress uniform: McAllister, 1996: 154–5). In these and other ways, McDonald's has sought to make children lifelong consumers of its products, indeed lifelong members of, and active contributors to, our consumer society.

McDonald's has also sought legitimacy by linking itself to social issues. The most notable example of this is Ronald McDonald House, a home for sick children. Through its association with this charity (and in other ways), McDonald's has attempted to portray itself as a philanthropic organization. While there is a measure of philanthropy in such acts, there is an even greater measure of commercialism. The goal is to have the McDonald's name associated with philanthropy, and not (as is the case) with helping to turn children into lifelong consumers or with commercialism more generally.

A similar objective is involved in McDonald's sponsorship of various kinds of sporting events. The most notable example is the McDonald's high school all-American basketball teams and the all-star games played by these teams. With such sponsorship, McDonald's hopes to link its name with one of America's most treasured sports, especially among the young people who are its biggest customers.

However, the most important critique of McDonald's from this point of view is that it is a leader in producing advertisements which, if they do not lie, almost always fail to tell the truth. The tobacco and alcohol industries are usually singled out for critique on this issue, but something needs to be said about the fast-food industry in this regard. Unlike tobacco and alcohol, it is difficult to attribute a specific number of deaths to excessive consumption of fast food. Nevertheless, it is clear that the kind of food served in fast-food restaurants – high in fat, cholesterol, calories, salt and sugar – is dangerous to the health of those who consume it on a regular basis. McDonald's certainly never tells us this in its advertisements and it may even state or imply that its food is healthy for us. By, for example, associating itself with all-American basketball players, McDonald's implies that such good health, even robustness, is associated with eating at its restaurants.

While the growth of McDonald's and other fast-food restaurants is associated with consumerism (and its attendant problems), the relationship of McDonaldization to all of this is a complex one. To the degree that McDonaldization encompasses most or all of the new means of consumption, then it can be seen as directly linked to consumerism. For example, the mega-mall can be seen as McDonaldizing consumption by, for example, making it more efficient to shop by combining many different types of shops and stores in one location. We have discussed (Chapter 8) how credit cards have served to McDonaldize the process of getting and using a loan. Involved in such new means of consumption as mega-malls and credit cards, McDonaldization is directly linked to consumerism.

However, McDonaldization can be differentiated from consumerism in a variety of ways. At its base, McDonaldization is a set of principles for the organization of consumption, work and many other activities. Those principles can be, and are being, extended to and employed in a variety of non-commercial undertakings. A non-profit organization, perhaps one involved with philanthropy or grant-giving, could well be attracted by the success of McDonald's and other McDonaldizing businesses and seek to learn and apply the principles that lie at the base of their success. Such a non-profit organization would be part of the process of McDonaldization but not involved (necessarily) in consumerism. Thus, McDonaldization, while deeply involved in consumerism is not coterminous with it.

Conversely, consumerism involves much more than McDonaldization. There is, for example, the importance of advertising, as well as the latter's increasing sophistication. Beyond that, there is the growth of infomercials, advertorials, direct marketing, telemarketing, and the like. However, some or all of these could be said to be McDonaldizing: for example, telemarketing has grown increasingly McDonaldized.

Stratification: Class, Race, Gender and Age

Most of the discussion of McDonaldization has a middle- and even an upper-class bias. A general focus on consumption, as well as a more specific concern with such means of consumption as credit cards and cruise lines, would seem supportive of such a bias. However, much of this analysis also applies to, and has direct and indirect implications for, those in the lower classes. It also has such connotations for other minority groups, including blacks, women and adolescents. The goal in this section is to suggest at least some of these implications.

Minority groups are, if anything, more affected by McDonaldization than majority groups. As we have seen, McDonaldized systems have tended to be those that offer low prices and often lesser-quality goods and services. It is those in the lower classes who are most likely to use such systems if, for no other reason than the fact that they cannot afford higher-priced and higher-quality non-McDonaldized alternatives. Conversely, those in the middle and upper classes have the resources to frequent non-McDonaldized alternatives. Of course, even they are lured by McDonaldized systems, but the difference is that they have the wherewithal to resist the pull when they so desire. It seems safe to hypothesize that those from the lower classes patronize McDonaldized systems to a disproportionate degree. (This, however, may change when more high-priced and quality settings become more McDonaldized.)

It is even clearer that those from the lower classes are more likely to work in McDonaldized systems; in other words to hold McJobs. Relatively few adult members of the middle and upper classes hold such jobs. (However, their children may well have McJobs, at least during a portion of their adolescence.) Members of such classes may well own one or more McDonaldized system, but they are highly unlikely to work in them. With little education, few skills and a dearth of alternatives, members of the lower classes may have little choice but to accept McJobs, or to find themselves among the unemployed. Their teenage children are at least as likely, and probably more likely, to hold such occupations than the children of the middle and upper classes. Furthermore, they tend to hold them longer, perhaps even well into their adult years.

These conclusions about patronage and work are also likely to hold for race, since blacks, Hispanics and other minorities are found disproportionately in the lower classes. There is certainly nothing about race *per se* that would predispose a certain group to work in, or patronize, a McDonaldized system. However, some McDonaldized systems may find it in their interest to zero in on certain races with specific products or with targeted advertising campaigns, which may lead certain minority groups to use McDonaldized systems to a disproportionate degree.

The issue of the relationship between gender and McDonaldized systems is more complex. For one thing, generalizations about social class hold, at least to a certain degree, for women. That is, middle- and upper-class women tend to use McDonaldized systems less than lower-class women. To the degree that we have witnessed a feminization of poverty, more women than men are likely to frequent those systems. For another, women across all social classes may be hypothesized to frequent such systems more than men in comparable class situations. For example, even with substantial changes in gender relations, women across class lines continue to shoulder most of the responsibility for providing the family with meals. However, many more women are working and thus have less time to prepare meals at home. The result is that they are more likely to be taking the family out to a fast-food restaurant, having a pizza delivered, or bringing home a pre-made meal from a fast-food restaurant or a supermarket salad bar. Because of a continuation of traditional gender roles, women, whatever their social class are still

saddled with the responsibility of providing them by frequenting McDonaldized systems of one type or another.

Large numbers of both males and females work in McJobs, especially as
teenagers. It may be, however, that the feminization of poverty causes more
adult women than men to work in such occupations. This hypothesis, as well
as the overall issue of the relationship between gender and McJobs, is
worthy of further study.

Overall, since we live in a society stratified on the basis of income, race
and gender, it should come as no surprise that there are differences along
these lines in susceptibility to McDonaldization. Another dimension, mentioned above, is age. Young people, in part because of their lack of means,
are more likely than older people to patronize and to work in McDonaldized
systems. And the products, the advertisements and the jobs are tailored to
the needs and interests of young people.

However, while there are certainly differences along class, race, gender
and age lines, what is truly striking about McDonaldization is the degree to
which it cuts across these demarcations; how it has managed to have a
profound impact on virtually everyone. One of the ways in which it has done
this is by driving out non-McDonaldized alternatives. In many places,
whatever one's class, race, gender or age, one has no alternative but to
utilize a McDonaldized system; there are no readily available non-
McDonaldized alternatives. Similarly, in some locations, and for at least
some groups, no jobs are available other than McJobs. This lack of
alternatives is the ultimate expression of Weber's iron cage and everyone,
whatever their particular characteristics, is locked in the cage together.

The other major way in which McDonaldization has come to affect
everyone is by becoming a prized component of our value system. That is,
people across all of these categories have come to value the efficiency,
predictability, calculability and control that characterize McDonaldized
systems. McDonald's, itself, has become a cultural icon, as have other
McDonaldized systems. All groups are affected by McDonaldization not
only because there are few alternatives, but also because they value the
process and the systems that represent it.

Before moving on, something needs to be said about all of this, especially
social class, and its relationship to the new means of consumption. Relatively few Americans have difficulty affording fast-food restaurants, at least
some of the time. This is not to say that there are not large numbers of poor
people, especially the homeless and illegal immigrants, who, unable to
afford a fast-food meal, go without or live off the discards of those who can.
Yet it seems likely that most of those in the lower classes in the United
States can afford a fast-food meal, at least now and then.

However, it is a different matter in other, less-developed, parts of the
world. In many nations, a meal at a fast-food restaurant is prohibitively
expensive for perhaps the vast majority of people. For many others, it is a
special treat that can be afforded only occasionally; a family meal at
McDonald's might cost a month's earnings. In some countries, a dinner date

at a fast-food restaurant is a sign of affluence and sophistication. Then, of course, there are the nations that are so badly off economically that there are few, if any, fast-food restaurants. The mainly poor denizens of such countries are completely "deprived" of the possibility of dining at McDonald's.

Most of the other new means of consumption are even more class linked. Many poor Americans do not qualify for credit cards, or if they do, it is only for the far less desirable "secured cards" that require that a set amount of money be on deposit with the credit card company. The more "prestigious" the card (gold, platinum, etc.), the further it is out of the reach of those in the lower classes. In order to obtain "credit" members of those classes must rely on loan sharks or old-fashioned installment buying.

Household Finance Co. (HFC) specializes in loaning money to working- and lower-class customers (Bailey, 1996). The company actively seeks out customers already deeply in debt to, say, their credit card companies. They might offer such customers a home equity loan at an interest rate far above that to be obtained at the local bank. They also offer credit cards carrying interest rates far higher than the norm. HFC engages in "sucker pricing," relying on the likelihood that their customers will not know that they are being charged a usurious rate and that a far lower one is readily available. Few middle- or upper-class people are targeted by companies like HFC.

The poor of most other countries are even less likely to have credit cards than poor Americans; indeed, they may not even have ever heard of credit cards, let alone the differences between a gold and a platinum card. Thus, the poor are likely to be deprived of the commodities obtainable through such mechanisms (as well as the life of perpetual indebtedness that often accompanies them).

Most of the other new means of consumption are aimed, as one would expect in a capitalistic society and world, at the middle and upper classes with the money to utilize them. Few members of the lower classes are likely to be frequent visitors to Las Vegas or regular users of cruise lines. Shopping malls and mega-malls are far more likely to be filled with middle- and upper- than with lower-class consumers. Most telemarketers concentrate on those with the money to afford their wares. And the new cybermalls are even more class-linked since only the relatively affluent are able to afford the technology that gives them access to the cybermalls.

This being said, some of the new means of consumption do focus on, perhaps prey upon, the lower classes. Some telemarketers do find those in the lower classes easier and more profitable targets. To take another example, some of the infomercials one sees on television seem to be aimed primarily at those on the economic margins.

The new means of consumption have been developed and put in place by capitalists interested in profits. Naturally, they have, in the main, developed means that are primarily attuned to the needs of people with economic resources (or in creating the need for their goods and services among such people). On the one hand, those with money are the beneficiaries of these new means of consumption. On the other hand, it is they who are most likely to be exploited by them. However, the plight of the poor is even worse. They are likely, as we have seen, to be largely excluded from the utilization of the new means of consumption. When they are not excluded, they usually come into contact with the most marginal of the new means (fast-food restaurants, questionable infomercials, fly-by-night telemarketers, HFC). As usual, the poor have the worst of both worlds.

A Modern Phenomenon in a Postmodern Age

Finally, I would like to return to the issue of the relationship between postmodernism and McDonaldization. Throughout this book I argued that modernism and postmodernism can be seen as alternative ways of looking at contemporary phenomena. As a complement to my modern analyses of fast-food restaurants and credit cards, I used postmodernism as a theoretical lens to examine the new means of consumption (including fast-food restaurants and credit cards). The issue could be left at that, but for the sake of discussion let us re-examine McDonaldization from another perspective on the relationship between modernism and postmodernism, which is that we are in the midst of a monumental historical change in which a postmodern society is in the process of supplanting modern society.

The issue, in this case, is the fate of modern phenomena and a modern process in a postmodern world. Let us assume that we can consider the fast-food restaurant and the McDonaldization process as modern phenomena and that we are currently undergoing a transformation to a postmodern society. Can the fast-food restaurant survive, perhaps even prosper, in a postmodern world? What is the fate of McDonaldization in such a world?

If rationality is the *sine qua non* of modern society, then non-rationality and/or irrationality occupies a similar position in postmodern society. Suppose the postmodernists are correct and we are on the verge of the emergence of a non-rational or irrational society. What are the prospects for McDonald's and McDonaldization in such a situation? For one thing, such rational phenomena could continue to exist in a postmodern world and coexist with the presumably dominant irrationalities. In that case, McDonaldized systems would be rational outposts in an otherwise irrational world. People would flock to McDonald's to escape, at least momentarily, the irrationalities that surround them. Visiting a McDonald's would be like frequenting a throwback to an earlier era (much like eating at a diner is today). But surviving in this way, in the interstices of an otherwise non-rational world, would be very different from being the master trend that McDonaldization, at least from a postmodern perspective, once was.

If one possibility is survival at the margins, a second is disappearance in an avalanche of irrationalities. This would be the scenario envisioned by many postmodernists. They would see rational McDonaldized systems as incompatible with the dominant irrational systems and likely, sooner or later, to be swamped by them. The long-term process of McDonaldization would finally come to an end as it grew increasingly unable to rationalize the irrational.

A third, and in many ways highly likely, possibility would be some sort of fusion of the irrational elements of postmodernity with the rational components of McDonaldization. In other words, the creation of a pastiche of modern and postmodern elements. While this appears, on the surface, to be a compromise, in fact such a pastiche is one of the defining characteristics of postmodernism. So this kind of fusion would represent another version of the triumph of postmodernity. Buttressing the case for this alternative is the fact that McDonaldized systems already are well described by many of the concepts favored by postmodernists – consumerism, simulacra, hyperspace, multinational capitalism, implosion, ecstasy, and many others. It could be argued that such systems are *already* pastiches of modernism and postmodernism and therefore already postmodern.

The fourth, and diametrically opposed, possibility, is that McDonaldization will not only resist the irrationalities of postmodernity, but will ultimately triumph over them. Thus, while at the moment we might be seeing some movement toward postmodernism and irrationality, this tendency is likely to be short-lived as it is repulsed by the master trend of increasing rationalization. In this scenario it is postmodernism, not rationalization, that is the short-lived phenomenon. This alternative would obviously be unacceptable to most postmodern thinkers largely because it means that the advent of a postmodern world would be stillborn. The triumph of McDonaldization means, by definition, the continuation, even acceleration, of modernity.

The logic of the McDonaldization thesis would, needless to say, favor the last of these scenarios. After all, following Weber, the rationalization process has existed and flowered over the course of many centuries. In the process it has encountered a series of monumental barriers and countertrends. In the end it has not only triumphed over them, but emerged even stronger and more entrenched. Postmodernism *may* prove to be a more formidable opponent; it *may* do what no social change before it has done – alter, halt or even reverse the trend toward increasing rationalization. While such things might occur, it is hard to argue against the continuation, indeed acceleration, of McDonaldization. If history is any guide, McDonaldized systems will survive, even proliferate, long after we have moved beyond postmodern society and scholars have relegated postmodernism to the status of a concept of little more than historical interest.

Note

1. The term "McDonaldization" has found its way into several sociological dictionaries including Abercrombie et al. (1994) and Jary and Jary (1995).

References

Abbott, Andrew (1988) *The System of the Professions*. Chicago: University of Chicago Press.

Abbott, Andrew (1993) "The Sociology of Work and Occupations," *Annual Review of Sociology*: 187–209.

Abercrombie, Nicholas, Hill, Stephen and Turner, Bryan S. (1994) *Dictionary of Sociology*, new edn. London: Penguin Books.

Ahrens, Frank (1996) "At Malls, the Trends of Change," *Washington Post*, 29 November: C1, C6.

Alexander, Jeffrey (1994) "How 'National' Is Social Theory? A Note on Some Worrying Trends in the Recent Theorizing of Richard Münch," *Theory: The Newsletter of the Research Committee on Social Theory*, Autumn: 2–7.

Alexander, Jeffrey and Colomy, Paul (1990) "Neofunctionalism Today: Reconstructing a Theoretical Tradition," in George Ritzer (ed.), *Frontiers of Social Theory: The New Syntheses*. New York: Columbia University Press, 1990. pp. 33–67.

American Banker (1991) "EFT Experts Look Ahead with Costs on Their Minds," 20 May: 22A.

Appadurai, Arjun (1990) "Disjunction and Difference in the Global Cultural Economy," in Mike Featherstone (ed.), *Global Culture: Nationalism, Globalization and Modernity*. London: Sage. pp. 295–310.

Archer, Margaret (1990) "Theory, Culture and Post-Industrial Society," in Mike Featherstone (ed.), *Global Culture: Nationalism, Globalization and Modernity*. London: Sage. pp. 97–120.

Bailey, Jeff (1996) "HFC Profits Nicely by Charging Top Rates on Some Risky Loans," *Wall Street Journal*, 11 December: A1, A6.

Bank, David (1996) "How Net Is Becoming More Like Television to Draw Advertisers," *Wall Street Journal*, 13 December: A1, A8.

Bannon, Lisa (1996) "Disney Decides World Isn't So Small, Creating Education Resort for Boomers," *Wall Street Journal*, 1 March: B1, B5.

Barber, Benjamin R. (1995) *Jihad vs. McWorld*. New York: Times Books.

Barker, Donald I. (1994–5) "A Technological Revolution in Higher Education," *Journal of Educational Technology Systems*, 23: 155–68.

Baudrillard, Jean (1968/1988) "The System of Objects," in Mark Poster (ed.), *Jean Baudrillard: Selected Writings*. Stanford, CA: Stanford University Press. pp. 10–28.

Baudrillard, Jean (1970/1988) "Consumer Society," in Mark Poster (ed.), *Jean Baudrillard: Selected Writings*. Stanford, CA: Stanford University Press. pp. 29–56.

Baudrillard, Jean (1972/1981) *For a Critique of the Political Economy of the Sign*. St Louis, MO: Telos Press.

Baudrillard, Jean (1973/1975) *The Mirror of Production*. St Louis, MO: Telos Press.

Baudrillard, Jean (1976/1993) *Symbolic Exchange and Death*. London: Sage.

Baudrillard, Jean (1979/1990) *Seduction*. New York: St Martin's Press.

Baudrillard, Jean (1980–85/1990) *Cool Memories*. London: Verso.

Baudrillard, Jean (1983) *Simulations*. New York: Semiotext(e).

Baudrillard, Jean (1983/1990) *Fatal Strategies*. New York: Semiotext(e).

Baudrillard, Jean (1986/1989) *America*. London: Verso.

Baudrillard, Jean (1990/1993) *The Transparency of Evil: Essays on Extreme Phenomena.* London: Verso.

Baudrillard, Jean (1993) Interviewed in Mike Gane (ed.), *Baudrillard Live: Selected Interviews.* London: Routledge. pp. 19–209.

Bauman, Zygmunt (1989) *Modernity and the Holocaust.* Ithaca, NY: Cornell University Press.

Bauman, Zygmunt (1991) *Modernity and Ambivalence.* Ithaca, NY: Cornell University Press.

Bauman, Zygmunt (1992) *Intimations of Postmodernity.* London: Routledge.

Bauman, Zygmunt (1993) *Postmodern Ethics.* Oxford: Basil Blackwell.

Beck, Ulrich (1992) *Risk Society: Towards a New Modernity.* London: Sage.

Belleville, Bill (1995) "Eco-Tourism Offers Cure for Evils Visited on Land," *Orlando Sentinel*, 26 February: C3.

Berger, Joseph, Zelditch, Jr., Morris and Anderson, Bo (eds) (1989) *Sociological Theories in Progress: New Formulations.* Newbury Park, CA: Sage.

Berger, Peter (1963) *Invitation to Sociology.* New York: Doubleday.

Berger, Peter and Luckmann, Thomas (1967) *The Social Construction of Reality.* Garden City, NY: Anchor.

Best, Steven (1980) "Jameson, Totality, and the Poststructuralist Critique," in Douglas Kellner (ed.), *Postmodernism: Jameson: Critique.* Washington, DC: Maisonneuve Press. pp. 333–68.

Beyer, Peter (1994) *Religion and Globalization.* London: Sage.

Bloland, Harland G. (1995) "Postmodernism and Higher Education," *Journal of Higher Education*, 66: 521–59.

Bourdieu, Pierre (1984a) *Homo Academicus.* Stanford, CA: Stanford University Press.

Bourdieu, Pierre (1984b) *Distinction: A Social Critique of the Judgment of Taste.* Cambridge, MA: Harvard University Press.

Bourdieu, Pierre (1990) *In Other Words: Essays Toward a Reflexive Sociology.* Cambridge: Polity Press.

Bourdieu, Pierre and Wacquant, Loic J.D. (1992) *An Invitation to Reflexive Sociology.* Chicago: University of Chicago Press.

Bourdieu, Pierre, Chamboredon, Jean-Claude and Passeron, Jean-Claude (1991) *The Craft of Sociology: Epistemological Preliminaries.* Berlin and New York: Walter de Gruyter.

Braverman, Harry (1974) *Labor and Monopoly Capital: The Degradation of Work in the Twentieth Century.* New York: Monthly Review Press.

Bryant, Adam (1992) "It Pays to Stick to Basics in Credit Cards," *New York Times*, 31 October: 35.

Bryman, Allan (1995) *Disney and His Worlds.* London: Routledge.

Bulkeley, William M. (1996) "Hold the Ketchup! Chic Restaurants Aim to Sell Haute Cuisine through Chains," *Wall Street Journal*, 1 April: B1, B8.

Burawoy, Michael (1979) *Manufacturing Consent: Changes in the Labor Process under Monopoly Capitalism.* Chicago: University of Chicago Press.

Burr, Steven W. (1995) "What Research Says about Sustainable Tourism Development," *Parks & Recreation*, September: 18ff.

Carey, Susan (1996) "Ersatz Isles Lack Local Color, but the Bathrooms Shine," *Wall Street Journal*, 16 February: B1, B5.

Carpenter, Richard P. (1994) "Memories Come Aboard on an SS Norway Cruise to Caribbean Islands," *Boston Globe*, 6 February: B1ff.

Chain Store Executive (1992) "Evaluating the Payments: More is Better," September: 28.

Clarke, Simon (1990) "The Crisis of Fordism or the Crisis of Social Democracy," *Telos*, 83: 71–98.

Consumer Reports (1992) "Hello, Central, Get Me 18005551696034858369394163859 0 504887659876," August: 7.

Cook, Karen, O'Brien, Jodi and Kollock, Peter (1990) "Exchange Theory: A Blueprint for Structure and Process," in George Ritzer (ed.), *Frontiers of Social Theory*. New York: Columbia University Press. pp. 158–171.

Cooper, Kenneth (1991) "Stanford President Sets Initiative on Teaching," *Washington Post*, 3 March: A12.

Coughlin, Ellen K. (1992) "Sociologists Confront Questions about Field's Vitality and Direction," *Chronicle of Higher Education*, 12 August: A6–A8.

Crenshaw, Albert B. (1991a) "Americans Putting Brakes on Borrowing," *Washington Post*, 8 March: A1, A14.

Crenshaw, Albert B. (1991b) "Keeping Tabs on Card Holders," *Washington Post*, 20 January: H4.

Crozier, Michel (1964) *The Bureaucratic Phemonenon*. Chicago: University of Chicago Press.

Damrosch, David (1995) *We Scholars: Changing the Culture of the University*. Cambridge, MA: Harvard University Press.

Davidson, Julie (1995) "Fair Game When the Chips Are Down," *Glasgow Herald*, 24 February.

Debord, Guy (1977) *The Society of the Spectacle*. London: Rebel Press.

Deleuze, Gilles and Guattari, Felix (1972/1983) *Anti-Oedipus: Capitalism and Schizophrenia*. Minneapolis: University of Minnesota Press, 1983.

Derrida, Jacques (1978) *Writing and Difference*. Chicago: University of Chicago Press.

Detweiler, Gerri (1993) *The Ultimate Credit Handbook*. New York: Plume.

Dezelay, Yves (1990) "The *Big Bang* and the Law: The Internationalization and Restructuration of the Legal Field," in Mike Featherstone (ed.), *Global Culture: Nationalism, Globalization and Modernity*. London: Sage. pp. 279–94.

Duhamel, Georges (1931) *America the Menace: Scenes from the Life of the Future*. Boston: Houghton Mifflin.

Duignan, Peter and Gann, Lewis (1992) *The Rebirth of the West: The Americanization of the Democratic World*. Oxford: Basil Blackwell.

Edelman, V. (1996) "Touch Goes High-Tech: Virtual Reality Sex," *Psychology Today*, 29: 59ff.

Edwards, Richard (1979) *Contested Terrain: The Transformation of the Workplace in the Twentieth Century*. New York: Basic Books.

Elger, Tony and Smith, Chris (eds) (1994) *Global Japanization? The Transnation Transformation of the Labour Process*. London: Routledge.

Elias, Norbert (1978) *What is Sociology?* New York: Columbia University Press.

Ewen, Stuart (1976) *Captains of Consciousness*. New York: McGraw-Hill.

Ewen, Stuart (1988) *All Consuming Images*. New York: Basic Books.

Ewen, Stuart and Ewen, Elizabeth (1982) *Channels of Desire: Mass Images and the Shaping of American Consumers*. New York: McGraw-Hill.

Faiola, Anthony (1996a) "Net Worth: It's Never Been Easier to Click and Go – But Does Travel Really Compute?," *Washington Post – Travel*, 11 February: E1, E6.

Faiola, Anthony (1996b) "Satisfying DC's Appetite: Dining Out Is In, and So Are Big National Restaurant Chains," *Washington Post – Washington Business*, 16 December: 12–13.

Featherstone, Mike (1990) "Global Culture: An Introduction," in Mike Featherstone (ed.), *Global Culture: Nationalism, Globalization and Modernity*. London: Sage. pp. 1–14.

Featherstone, Mike (1991) *Consumer Culture and Postmodernism*. London: Sage.

Feifer, M. (1985) *Going Places*. London: Macmillan.

Fine, Gary (1990) "Symbolic Interactionism in the Post-Blumerian Age," in George Ritzer (ed.), *Frontiers of Social Theory*. New York: Columbia University Press. pp. 117–57.

Fjellman, Stephen (1992) *Vinyl Leaves: Walt Disney World and America*. Boulder, CO: Westview Press.

Foote, Nelson (1953) "The Professionalization of Labor in Detroit," *American Journal of Sociology*, 58: 371–80.

Ford, Henry (1922) *My Life and Work*. Garden City, NY: Doubleday, Page.

Foucault, Michel (1979) *Discipline and Punish: The Birth of the Prison*. New York: Vintage.

Fowles, Jib (1996) *Advertising and Popular Culture*. London: Sage.

Fox, Larry and Radin, Barbara (1996) "Your Destiny Awaits," *Washington Post*, 8 December: E4.

Friedman, Jonathan (1990) "Being in World: Globalization and Localization," in Mike Featherstone (ed.), *Global Culture, Nationalism, Globalization and Modernity*. London: Sage. pp. 311–28.

Friedman, Jonathan (1994) *Cultural Identity and Global Process*. London: Sage.

Friedman, Jon and Meehan, John (1992) *House of Cards: Inside the Troubled Empire of American Express*. New York: G.P. Putnam's Sons.

Friedrichs, Robert (1970) *A Sociology of Sociology*. New York: Free Press.

Furfey, Paul (1953/1965) *The Scope and Method of Sociology: A Metasociological Treatise*. New York: Cooper Square.

Gabriel, Yiannis and Lang, Tim (1995) *The Unmanageable Consumer: Contemporary Consumption and Its Fragmentation*. London: Sage.

Galanoy, Terry (1980) *Charge It: Inside the Credit Card Conspiracy*. New York: G.P. Putnam's Sons.

Gane, Mike (1991) *Baudrillard and Critical and Fatal Theory*. London: Routledge.

Gane, Mike (ed.) (1993) *Baudrillard Live: Selected Interviews*. London: Routledge.

Genosko, Gary (1992) "The Struggle for an Affirmative Weakness: de Certeau, Lyotard, and Baudrillard," *Current Perspectives in Social Theory*, 12: 179–94.

Genosko, Gary (1994) *Baudrillard and Signs: Signification Ablaze*. London: Routledge.

Gerth, Hans and Mills, C. Wright (1953) *Character and Social Structure*. New York: Harcourt, Brace and World.

Gibson, Richard (1996a) "McDonald's Accelerates Store Openings in US and Abroad, Pressuring Rivals," *Wall Street Journal*, 18 January: A3.

Gibson, Richard (1996b) "Some Franchisees Say Moves by McDonald's Hurt Their Operations," *Wall Street Journal*, 17 April: A1, A10.

Giddens, Anthony (1984) *The Constitution of Society: Outline of the Theory of Structuration*. Berkeley, CA: University of California Press.

Giddens, Anthony (1990) *The Consequences of Modernity*. Stanford, CA: Stanford University Press.

Giddens, Anthony (1991) *Modernity and Self-Identity: Self and Society in the Late Modern Age*. Stanford, CA: Stanford University Press.

Giddens, Anthony (1992) *The Transformation of Intimacy: Sexuality, Love and Eroticism in Modern Societies*. Stanford, CA: Stanford University Press.

Goffman, Erving (1961) *Asylums*. Garden City, NY: Anchor Books.

Goldman, Steven L., Nagel, Roger N. and Preiss, Kenneth (1994) "Why Seiko Has 3,000 Watch Styles," *New York Times*, 9 October: 9.

Gouldner, Alvin (1970) *The Coming Crisis in Western Sociology*. New York: Basic Books.

Green, Kenneth C. and Gilbert, Steven W. (1995) "Great Expectations: Content, Communications, Productivity, and the Role of Information Technology in Higher Education," *Change*, 27: 8

Grochowski, John (1995) "Vegas' Virtual Reality: The City of Illusion Keeps Gambling on Reinvention," *Chicago Sun-Times*, 8 October: Travel section, p. 1.

Habermas, Jürgen (1981) "Modernity versus Postmodernity," *New German Critique*, 22: 3–14.

Habermas, Jürgen (1987) *The Philosophical Discourse of Modernity: Twelve Lectures*. Cambridge, MA: MIT Press.

Hage, Jerald and Powers, Charles H. (1992) *Post-Industrial Lives: Roles and Relationships in the 21st Century*. Newbury Park, CA: Sage.

Hannerz, Ulf (1990) "Cosmopolitans and Locals in World Culture," in Mike Featherstone (ed.), *Global Culture: Nationalism, Globalization and Modernity*. London: Sage. pp. 237–52.

Hansell, Saul (1994) "Into Banking's Future, Electronically," *New York Times*, 31 March: D1, D13.

Harvey, David (1989) *The Condition of Postmodernity: An Inquiry into the Origins of Cultural Change*. Oxford: Basil Blackwell.

Heywood, Ian (1994) "Urgent Dreams: Climbing, Rationalization and Ambivalence," *Leisure Studies*, 13: 179–94.

Hill, Brian J. (1995) "A Guide to Adventure Travel," *Parks & Recreation*, September: 56.

Hochschild, Arlie R. (1983) *The Managed Heart: Commercialization of Human Feelings*. Berkeley, CA: University of California Press.

Hockstader, Lee (1995) "Attack on Big Mac," *Washington Post*, 8 August: A13.

Houser, Dave G. (1994) "In Expeditions at Sea, Passengers Get Excitement without Loss of Comfort," *Baltimore Sun*, 20 February: 1M.

Howard, Elizabeth G. (1996) "Satellite Solution: Popping up like Dandelions, Satellite Campuses Tighten Bond of Learning, Students," *Kansas City Business Journal*, 14: 7 (sec. 1).

Jacobson, Michael F. and Mazur, Laurie Ann (eds) (1995) *Marketing Madness: [A Survival Guide for a Consumer Society]*. Boulder, CO: Westview Press.

Jameson, Fredric (1984) "Postmodernism, Or, The Cultural Logic of Late Capitalism," *New Left Review*, 146: 59–92.

Jameson, Fredric (1989) "Afterword – Marxism and Postmodernism," in Douglas Kellner (ed.), *Postmodernism, Jameson, Critique*. Washington, DC: Maisonneuve Press. pp. 369–87.

Jameson, Fredric (1991) *Postmodernism, or, The Cultural Logic of Late Capitalism*. Durham, NC: Duke University Press.

Jary, David and Jary, Julia (1995) *Collins Dictionary of Sociology*. Glasgow: HarperCollins.

Kalberg, Stephen (1980) "Max Weber's Types of Rationality: Cornerstones for the Analysis of Rationalization Processes in History," *American Journal of Sociology*, 85: 1145–79.

Kantrow, Yvette (1989) "Fewer Paying Off Card Balances, ABA Survey Finds," *American Banker*, 19 September: 1, 22.

Katz, Lawrence F. and Krueger, Alan B. (1992) "The Effect of the Minimum Wage on the Fast-Food Industry," *Industrial and Labor Relations Review*, October: 6.

King, Anthony (1990) "Architecture, Capital and the Globalization of Culture," in Mike Featherstone (ed.), *Global Culture: Nationalism, Globalization and Modernity*. London: Sage. pp. 397–411.

King, Margaret J. (1980) "McDonald's and the New American Landscape," *USA TODAY*, January.

King, Margaret J. (1983a) "Empires of Popular Culture: McDonald's and Disney," in Marshall Fishwick (ed.), *Ronald Revisited: The World of Ronald McDonald*. Bowling Green, OH: Bowling Green University Press. pp. 106–19.

King, Margaret J. (1983b) "McDonald's and Disney," in Marshall Fishwick (ed.), *Ronald Revisited: The World of Ronald McDonald*. Bowling Green, OH: Bowling Green University Press.

Knights, David (1990) "Subjectivity, Power and the Labour Process," in David Knights and Hugh Willmott (eds), *Labour Process Theory*. Basingstoke: Macmillan. pp. 297–335.

Knights, David and Willmott, Hugh (eds) (1990) *Labour Process Theory*. Basingstoke: Macmillan.

Kowinski, William Severini (1985) *The Malling of America: An Inside Look at the Great Consumer Paradise*. New York: William Morrow.

Kraft, Scott (1994) "Agog at Euro Disneyland," *Los Angeles Times*, 18 January: H1.

Kroc, Ray (1977) *Grinding It Out*. New York: Berkeley Medallion Books.

Kuhn, Thomas (1962/1970) *The Structure of Scientific Revolutions*. Chicago: University of Chicago Press.

Kuisel, Richard (1993) *Seducing the French: The Dilemma of Americanization*. Berkeley, CA: University of California Press.

Lancaster, J. (1995) "Jerusalem's Beef: Is McDonald's One Americanization Too Many?" *Washington Post*, 1 August: A14.

Leidner, Robin (1993) *Fast Food, Fast Talk: Service Work and the Routinization of Everyday Life*. Berkeley, CA: University of California Press.

Lemert, Charles (ed.) (1981) *French Sociology: Rupture and Renewal since 1968*. New York: Columbia University Press.

Levine, Arthur (1993) "Student Expectations of College," *Change*, September/October: 4.

Levine, Donald (1981) "Rationality and Freedom: Weber and Beyond," *Sociological Inquiry*, 51: 5–25.

Lewis, Michael (1995) "The Rich: How They're Different . . . Than They Used to Be," *New York Times Magazine*, 19 November: 67.

Liska, Allen (1990) "The Significance of Aggregate Dependent Variables and Contextual Independent Variables for Linking Macro and Micro Theories," *Social Psychology Quarterly*, 53: 292–301.

Littler, Craig R. (1990) "The Labour Process Debate: A Theoretical Review 1974–1988," in David Knights and Hugh Willmott (eds), *Labour Process Theory*. Basingstoke: Hampshire. pp. 46–94.

Los Angeles Times (1993) "Road to Cashlessness Paved with Plastic," 20 December: C1.

Love, John (1986) *McDonald's: Behind the Arches*. Toronto: Bantam Books.

Loving, Bill (1996) "Tripping on the Internet: Virtual Journeys," *Star Tribune*, 7 January: 1Gff.

Luxenberg, Stan (1985) *Roadside Empires: How the Chains Franchised America*. New York: Viking.

Lyotard, Jean-François (1979/1984) *The Postmodern Condition: A Report on Knowledge*. Minneapolis, MN: University of Minnesota Press.

Lyotard, Jean-François (1988/1992) *The Postmodern Explained*. Minneapolis, MN: University of Minnesota Press.

McAllister, Matthew P. (1996) *The Commercialization of American Culture*. London: Sage.

MacCannell, Dean (1976) *The Tourist: A New Theory of the Leisure Class*. New York: Schocken.

McCreary, Edward A. (1964) *The Americanization of Europe: The Impact of Americans and American Business on the Uncommon Market*. Garden City, NY: Doubleday.

Macdonald, Keith M. (1995) *The Sociology of the Professions*. London: Sage.

McDonald's (1996) *The Annual: McDonald's Corporation 1995 Annual Report*. Oak Brook, IL: McDonald's Corporation.

McDowell, Edwin (1995) "Hotel Franchise Company Looks to House Sales," *New York Times*, 17 June: 35.

McEnery, Mary Anne (1995) "Stores Give Way to a Bargain Hunter's Nirvana," *Bergen Record*, 5 October: H1.

McHugh, Josh (1996) "A Shoe that Really Fits," *Forbes*, 3 June: 126–7.

McKay, Betsy (1996) "In Russia, West No Longer Means Best: Consumers Shift to Home-Grown Goods," *Wall Street Journal*, 9 December: A9.

Mandell, Lewis (1990) *The Credit Card Industry: A History*. Boston: Twayne.

Mannheim, Karl (1929/1936) *Ideology and Utopia*. New York: Harcourt, Brace and World.

Mannheim, Karl (1935/1940) *Man and Society in an Age of Reconstruction*. New York: Harcourt, Brace and World.

Marx, Karl (1867/1967) *Capital: A Critique of Political Economy*, vol. 1. New York: International Publishers.

May, Tony (1995) "Millions Journey among the Junk-Food Mountains to Give Their Sensations a Whirl," *Guardian*, 19 August: 35.

Mead, George Herbert (1934/1962) *Mind, Self and Society: From the Standpoint of a Social Behaviorist*. Chicago: University of Chicago Press.

198   *References*

Meier, Barry (1992) "Credit Cards on the Rise in High Schools," *New York Times*, 5 September: 9.

Mills, C. Wright (1959) *The Sociological Imagination*. New York: Oxford University Press.

Monaghan, Peter (1996) "Mixing Technologies: Northern Arizona U. Uses TV and Internet to Reach Students Who Live Far Away," *Chronicle of Higher Education*, 29 March: A21ff.

Mullins, Nicholas (1973) *Theories and Theory Groups in Contemporary American Sociology*. New York: Harper and Row.

Münch, Richard (1981) "Talcott Parsons and the Theory of Action I: The Structure of the Kantian Lore," *American Journal of Sociology*, 86: 709–39.

Münch, Richard (1982) "Talcott Parsons and the Theory of Action II: The Continuity of the Development," *American Journal of Sociology*, 87: 771–826.

Münch, Richard (1991)"American and European Social Theory: Cultural Identities and Social Forms of Theory Production," *Sociological Perspectives*, 34: 313–336.

Münch, Richard (1993) "The Contribution of German Social Theory to European Sociology," in Birgitta Nedelmann and Piotr Sztompka (eds), *Sociology in Europe: In Search of Identity*. Berlin: Walter de Gruyter. pp. 45–66.

Münch, Richard and Smelser, Neil (1987) "Relating the Micro and Macro," in Jeffrey C. Alexander, Bernhard Giesen, Richard Münch and Neil Smelser (eds), *The Micro–Macro Link*. Berkeley: University of California Press. pp. 356–87.

Munt, Ian (1994) "The 'Other' Postmodern Tourism: Culture, Travel and the New Middle Classes," *Theory, Culture and Society*, 11: 101–23.

Myerson, Allen R. (1996) "America's Quiet Rebellion against McDonaldization," *New York Times*, 28 July: E5.

Nedelmann, Birgitta (1991) "Individualization, Exaggeration and Paralysation: Simmel's Three Problems of Culture," *Theory, Culture and Society*, 8: 169–94.

Newbern, Kathy M. and Fletcher, J.S. (1995) "Leisurely Cruise the Caribbean," *Washington Times*, 27 August: Travel section: E1.

Pacelle, Mitchell (1996) "More Stores Spurn Malls for the Village Square," *Wall Street Journal*, 16 February: B1, B3.

Parker, Martin and Jary, David (1995) "The McUniversity: Organization, Management and Academic Subjectivity," *Organization*, 2: 1–20.

Parrinello, Giuli Liebman (1993) "Motivation and Anticipation in Post-Industrial Tourism," *Annals of Tourism Research*, 20: 233–49.

Parsons, Talcott (1937) *The Structure of Social Action*. New York: McGraw-Hill.

Pierce, Roger L. (1990) "Seeking New Opportunities in Tomorrow's Payment-Systems World," *American Banker*, 5 July: 11A.

Pieterse, Jan Nederveen (1994) "Globalisation as Hybridisation," *International Sociology*, 9: 161–84.

Pine, Joseph (1993) *Mass Customization: The New Frontier in Business Competition*. Cambridge, MA: Harvard Business School Press.

Piskora, Beth and Kutler, Jeffrey (1993) "ATMs, Debit Cards and Home Banking: Finally, Many Bank Customers Seem to Be Ready for the Future," *American Banker*, 27 September: 1A.

Plater, William M. (1995) "Future Work: Faculty Time in the 21st Century," *Change*, 27: 22

Postman, Neil (1985) *Amusing Ourselves to Death: Public Discourse in the Age of Show Business*. New York: Viking.

Pressler, Margaret Webb (1995a) "New Lease on Life in the Great Indoors," *Washington Post*, 14 March: D1, D6.

Pressler, Margaret Webb (1995b) "Putting a New Tag on Retailing," *Washington Post*, 13 June: D1, D5.

Prichard, Craig and Willmott, Hugh (1996) "Just How Managed is the McUniversity?" Paper presented at Dilemmas of Mass Higher Education conference, Staffordshire University, April.

Quint, Michael (1990) "D'Agostino to Accept Debit Cards for Purchases," *New York Times*, 19 May: 43.

Richman, Phyllis C. (1996) "The Golden Years Arches: McDonald's Mature Burgers Don't Cut the Mustard," *Washington Post*, 10 May: D1.

Riding, Alan (1992) "Only the French Elite Scorn Mickey's Debut," *New York Times*, 13 April: A13.

Ritzer, George (1975/1980) *Sociology: A Multiple Paradigm Science*. Boston: Allyn and Bacon.

Ritzer, George (1981) *Toward an Integrated Sociological Paradigm: The Search for an Exemplar and an Image of the Subject Matter*. Boston: Allyn and Bacon.

Ritzer, George (1983) "The McDonaldization of Society," *Journal of American Culture*, 6: 100–7.

Ritzer, George (1988) "Problems, Scandals and the Possibility of 'TextbookGate': An Author's View," *Teaching Sociology*, 16: 373–80.

Ritzer, George (1990) "The Current Status of Sociological Theory: The New Syntheses," in George Ritzer (ed.), *Frontiers of Social Theory: The New Syntheses*. New York: Columbia University Press. pp. 1–30.

Ritzer, George (1991) *Metatheorizing in Sociology*. Lexington, MA: Lexington Books.

Ritzer, George (ed.) (1992) *Metatheorizing*. Newbury Park, CA: Sage.

Ritzer, George (1993) *The McDonaldization of Society*. Thousand Oaks, CA: Pine Forge Press.

Ritzer, George (1995) *Expressing America: A Critique of the Global Credit Card Society*. Thousand Oaks, CA: Pine Forge Press.

Ritzer, George (1996a) *The McDonaldization of Society*, revised edn. Thousand Oaks, CA: Pine Forge Press.

Ritzer, George (1996b) *Sociological Theory*, 4th edn. New York: McGraw-Hill.

Ritzer, George (1997) *Postmodern Social Theory*. New York: McGraw-Hill.

Ritzer, George (forthcoming) *Revolutionizing the Means of Consumption*. Thousand Oaks, CA: Pine Forge Press.

Ritzer, George and Walczak, David (1988) "Rationalization and the Deprofessionalization of Physicians," *Social Forces*, 67: 1–22.

Robertson, Roland (1990) "Mapping the Global Condition: Globalization as the Central Concept," in Mike Featherstone (ed.), *Global Culture: Nationalism, Globalization and Modernity*. London: Sage. pp. 15–30.

Robertson, Roland (1992) *Globalization: Social Theory and Global Culture*. London: Sage.

Rojek, Chris (1993) "Disney Culture," *Leisure Studies*, 12: 121–35.

Rojek, Chris (1995) *Decentring Leisure: Rethinking Leisure Theory*. London: Sage.

Rupkey, Christopher S. (1979) "The 'Have It All Now' Generation," *New York Times*, 13 May: 26.

Schaaf, Dick (1994) "Inside Hamburger University," *Training*, December: 18–24.

Schutz, Alfred (1932/1967) *The Phenomenology of the Social World*. Evanston, IL: Northwestern University Press.

Seattle Times (1994) "Shopping Vacations: Millions Make Pilgrimages to New Mega-Mall Meccas," 13 November: K5.

Servan-Schreiber, J.-J. (1968) *The American Challenge*. New York: Atheneum.

Seymour, Daniel (1995) *Once Upon a Campus: Lessons for Improving Quality and Productivity in Higher Education*. Phoenix, AZ: The Oryx Press.

Sharpe, Anita (1996) "Medical Entrepreneur Aims to Turn Clinics into a National Brand," *Wall Street Journal*, 4 December: A1, A11.

Shelton, Allen (forthcoming) "Writing McDonald's, Eating the Past: McDonald's as a Postmodern Space."

Shiver Jr., Jube (1988) "Scoring System for Loan Seekers Stirs Debate," *Los Angeles Times*, 30 October, Pt. 4: 5.

Simmel, Georg (1907/1978) *The Philosophy of Money*. London: Routledge and Kegan Paul.

Simmel, Georg (1991) "Money in Modern Culture," *Theory, Culture and Society*, 8: 17–31.

Simon, William E. (1996) "The Dumbing Down of Higher Education," *Wall Street Journal*, 19 March: A18.

Singletary, Michelle (1996) "Borrowing by the Touch," *Washington Post*, 30 March: C1, C2.

Smart, Barry (1994) "Sociology, Globalisation and Postmodernity: Comments on the 'Sociology for One World' Thesis," *International Sociology*, 9: 149–59.

Smith, Anthony D. (1990) "Towards a Global Culture," in Mike Featherstone (ed.), *Global Culture: Nationalism, Globalization and Modernity*. London: Sage. pp. 171–92.

Smith, Vicki (1994) "Braverman's Legacy: The Labor Process Tradition at 20," *Work and Occupations*, 21: 403–21.

Sorokin, Pitirim (1956) *Fads and Foibles in Modern Sociology and Related Sciences*. Chicago: Regnery.

Specter, Michael (1995) "Borscht and Blini to Go," *New York Times*, 9 August: C1, C3.

Stephanson, Anders (1989) "Regarding Postmodernism: A Conversation with Fredric Jameson," in Douglas Kellner (ed.), *Postmodernism: Jameson: Critique*. Washington, DC: Maisonneuve Press. pp. 43–74.

Stille, Alexander (1995) "Virtual Antiquities Could Help Real Icons Stand Test of Time," *Washington Post*, 25 December: A3ff.

Strinati, Dominic (1990) "A Ghost in the Machine? The State and Labour Process Theory in Practice," in David Knights and Hugh Willmott (eds), *Labour Process Theory*. Basingstoke: Macmillan. pp. 209–43.

Strom, Stephanie (1993) "Holiday Shoppers Are Whipping Out the Plastic," *New York Times*, 18 December: 45.

Sullivan, Barbara (1995) "McDonald's Sees India as Golden Opportunity," *Chicago Tribune*, 5 April: Business section, p. 1.

Sulski, Jim (1995) "Colleges Set Up Shop in Suburbs: Location is Big Lure for Students at Satellite Campuses," *Chicago Tribune*, 8 October: C3ff.

Takaki, Ronald (1990) *Iron Cages: Race and Culture in 19th-Century America*. New York: Oxford University Press.

Talbott, Shannon Peters (1996) "Global Localization of the World Market: Case Study of McDonald's in Moscow," *Sociale Wetenschappen*, December: 31–44.

Tannenbaum, Jeffrey A. (1996) "Chicken and Burgers Create Hot New Class: Powerful Franchisees," *Wall Street Journal*, 21 May: A1, A8.

Taylor, Frederick W. (1947) *The Principles of Scientific Management*. New York: Harper and Row.

Tazzioli, Terry (1995) "Gay Odyssey: Learning to Respect Personal Style within a 'Lifestyle'," *Seattle Times*, 7 May: K2ff.

Timothy, Dallen and Butler, Richard W. (1994) "Cross-Border Shopping: A North American Perspective," *Annals of Tourism Research*, 22 (1): 16–34.

Tiryakian, Edward A. (1991) "Pathways to Metatheory: Rethinking the Presuppositions of Macrosociology," in George Ritzer (ed.), *Metatheorizing*. Newbury Park, CA: Sage. pp. 69–87.

Touraine, Alain (1995) *Critique of Modernity*. Oxford: Basil Blackwell.

Travel Weekly (1995) "One Big Happy Family," 16 March: 54.

Turner, Bryan (1986) "Simmel, Rationalisation and the Sociology of Money," *Sociological Review*, 34: 93–114.

Updegrave, Walter L. (1987) "How Lenders Size You Up," *Money*, April: 145ff.

Urry, John (1987) "On the Waterfront," *New Society*, 14 (August): 12–14.

Urry, John (1990a) *The Tourist Gaze: Leisure and Travel in Contemporary Societies*. London: Sage.

Urry, John (1990b) "'Consumption' of Tourism," *Sociology*, 24: 23–35.

Urry, John (1992) "The Tourist Gaze and the 'Environment'," *Theory, Culture and Society*, 9: 1–26.

Urry, John (1994) "Cultural Change and Contemporary Tourism," *Leisure Studies*, 13: 233–8.

Van Giezen, Robert W. (1994) "Occupational Wages in the Fast-Food Restaurant Industry," *Monthly Labor Review*, August: 24–30.

Varney, Kenneth R. (1994) "Automated Credit Scoring Screens Loan Applicants," *Washington Post*, 15 January: E1, E13.

Virilio, Paul (1986) *Speed and Politics*. New York: Semiotext(e).

Wacquant, Loic J.D. (1992) "Toward a Social Praxeology: The Structure and Logic of Bourdieu's Sociology," in P. Bourdieu and L.J.D. Wacquant, *An Invitation to Reflexive Sociology*. Chicago: University of Chicago Press. pp. 2–59.

Wagner, Peter (1994) *A Sociology of Modernity: Liberty and Discipline*. London: Routledge.

Wallerstein, Immanuel (1974) *The Modern World-System: Capitalist Agriculture and the Origins of the European World-Economy in the 16th Century*. New York: Academic Press.

Wallerstein, Immanuel (1980) *The Modern World-System II: Mercantilism and the Consolidation of the European World-Economy, 1600–1750*. New York: Academic Press.

Wallerstein, Immanuel (1989) *The Modern World System III: The Second Era of Great Expansion of the Capitalist World-Economy, 1730–1840*. New York: Academic Press.

Walsh, John P. (1993) *Supermarkets Transformed: Understanding Organizational and Technological Innovations*. New Brunswick, NJ: Rutgers University Press.

Waters, Malcolm (1996) "McDonaldization and the Global Culture of Consumption," *Sociale Wetenschappen* December: 17–30.

Weber, Max (1921/1958) *The Rational and Social Foundations of Music*. Carbondale, IL: Southern Illinois University Press.

Weber, Max (1921/1968) *Economy and Society*, 3 vols. Totowa, NJ: Bedminster Press.

Weeks, Linton and Roberts, Roxanne (1996) "Amusement Mall," *Washington Post*, 7 December: C1, C5.

Weinstein, Deena and Weinstein, Michael A. (1993) *Postmodern(ized) Simmel*. London: Routledge.

Whitefield, Debra (1987) "Money Talk: Credit Vendors Target the Colleges," *Los Angeles Times*, 21 May: 4: 3.

Williams, Francis (1962) *The American Invasion*. New York: Crown.

Winerip, Michael (1994) "All Under One Roof: Stores and Education," *New York Times*, 2 May: B8.

Witchel, Alex (1994) "By Way of Canarsie, One Large Hot Cup of Business Strategy," *New York Times*, 14 December: C1, C8.

Womack, James P., Jones, Daniel T. and Roos, Daniel (1990) *The Machine that Changed the World*. New York: Rawson Associates.

Worsley, Peter (1982) *Marx and Marxism*. Chichester: Ellis Horwood.

Name Index

Subject Index